ON THE WATERFRONT

To Rob

J. D. Parke.

July 4th 2005 .

The Rev. J.D. Parker as leader of the Witness for Peace Movement.

On The Waterfront

Joseph D. Parker

The Pentland Press Limited
Edinburgh · Cambridge · Durham · USA

First published in 2000 by
The Pentland Press Ltd.
1 Hutton Close
South Church
Bishop Auckland
Durham

British Library Cataloguing in Publication Data.
A catalogue record for this book is available
from the British Library.

ISBN 1 85821 737 7

Typeset by George Wishart & Associates, Whitley Bay.
Printed and bound by Antony Rowe Ltd., Chippenham.

For Dorothy

*– who more than most
helped make it happen*

AUTHOR'S NOTE

All profit derived from the sale of this book is designated by the author for the sole purpose of promoting volunteer service with the Missions to Seamen on a world wide basis by the Society's Central Office in London, UK.

CONTENTS

INTRODUCTION

My retirement in June 1993 brought to a conclusion a Ministry on the waterfront which spanned a period in excess of thirty years, during which time I served in the ports of Dublin in the Republic of Ireland, Belfast, Northern Ireland and Vancouver, British Columbia, Canada. I had lived an active life and now like most retirees I was beginning to wonder what I would do with my time, but not for long. Soon my daughter said to me, 'Dad, you have lived a very full and interesting life so why not share some of your experiences? Now you have time to write.'

While there are certain aspects of my Ministry which are absolutely confidential and must remain so, nevertheless over the years I recorded a number of experiences and stories about my work which I found wholly absorbing, though not with this purpose in mind. However when my daughter made this suggestion it seemed logical that I should gather all of them together in book form, together with one or two other articles worth including.

Seafarers rarely make headline news unless tragedy or misfortune turns the spotlight on them. Rather sadly, except for family, friends and people who reside in predominant seafaring communities, so far as society is concerned it is largely a question of 'out of sight out of mind'. The world should know more about these men who form the lifeline between the nations of the world and be encouraged to recognize the debt we owe them by lending support to those charitable societies which seek to serve them of which the Missions to Seamen is but one.

This book is comprised of a series of stories and incidents about seafarers and their families, the struggles and the joy in fulfilling their needs under the auspices of the Flying Angel flag of the Missions to Seamen, the involvement of a Padre and his family with them for over thirty years and a record of the immeasurable contribution of the Missions' volunteer workers who helped care for these strangers in our midst. As with all human stories there is joy, sorrow, tragedy, frailty and frustration reflected in this book. In one respect the life of the seafarer is almost unique. It is lived for the most part separated from family and friends which makes it difficult for both in times of crisis.

I have dedicated this book to my wife, Dorothy, without whose loyalty and support throughout my Ministry it might never have happened. She married a business man, who later found his vocation to the Priesthood while serving as a volunteer worker with the Missions to Seamen and despite the sacrifices this change called for Dorothy stayed the course as wife and mother. Mother not only to her own family but to countless seafarers from many lands.

EARLY DAYS, GROWTH AND DEVELOPMENT

When I first served with the Missions to Seamen in the port of Dublin, the Rev. Don Lewin, Senior Chaplain, had a saying which he frequently used. Whenever a trainee would appear to have come under the spell of a particular form of thinking he would plead for a fair and proper analysis of the subject by saying, 'Hasten slowly.' It is a discipline which if exercised with honesty and integrity can be of real benefit in our approach to life.

One of the short-comings in Irish national life is 'Brit Bashing'. It is almost a way of life for some people who can find no redeeming feature in the British. Here I'm not seeking to defend the overall objectives of the Empire but merely asking that we hasten slowly in our analysis of history lest through prejudice we overlook many enlightened and positive developments.

One such development in the year 1856 was the foundation of the Missions to Seamen in London, England. The Royal Navy and the British Merchant Navy encompassed a formidable share of the world's shipping fleet at this time and some today may be tempted to say that the growth and development of the Missions to Seamen was very self serving for this reason. While this claim may indeed have been true in the initial stages and to what degree I cannot be sure, nevertheless, I can vouch from personal experience that in time the Society's doors were opened to all seafarers irrespective of race, creed or colour. In my lifetime I've never known it any other way.

It is to the great credit of the Church of England and to the credit of the Churches in communion with it throughout the British Isles that foreign seafarers also found a home away from home in these isles and that the money was raised to extend this caring ministry into the ports of the world.

I was born in 1928 in the Irish Free State, later to be declared the Republic of Ireland, an Anglican by faith. I can recall how as a boy in Sunday School we were constantly reminded that as followers of Jesus Christ we had a special duty to care for the stranger in our midst. Most Church people looked forward to having a visiting preacher to tell us all about the work of the Missions to Seamen, largely because he had so much to tell us about the practical application of the Christian faith as opposed to dogma.

The visiting preacher whom we called the Deputation Secretary would not only preach but would solicit donations from individuals and parish funds. He would encourage the growth and development of vocations, Lay-workers and Chaplains to serve with the Society at home and overseas. He would seek to recruit volunteers in parishes within easy reach of the local club. Above all he would try to find a volunteer amongst the parishioners to act as Hon. Secretary and if possible form a support group in the area.

It seems difficult to believe that it was from such a humble beginning throughout the British Isles that the Society came to plant its flag in the major ports of the world. At home and overseas Chaplains and volunteers of the Society earned a reputation for caring which spread to the management of most good shipping companies, bringing forth a response in terms of financial support and assistance. Over the years the Society has acquired a host of benefactors and friends throughout the world.

Originally as the work spread overseas it came to be directed by a priest whose title was that of Superintendent, later General Secretary and finally with the grand title of Secretary General. He functions with a back up staff from a Central Office in London, England. The Superintendent or General Secretary in London acted as a sort of Director General for many years and most Chaplains at his request were posted and licensed by local Bishops world wide throughout the Anglican Communion.

Over time many provinces of the Anglican Communion overseas became of age and not unnaturally wanted to control their own affairs. In these countries the work is financed at local level and Chaplains are being appointed from the local churches, instead of being drawn from a central pool selected by a candidates committee in London of which the General Secretary is a member. Where the latter changes have already taken place the House of Bishops in these provinces usually appoint one of their number to act as liaison between Diocesan Bishops, Port Chaplains and the Central Office in London (formally known as Head Office). These changes continue to be implemented and improved upon.

The role of the former General Secretary has undergone a more radical change from that of a sort of Director General whose word was almost regarded as law to that of a liaison officer between the Bishops in whose Diocese the society is at work, Port Chaplains and the Central Office in London, though he holds the impressive title of Secretary General. Under the old system a General Secretary was not only chosen for his administrative skills but for his pastoral experience in service at home and overseas.

Another development over the years has been ecumenical collaboration and cooperation which has taken place extensively world wide. Societies or religious denominations cooperate together in service to the seafarer from under one roof. While the Roman Catholic Church only became officially involved in this work within the past eighty years or so with the foundation of the Apostleship of the Sea there were already a number of Non-Conformist Church bodies together with the Anglican Missions to Seamen operating world wide. Now in many ports, to avoid duplication and unnecessary waste, all of our resources are being pooled and we work together.

My career with the Missions to Seamen began prior to most of these latter developments and spanned the history of these changes, before the birth or independence of many nations and before modern economics began to revolutionize the shipping industry, with larger and larger ships being launched every year, manned by fewer and fewer crew, the advent of the modern container ship with a rapid turn around in port arriving and departing within hours, the registration of ships under flags of convenience to avoid taxation and the employment of crews from under developed countries for lower wages. Most of these conditions in one form or another find a place in the stories I relate.

While conditions of employment may change from one company to another, from one country to another, or serving under one flag or another there is one aspect of life which for the seafarer and his family never changes: 'separation', which every generation has to learn to cope with and endure.

What's in a Name?

What's in a name? A lot more than one would think on first hearing. This is especially true of biblical names when originally used. I suppose if one were to ask a parent why they chose that name for their child you would receive a variety of answers but most of them would have an association of one kind or another.

This question brings to mind a very funny incident which occurred before my wife and I were married. We were in the midst of marriage preparation by the parish priest who had baptized Dorothy as a baby and had known her all her life. He was very protective of her and I was a comparatively new arrival on the scene. He was determined to impress upon me the treasure which he felt I would be receiving in my future bride. Turning to me he enquired, 'Joe, do you know what Dorothy's name means?' A little humiliated, I had to confess that I did not know. 'Consider yourself a very lucky lad, for it means the gift of God,' replied the Archdeacon. Smarting a little as a result of having to declare my ignorance I thought to myself, two can play that game, so I asked, 'Archdeacon, do you know what my name means?' 'Joseph, I'm ashamed to say I don't and it's a biblical name too.' Feeling very proud of myself I replied, 'And he shall multiply.' As quick as a flash the Archdeacon replied, 'Don't tell her that now or she may never marry you at all.'

The name we choose to function under eventually acquires a meaning and a quality of its own. In the Christian sense the word 'Mission' was originally used to denote a person or a body of people 'Sent'. So the title Missions to Seamen denotes or represents a body of people commissioned by the Anglican church to share with seafarers the Good News of Jesus Christ under the emblem of the Flying Angel flag of the Missions to Seamen, an emblem inspired by a passage of scripture in the Christian bible. Chapter 14 v6 of the book of the Revelation of St. John the Divine. 'I saw another angel fly in the midst of heaven having an everlasting gospel to preach unto them that dwell upon the earth, and to every nation and kindred and people.'

I believe it's true to say that when our Missions first began the main emphasis was on preaching, a verbal proclamation of how Jesus Christ had died for the sins of the whole world and on the third day rose again from the dead to offer the gift of eternal life to all those who repent and believe in His name. While this proclamation may have made some sense to those on the periphery of the Christian faith, to most of those outside it made no sense at all, a fact which even that giant of a Christian missionary Paul had already discovered. In his first letter to the Corinthians Chapter 3 v2 he writes, 'I have fed you with milk, and not with meat: for hitherto ye were not able to bear it, neither yet now are ye able.' In this sense as we ventured out into the ports of the world in the name of Jesus Christ and saw the conditions under which many seafarers lived, our emphasis had to change to one of a proclamation of the total Good News of Jesus Christ which included His concern for man's body as well as his soul. Jesus fed the hungry, healed the sick, comforted the sorrowful, and died for all. As He once said, 'In as much as you do unto the least of these my brethren you do unto Me.'

The word mission seems to have been used down the years to describe a variety of activities. During wartime people were sent on missions of one kind or another; in today's commercial world companies produce mission statements to inform people what they are about; likewise various welfare agencies and secular bodies of one kind or another. Of course those of us with a Christian background would claim the word has its roots in early Christianity. However, even here, this word over time came to have a variety of associations, one being that it became associated with the making of instant Christians, under the influence of powerful and persuasive preachers, from whom it was difficult to escape without favouring them with a decision. Seafarers do not take to this lifestyle. Today the overwhelming majority of our Clubs are known as Flying Angel Clubs which distinguishes them for what they are, though many seafarers and Mission staff, myself included, frequently revert to the use of the word Mission to describe the Club.

In the name of Jesus Christ seafarers of every race, creed and colour are welcomed at the Flying Angel Club. While we would like to welcome everyone into membership of the Christian faith this is not obligatory to enjoy the hospitality offered there. Those who come to our Clubs and seek to become members of the Christian church must do so freely without any pressure having been applied on our part.

Chaplains head a team of volunteers who play a vital role in the life of the Society world wide. Were the Society to have to pay staff to achieve what is achieved by voluntary help, its outreach would be a fraction of what it is today. It's no overstatement to say that in whatever currency is chosen, volunteered time amounts to millions in the life of the Missions to Seamen.

In most countries, of necessity, the facilities for entertainment and other services available in a Club depend upon the funds available. Without bankrupting a Club most Chaplains continue to try and improve these. Grants are sought at local and international levels for this purpose.

An old hand at the game, I have to admit that in my experience nothing in the way of entertainment compares with providing the seafarer with an opportunity to meet, talk and socialize with those who live ashore. In my time in the Clubs where I've served we ran dances and social functions on a regular basis. These were so popular that we could never organize enough or recruit enough girls to act as hostesses.

'Give a dog a bad name and it will stick to him.' This old saying has been particularly applied to seafarers. While I suppose a bad name has been deserved in some instances nevertheless it is grossly unfair to label every seafarer thus. This label mitigated against us too as we tried to recruit hostesses. I'm not attempting to say that every seafarer is a paragon of virtue, which would not be true, but merely to say that seafarers are no different from the rest of society, having their share of good and bad points.

I could count on the fingers of two hands the number of unruly incidents involving bona-fide seafarers which took place in our Clubs during my career with the Missions to Seamen spanning over thirty years. Many, many times I have been informed by hostesses that they would much prefer to dance in our Club than in places downtown where they got fed up being propositioned by one patron after another.

DUBLIN,

THE REPUBLIC OF IRELAND

INTRODUCTION AND INITIATION

In the previous chapter I have tried to provide the reader with a condensed history of the growth and development of the Missions to Seamen. Before going any further it is incumbent upon me to say that I have no qualifications as an official historian on behalf of the Society but have written thus to enable the reader to fit us into the picture. Though I believe it is not so, nevertheless if there are any serious mistakes or omissions I must apologize. My excuse must be that like others who have served with the Missions to Seamen, the work was so totally absorbing that I never found time to devote to historic research.

I was first introduced to this Ministry during a sermon preached in our Parish Church by the Rev. Don Lewin, Senior Chaplain in the port of Dublin. The seafarer by virtue of his job had to spend long periods separated from family and friends. During the course of business I had to remain away from home, though only days at a time. This gave me a natural empathy with the seafarer who had to endure long periods of separation from loved ones, with the result that I became a volunteer at the Mission.

It was all so matter of fact at the time that I can hardly believe how our lives progressed from this point. I was extremely happily married, we were buying our own home on very favourable terms, we had two beautiful and healthy sons, in my business career I was a rising star, yet for some strange reason fulfilment seemed to elude me. My vocation lay elsewhere. Eventually after much heart searching and enormous sacrifice on the part of my wife, I resigned my business career to join the Missions to Seamen as a lay worker. Personally this move did not involve much sacrifice on my part as I would be doing what I wanted to do more than anything else with my life. On the other hand it was to be quite different for my wife. Her husband would now have to work long and irregular hours for a fraction of his previous salary (anti social hours too). We would no longer possess an automobile which was a great luxury in those days. We had to sell the interest in our own home which we were buying and move into accommodation provided by the Missions to Seamen and become birds of passage. These were but a few of the sacrifices which my wife made at this stage to enable me to pursue what I considered to be my vocation. She had married a business man but was true to her marriage vow 'for better or for worse' and stayed the course.

The first Chaplain I served with was Don Lewin who introduced me to the Missions to Seamen. As members of the Church of Ireland we shared the same philosophy, 'A house going parson makes a Church going people.' In our circumstances, it was ships we had to visit and they changed from day to day. How else was the seafarer to know that we existed unless we visited him day by day? Ship visiting was to become my rule of life throughout my career with the Missions to Seamen.

While ship visitation was always a priority, the daily ritual rarely changed. First thing upon arrival at the Club in Dublin and Belfast was to share Morning Prayer with all the staff. Indeed I can recall how the janitorial staff would await our arrival for prayers before going home. None of us thought that we were any holier for this but we all had a healthy respect for the Almighty as a power giver which most of us could use. Now the mail was opened to ensure there were no welfare cases from overseas which called for immediate attention. Ships due to be visited were then divided amongst the staff. We then had coffee together before setting out to visit the ships. This was to be my daily routine with some adjustments for over thirty years on the waterfront.

Spiritual indigestion would probably best describe my feelings the first time I went ship visiting. There welled up inside me an overwhelming sense of vocation in terms of the task in hand. What I failed to realize was that the Almighty had called Joe Parker to do this work because he was as he was. In other words all I was expected to do was dedicate myself and be myself. Instead I had already ascended cloud nine!

Don Lewin was a wise man and he handled the situation in his own unique style. He stopped the car at an entrance gate on Ringsend Road which did not look at all like where ships would berth, though there was a path which led in the direction of the waterfront. To use a nautical term Don took off walking at such a rate of knots along this path that I had difficulty keeping up with him. He became uncommunicative and kept on walking through what is described in local dialect as a knacker's yard. Strewn all over the ground was a variety of dead animal parts which stank to high heaven: guts, hoofs, hides, etc. Don moved fast while in his wake my stomach almost turned inside out. I could even feel my colour changing. The smell was so foul that after all these years I still feel like throwing up every time I recall the incident.

Breaking his silence Don turned to me and said, 'Sorry, Joe, but sometimes it's like this on the waterfront,' and then with a leap he vaulted over a wall into where a ship was berthed on the adjoining property. His ruse worked. By now I'd already come down from cloud nine. There was of course a more direct route to reach this shipping berth.

Many traditions are observed at sea. I have always felt that my initiation to ship visiting could be compared with the ceremony laid on for seafarers crossing the equator for the first time.

There was a sequel to this story which even now I also find it difficult to recall. One stormy afternoon a couple of years later Don got involved in a deep theological discussion with a Dutch seafarer on a small coaster. There was a ferocious gale blowing outside and though the little vessel was tied up alongside the quay she was being tossed about in no uncertain manner. While the cook continued to prepare the meal everyone on board had assembled in the small galley to hear the discussion. With so many of us packed into this small area, the heat, smell of cooking and the continuous swaying of the small vessel I began to feel queasy and in need of air. The top half of the galley door on this type of vessel is usually left open so I decided to tactfully make my way there for a breather. Sticking my head over the top of the door I took one deep breath and darn near died on the spot. The wind was blowing in the wrong direction and again I filled my lungs with the knacker's yard.

Céad Mile Fáilte

'*Céad mile fáilte*' . . . Translated into English it means 'A hundred thousand welcomes'. This is I understand the favoured sales promotion slogan of the Irish Tourist Board. One could not find more appropriate words to describe the nature of the welcome extended to seafarers upon arrival in the port of Dublin, where I first joined the Missions to Seamen. The Republic of Ireland is not a wealthy country and the Anglican church population is but a tiny percentage of the total population, nevertheless with help from friends and neighbours the maintenance of the Flying Angel Club was very much part of our tradition.

In those days the Flying Angel Club was located on Eden Quay. I have no idea from where the quay derived its name but it seemed appropriate that we should be located there considering our connection with the biblical Garden of Eden.

Security was always a problem

Money wasn't too plentiful in those days and a part of one's training of necessity had to include instruction on how best to fulfil the role of 'Man Friday'. Don Lewin who was responsible for my training took this business very seriously and went to great lengths to share his knowledge with me. I owe him a great debt in this respect. A lot of people roamed this Garden of Eden, the vast majority not being seafarers. 'Forbidden fruit tastes good', so we always had security problems. One had to learn how to quickly spot an intruder, i.e. a non bona-fide person who was not a seafarer. It was possible to walk straight into the club from the street yet we could not afford to employ someone exclusively to keep a check upon everyone coming through the door. Just as dogs can be trained to sniff out dope we were trained in the methods to ferret out impostors. We kept an updated list of ships in port, details of ships scheduled to arrive and time of arrival. When our suspicions were aroused we would enquire of the suspect the name of his ship? If the reply was phony and the ship was not listed we had trapped an impostor and would ask him to leave. Ever vigilant as taught, on one occasion I looked across the room at this big guy whom I had detected spoke with a local accent. Summoning up all the courage I could muster I went over to him and popped the question. 'What's the name of your ship?' Poker faced he replied, 'Hardship.' Now I moved in for the kill. 'Strange but I can't remember seeing that name on today's shipping list.' 'Is that so?' he said with a broad grin on his face and stood his ground. Hardship, I thought, what a strange name for a ship. It was then that the penny dropped. A new hand on the job, he could not resist the temptation to pull my leg. He was of course a bona-fide seafarer.

All sorts and conditions of men

We will call him John Joe (not his real name). He was a frequent visitor to the Flying Angel Club in Dublin. John Joe had a problem in that he lifted the elbow a bit too frequently and however hard we tried to work on him we met with little success save that we retained his friendship. One evening following closing time in the local pubs John Joe struggled through the door of the club very unsteady on his feet, a danger to nobody but himself. In his sober moments he was quite an entertainer and something of a wit. He had no teeth and had a very long nose; one of his favourite turns was to create the most extraordinary shapes with his mouth. On this occasion with quite a struggle he made it to the centre of the lobby and began in a mindless fashion to make these extraordinary shapes with his mouth while he slowly tilted his head upwards to the floor above from where he could hear the noise of dancing. Suddenly the plaster on the ceiling came tumbling down on the open mouthed John Joe. His face was a study at this moment as he tried to analyze why this had occurred. Was it a message about heaven or a warning about hell? Yet, for all his problems with the booze, John Joe would not harm a fly and was kindness personified. He was a truly lovable character though somewhat unorthodox, to say the least.

Heart to Heart

As I mounted the gangway of this rust covered deep sea ship I met the local agent on his way down. He said to me, 'You're wasting your time here; I think they are all followers of Buddha.' He then showed me a number of pictures of Buddha which had been given him on board. I replied with the one liner we used on these occasions, 'Whatever they are they will be welcome at our place.'

On board I could not find a single person who could speak English so the only thing I could do in the circumstances was to saturate the place with copies of our map/brochure in the hope that someone would translate for everybody.

The next day was Sunday and as we were about to enter Chapel for the morning service of Holy Communion a taxi drew up at the front door of the club and though it was mid winter, out stepped a gentleman magnificently dressed in a sky blue suit. He turned out to be the Chief Engineer who had come to join us for service. He spoke pidgin English which he had learned during the voyage. We understood from him that the Captain could read and write English, but had difficulty speaking the language. They were all from mainland China but owing to the political upheaval they had re-settled in Taiwan.

We Anglicans share a common cup at the Holy Communion. It is customary for us to receive the sacrament in both kinds (bread and wine) kneeling before the Altar at the communion rail. The Chief joined us kneeling before the Altar and all went well until he drank the almost full Chalice of consecrated wine instead of taking a sip from it. Tactfully the Chaplain consecrated more wine and the remainder of the congregation was communicated. The Chief was not unmoved by this experience, as we shall learn later, though I should add we never found out to what Christian denomination he belonged.

When the Chief got back on board ship having checked the place out he obviously made a good report to everyone, as from this time forth until the ship sailed our club became their most attractive place to visit ashore, home away from home. I will always remember the generosity of individual members of the crew to each one of us; almost daily they would arrive with gifts of one kind or another to the point that we became embarrassed in the face of such generosity.

It did not end here. A special dinner party was arranged on board for everyone associated with the Mission, and with genuine Chinese food on the menu everyone attended. A very funny incident occurred during the evening which is worth repeating. Through the bush telegraph one of the local papers heard about the party and sent a photographer along to take a picture. The nautical background on the ship's bridge appealed to him and with the permission of the Captain he settled for this spot. Over the years many folk directing seafarers to the Flying Angel Club would say, 'Close to the bridge,' (meaning O'Connell Bridge, almost centre of the city where most buses stopped). When the word bridge was mentioned a number of the crew immediately grabbed a coat and headed down the gangway for O'Connell Bridge until someone explained the confusion. They wanted to be sure that they were in the picture.

We were so touched by the trouble taken to entertain and feed us on board that it was agreed to do something special to return their hospitality before their ship sailed. We made enquiries and found that the ship was scheduled to put to sea after midnight. That afternoon we took as many of the crew as were available on a tour of the Dublin mountains in a fleet of cars. We returned to the Club for a typical Irish meal of bacon, cabbage and potatoes.

The night in question happened to be one of our regular dance nights which was particularly fortunate in that we went from the meal to the dance. Just before the conclusion of the dance, out stepped the Chief onto the floor and signalled for silence. He began by saying something like this in his pidgin English. 'We very sorry, no ready... tomorrow you get...' and now with a hand upon his chest went on to say obviously with all the sincerity he could muster, 'from our hearts to your hearts' and handed Padre Lewin a small docket to pick up a present from a local jeweller's next day.

Our custom was to end the day with family prayers in Church when we also commended to Almighty God's gracious keeping all those who go down to the sea in ships. They joined us for the occasion as they had done while in port knowing that tomorrow when they themselves were at sea we would be remembering them.

What was this mysterious gift 'from our hearts to your hearts'? By morning our curiosity was insatiable – we had to know the answer. An early visit to the jeweller satisfied our curiosity. It turned to be a large Challenge Cup with two handles. Obviously the Chief had persuaded his shipmates that our Chalice was far too small and it needed handles for a good grip if you were going to take a good sip!

LASTING IMPRESSIONS

My father died when I was very young and I've no idea what he looked like apart from images gleaned from photographs and what my mother said about him. So my mother was my only parent and guardian to whom I owe the foundation of my faith. She had an extraordinary sense of duty and was totally dedicated to doing what she believed to be right. She was a committed member of the Anglican church and though long since dead, even to this day her example continues to have an extraordinary influence over my life.

It's been said that the cradle of Christianity is a mother's knee and how very true. In my wife I was fortunate to have found a fellow traveller with my mother, and having set out upon a new course in life we were agreed upon the direction we should take. On this journey I would meet others who would also make a lasting impression.

A giant of a man

A giant in the faith, he was about four feet nothing in height and a voluntary worker at the Flying Angel Club in the port of Dublin. He was described as a totally insignificant person by some people who did not know any better, but was always available to lend a helping hand even if it caused personal inconvenience. Anything that needed doing to forward the aims of the Missions to Seamen he was first to quietly volunteer.

Small in stature he took a fair ribbing from acquaintances, yet he was incapable of a hasty word or a nasty deed when in the eyes of many he might well have been justified to reply in kind but this was not his style. Every Sunday he operated the film projector and fulfilled a host of other jobs between times. He also played in the Mission band. Though no genius when it came to musical talent nevertheless what he had he had to share. In his spare time he taught poor boys to play the piano accordion who could not afford to pay a tutor. I do believe our little giant saw the face of Jesus in everyone who approached. 'In as much as you do it unto the least of these my brethren you do it unto Me.' (The words of Jesus.)

Another servant of all

These were formative years for me as I entered into a lifetime of service with the Missions to Seamen. The Most Rev. Dr G.O. Simms as Archbishop of Dublin was President of the Missions to Seamen in Dublin. A renowned scholar during his lifetime he was probably the greatest living authority on the world famous *Book of Kells*, a bound illuminated biblical manuscript which is preserved in the library of Trinity College, Dublin where it can be viewed today.

Whenever I celebrated Christmas during my career with the Missions to Seamen I recalled my first Christmas with the Society. Before sitting down to dinner with them the fragile figure of the Archbishop in his purple cassock could be seen as he mingled with our seafaring guests drawn from many nations, differing creeds and colour. Something of a linguist, he attempted to communicate with all, most certainly making everyone feel welcome.

Years later while serving on the other side of the world I met a seafarer who had been present on this occasion. He expressed his profound appreciation of the Archbishop's visit. He was deeply impressed by the fact that an Archbishop with the many demands of his office and a wife and family could still make time to spend with strangers on Christmas Day. 'I had never seen it like this before nor since, have you?' I felt bound to reply, 'Nor me either.'

The Archbishop's pastoral concern for the welfare of seafarers has remained with me throughout my life. Whatever the circumstances I can still hear him say, 'Yes, yes, but we must not forget.'

Later I began to have problems vocation wise and needed someone to talk to for guidance. Unappreciative of his enormous responsibilities and the demands made upon his time I troubled him much in those days. He never complained and was always patient and kind. People were people in his eyes and the bureaucracy never prevented him from being a true 'Father in God'.

Christmas in Dublin all those years ago and the tragic sequel which was to follow

First impressions of a new and important experience usually stay with us for life. Though I had been ship visiting for a good portion of the day, unlike the seafarer I would still be able to spend time with my family and sleep in my own home. By contrast the seafarer when he went ashore was a stranger in a strange land surrounded by closed doors, behind which families celebrated as he would have done were he at home. This was a day more than any other when I felt the Flying Angel should be active: on this day especially when we recall that there was no room in the Inn.

We served dinner in the evening. A member of staff or a volunteer sat at the head of each banquet table. We had just taken our seats when a man one side of me was called to the telephone. He had booked a call to his family in Finland which came through at this very moment. When he returned his eyes were very bright as he proceeded to tell us in great detail about the celebrations in his home, the presents his children had received and their reaction. Nobody had the heart to say stop as he went on and on so this conversation occupied our mealtime.

We had arranged a social evening of dancing and games to follow dinner. Our Finnish friend turned out to be the Chief Radio Officer on a large freighter chartered to transport coal from the USA to the Republic of Ireland. A professional musician before his change of career, he played both the oboe and the saxophone. For this evening he had volunteered his services to play with the Mission band and had brought his instruments along with him.

The Chief's performance won such wide acclaim during the dance which followed dinner that we were inundated with requests that he be invited to join the band for the dance scheduled for the next evening. Padre Lewin asked me to call on board ship and invite him to play again. I knocked upon his cabin door, waited a long time and as I was about to walk away he opened the door wearing a dressing gown. He apologized for the delay in responding to my knock by explaining that he had been dressing his leg when I knocked. He then showed me his leg and other areas of his body, all of which looked very sore and and angry. He went on to say that he was suffering from melanoma and intended to go on working for as long as possible to support his wife and young family. I tried to persuade him to forget all about the dance that evening but he would not be persuaded, insisting that he would be present to make his contribution. I informed Padre Lewin about his condition upon my return to the Mission but neither of us realized how seriously ill he was at the time.

Traffic on the waterfront rarely changes but on this occasion there was a significant change. We noticed in the distance as we drove towards a ship which looked familiar that there was a hearse (funeral car) parked alongside on the quay. It was our friend the Chief's ship and the hearse was waiting to take his body ashore as he had died at sea towards the latter part of the voyage.

It might as well have been one of the family who had died for we had shared so much together on his last Christmas in this world. Padre Lewin working in unison with the local shipping agents made arrangements for the widow to travel from Finland for the funeral and burial which it had been agreed would take place in Dublin. It was arranged for a Lutheran pastor from Finland to travel over from London to conduct the funeral service in the Mission Chapel and officiate at the grave-side. The burial took place in the Missions to Seamen's plot in a local cemetery. The final scene is one I'm unlikely to forget. At the graveside when the casket had been lowered into the grave the widow stepped forward to the graveside and after a prolonged search in her purse during which time she seemed to take out everything but what she was looking for she withdrew the object of her search: a small packet covered in white tissue paper which contained Finnish soil which she then sprinkled on the casket. The only woman present, she was surrounded by her late husband's shipmates, local agents and Missions to Seamen personnel. There was not a dry eye amongst those who witnessed this scene.

We were privileged to have shared this Christmas with our departed friend, if for no other reason than to be able to inform his wife of this happy time together and how much he had contributed to the happiness of others.

These days made a lasting impression
I recall another occasion when the Chaplain was not available and I had to visit a home to inform a wife that her husband was missing, not having returned on board ship the previous night where his ship was docked in France.

She had a young family and very bravely kept up a front for their sake, no doubt hoping and praying that I would return next day with better news but alas it was not to be.

Next day I had to return the bearer of sad tidings. When the ship moved out from its berth and as it was about to sail his body surfaced from beneath the ship, he having been drowned by accident obviously having fallen into the water upon his return from being ashore.

On this occasion the mother broke down and cried. One of her little boys, very protective of Mum, walked across the room to where I was sitting and kicked me on the shins for making his Mum cry.

These were early days in my ministry with the Missions to Seamen but they were of such significance that I knew in my heart that it was in this ministry I wanted to be. I didn't keep a log in those days but these years of training confirmed where my future would lie.

INTERLUDE

Though convinced that my vocation lay with the Missions to Seamen yet in a sense I still felt incomplete working as a layman. I enjoyed an excellent relationship with the Chaplains with whom I worked but somehow felt I was unable to reach my full potential and was in the need of further training.

Before joining the Missions to Seamen I had contemplated taking Holy Orders but was reluctant to proceed for a few reasons. Academically I had some doubt about my ability to make it and the thought of having to begin study all over again did not appeal to me. A commitment to ordination according to my tradition had to be for life. When the vacancy occurred at the Missions to Seamen for a lay-worker at the time this had seemed to be exactly what I had been waiting for but now I felt that something more was required of me.

I had attended a series of lectures at Trinity College, Dublin for a Diploma in Biblical Studies before I joined the Missions to Seamen but never sat the examination. I needed someone who would be capable of analyzing my feelings and help me find a sense of direction. The obvious choice was the Bishop of the Diocese, Archbishop Simms, who was also President of the Missions to Seamen. Having bared my soul to the Archbishop who was a good listener and was both sympathetic and kind, he suggested that we move one step at a time. First I was to study for and sit the examination for the Diploma in Biblical Studies. He appointed someone to direct my studies, which to my surprise I passed with distinction. This exercise helped rid me of the underlying fear of having to return to study in preparation for ordination.

The Archbishop felt I had a call to the Priesthood and nominated me for training at Trinity College, Dublin as an Extern Student in Theology. Now we faced problems of another kind. I had a wife and two sons to support. We would have nowhere to live while I pursued my studies and I would be required to terminate all connection with the Missions to Seamen for two years following ordination.

How often had I heard that saying when the odds seem to be stacked against us: 'Where there is a will there is a way.' Between them, my wife and the Missions to Seamen had the will and found the way. The headquarters of the Missions to Seamen in London, England and the local branch of the Society in Dublin permitted me to remain with the Society and serve on a part time basis in the port of Dublin and we were permitted to remain on in the Mission house. Dorothy took in boarders to make good the further loss we had suffered in income in addition to caring for the children.

I worked full time with the Mission during vacation times and Sundays only during term. I was required to live a communal life away from home Monday to Friday at the Divinity Hostel during term with other students. This was particularly hard on my wife as the only evening we could count upon being together was Saturday.

These were difficult years and to add to our problems Dorothy discovered that she was pregnant. Our difficulties did not end here for Dorothy developed toxaemia and had to be hospitalized for ten weeks before the birth of our daughter. My mother came to the rescue to keep house and look after our two boys. I was released from the obligation to live in the Divinity Hostel, to assist my mother. Our cash reserve was nil by now but when I enquired of the hospital how much we owed them a pleasant surprise awaited me. Some anonymous and kind person had already paid our account in full. To this day we have no idea who our kind benefactor was.

Looking back over those years we sometimes laugh about some of the circumstances in which we found ourselves, though we did not laugh at the time. As I said earlier, money was a scarce commodity as we reached our final goal. In terms of clothes and vestments I could almost have claimed to have been a reincarnation on the day of my ordination but this did not concern us too much. God had been good and we made it through the wilderness.

It was mandatory that all newly ordained clergy had to spend the first two years of their ministry in a parish before we could enter a specialized ministry. The Missions to Seamen in the port of Dublin had become so much a part of my life that I feared it would be very difficult for me to serve in a Dublin parish and have loyalty to a parish so close to the waterfront. My heart would be in the port and my loyalty divided. I decided to make my feelings known to Archbishop Simms and he completely understood. He recommended that I should make a clean break with the Diocese of Dublin and commence my ordained ministry in Northern Ireland.

I had about ten days vacation immediately following my ordination, my first in over two years, during which time we made the rounds of friends

Kneeling, the Rev. J.D. Parker is ordained in St. Molua's Church, Belfast.

and relations and did those things that required doing before moving away on what looked like a permanent basis. A pleasant get together organized before our departure was to attend a function at the Missions to Seamen at which we received the gift of a handsome cheque which was a tremendous help during the lean days before I would receive my first salary. As I was their first married Curate Assistant the parish purchased a house where we would live. Though I had a wife and three children I was paid the same stipend as a single man but in those early days for married Assistants to be provided with a house was considered a real perk. I travelled ahead of Dorothy to Belfast to await the arrival of our furniture from Dublin.

In some respects there is the world of difference between Northern Ireland, which is part of the United Kingdom, and the Republic of Ireland. Protestant religious groups take pride in proclaiming the word of God by reproducing passages of Scripture on the gable ends of houses, bill boards and other vantage points to ensure that some will take note and hopefully act upon it. When Dorothy arrived in Victoria Station, Belfast, accompanied by the children and put her head out of the window she got a bit of a surprise. There to greet her on a bill board were the words 'PREPARE TO MEET THY GOD'. This was a surprise; she wasn't quite sure where she had landed.

Over the next two years I was to serve as a Curate Assistant in a large semi-industrial parish in east Belfast within sight of the famous Harland and Wolff shipyards. We received a wonderful welcome as a family and always during the course of parish visiting and social functions we were made to feel quite at home. A number of the men worked in the shipyards and quite a few were former seafarers who with my background I was always glad to meet. My special responsibility was to look after the youth who congregated in great numbers around the parish Church and Parochial Hall. They were a most responsive and enthusiastic group of young people from whom I too learned much.

Many times as I look back over life and the way things have planned out, I am reminded of the opening words of a hymn: 'Thy hand, O God, has guided Thy flock, from age to age.' One busy evening in the Parochial Hall I became aware of the presence of a man who seemed to be watching my every move. I had no idea who he was but finally my curiosity got the better of me and I decided to do a little probing by tactfully asking a few questions. When it looked as if I was about to strike oil he turned to me and said, 'I'm a member of the local committee of the Missions to Seamen in Belfast. Our Chaplain was posted overseas some time ago and we're having difficulty replacing him and we have decided to talk to you if you're interested.' I informed him that I had yet to complete my mandatory two years in the parochial ministry and that my Bishop would probably throw a fit at the idea if I were even to approach him. He insisted that at very least I should agree to meet with the committee.

I concluded as a matter of courtesy that nothing would be lost by my agreeing to meet the committee. When we met I was informed that I filled the profile of the type of person for whom they had been looking. 'Subject to the agreement of our respective Diocesan Bishops as far as we are concerned the position is yours. Talk to your Bishop and then come back to see us.'

I was interested all right as I felt the Missions to Seamen was in my blood. I had known about the vacancy but had not entertained the thought of applying as I considered it might be too soon after ordination. However I did as the Committee had suggested and made an appointment to see my Diocesan Bishop. He did not throw a fit as I had expected but went through every aspect of the position in great detail. He had an intimate knowledge of the working of the Mission which quite frankly amazed me for someone who had never served in the Missions to Seamen. 'I want you to go home now and over the next three weeks think and pray about the various aspects we have discussed and then come and see me again.' Returning three weeks later having done as he had suggested, when we sat down he asked, 'Now tell me how you feel.' He did not bat an eyelid when I replied. 'If I don't agree to go when I'm free to do so then I believe I would be running away from what I should do with my life.' 'I will be very sorry to lose you from the Diocese but if this is how you feel I believe you must return to the Missions to Seamen.' Somehow I was not surprised by what the Bishop had said as deep down within me this is where I felt that I belonged. 'You will go with my blessing immediately you have completed your mandatory period in parochial life.'

In passing I should say that the first Rector under whom I served in the parochial ministry only lasted a week or two, though I hasten to add it was not because he wanted to get away from me but due to the fact that he was appointed to another parish. I was left on my own in this large and busy parish for several months before his successor was appointed. When news reached me of the appointment of his successor and that he was a member of the Orange Order, with my Southern Irish background I very nearly had a heart attack on the spot. I looked forward to the date of his institution with fear and trepidation. I need not have worried for I have yet to meet a more faithful pastor or a more efficient administrator. Once again I had been blessed by having someone of his calibre to instruct me at this crucial time in my life and to this day I'm grateful for the many things he taught me. In those days it used to be said that no matter what you did as a Curate it helped to keep in with the Rector's wife as you never knew when you might need a friend in court to plead your cause with 'Old Man' Rector. In this household one did not have to try very hard for the Rector's wife was a lovely lady and kindness personified. She made the most wonderful coffee cake I have ever tasted. Attendance at all staff meetings was always 100 per cent in the hope that this cake would be served with coffee.

BELFAST,

NORTHERN IRELAND

BACK IN HARNESS

When I returned to the Missions to Seamen in Belfast as Senior Chaplain there was probably nobody more surprised than myself. Belfast had a great tradition of service and my predecessor was held in very high esteem. I had very big shoes to fill.

On the other hand I had not gone out of my way to seek this appointment; if anything the Society had sought me rather than me seeking them. I recalled a message given to us by the Priest who conducted our pre-ordination retreat. Some of us were getting a little jittery and feeling inadequate as the big day approached which would commit us for life. He took the matter in hand. 'If Almighty God did not want you here now you would not be here,' he said. This assumption I felt was equally valid in the present circumstances. My heart and soul belonged to the Missions to Seamen so why not return now? So having contemplated my appointment in depth I came to terms with my fears. As St. Paul would have said, 'One plants, another waters but God gives the increase.' God required of each one of us to build upon the foundation of those who had gone before. I had no difficulty with this philosophy and could soon get on with the job.

Achieving this goal so soon after ordination seemed to vindicate the years of struggle that went before, especially for my wife. Now infinitely more relaxed she could get on with the business of living more freely and raising her family while, more adequately qualified, I could get on with the business of fulfilling my vocation. Our faith had been well tested of recent years, life had not been plain sailing but God had not failed us. To go forward in faith we could look back with confidence.

The City of Belfast had continued to grow in the years prior to my appointment and traffic congestion in some areas had become something of a nightmare. My predecessor had found it impossible to respond quickly to emergency calls from his home. This was considered a serious development: shipping forecasts envisaged a much faster turn around in port arrivals and departures on the same day with the development of a container trade. My predecessor had advised the local committee of this difficulty and of future shipping forecasts and counselled that a new residence unaffected by this problem should be purchased for his successor.

We as a family were given the privilege of selecting the new residence.

*Impressive mural painted by the late Raymond Piper in the Chapel of the
Flying Angel Club, Belfast. Note: Harvest Thanksgiving.*

We chose a beautiful family home in a quiet residential district surrounded
by a small lawn (yard in Canada) front and rear. During peak traffic
conditions it took twenty minutes by car to reach the port without breaking
the speed limit and at night even less when there was little traffic on the
road. In those days it was considered a must for a Priest to reside in close
proximity to those to whom he was called to minister.

The Flying Angel Club in Belfast was a modern well appointed club and
housed one of the most beautiful little Chapels I have ever seen. A special
feature of this Chapel was a mural painted on the wall immediately behind
the Altar by Raymond Piper, a local artist. This mural had a powerful
message and lent atmosphere to the little Church: Christ the light of the
world. It depicted the consummation of all things when one day the sea
would give up its dead and the representatives of all races would be drawn
towards the Christ the light of the world. The club was furnished in
excellent taste and reflected throughout the genuine care and concern of the
people of Northern Ireland for the stranger in their midst, a living witness
to their Christian concern. I had entered into a noble tradition. My
predecessor had been a man of substance too.

Belfast is legendary in the annals of history for its ship building industry.

In the yards of Harland and Wolff many of the world's famous vessels were built including the ill-fated *Titanic*. Throughout the province of Northern Ireland there were few families who did not have either a relative or a friend employed at sea. The population in general knew all about the lonely life of the seafarer, a stranger in every port but his own. Many had grown up with a natural empathy for the seafarer and knew what the work of the Missions to Seamen was all about. They were generous in their financial support of the Mission and many were willing volunteer helpers in the club.

I was fortunate to have succeeded in office one who had a number of years experience as a Chaplain serving both at home and overseas. He was the Senior Chaplain when the present club was designed and built and his experience and input were reflected throughout. The words of the Rev. Don Lewin with whom I had trained came to mind when I first contemplated how I would set about exercising my new responsibilities: 'Hasten slowly,' Don would have said and this I resolved to do, save in those areas where as a former businessman I felt more qualified to lead.

In his final address to the Annual General Meeting of the Society my predecessor had said, 'In my work here in Northern Ireland I have two duties, firstly the Chaplaincy of the port of Belfast and secondly the organizing work. It is difficult to divide one's time adequately between the two sides of the work.' The organizing work of which he spoke had to do with promoting the aims of the Society and with fund raising. The year in question had ended with a deficit of £1,100 as indicated on the income and expenditure section of the audited statement of accounts. I fully sympathized with the sentiment expressed by my predecessor but as a new broom with a degree of experience in administration acquired during my business career I felt the situation called for a new approach. It seemed to me that responsibility for much of the organizing work could be delegated for others to carry out on a day to day basis while I retained oversight. Our local committee was in full agreement and assured me of their full support.

Our reorganization in this area was timely. Mr John W. Bull, a senior inspector with the Board of Trade who had just retired, offered his services to the Mission free of charge on a part-time basis. A former ship's Chief Engineer, there was little we could tell him about seafaring. In an instant he became our Public Appeals Organizer with responsibility for organizing flag days and house to house collections throughout the province. His efforts met with immediate success and before finally deciding to take his full retirement he had laid a foundation upon which others would build.

Another volunteer and a former student helper in the Mission, Mr

Sidney Stewart, a graduate of Trinity College, Dublin and a licensed Lay
Reader in the Church of Ireland, volunteered his services to preach on our
behalf in parish churches. This meant that Church people throughout the
province were constantly being informed about our work. He was later
joined by Denis Trueman, also a licensed Lay Reader who was paid a small
honorarium. He had taken over responsibility for public appeals when John
Bull finally decided to take his full retirement.

One of my god-parents was named Dorothy, I married a Dorothy and
right now up comes another Dorothy, willing and ready to take a great
load off my shoulders. It seems no matter where I go, Dorothys always
bring blessings into my life. I met Dorothy Gunning soon after I returned
to the Missions to Seamen in Belfast. Her husband who had been
Treasurer of the Mission for a number of years had just died. Their Rector,
a great family friend, was overseas and was not available to officiate at the
funeral service so I was asked to take his place. In addition my wife had
been at school with their daughter. Their son was an executive officer in
the Royal Navy and all of the family were dedicated supporters of the
Missions to Seamen.

Now, with the passing of her husband, Dorothy Gunning had time on
her hands and that time unreservedly became the time of the Missions to
Seamen. She had few equals and anybody who has ever worked with her
will bear me out when I say that her enthusiasm and dedication were
incomparable. Utterly reliable, her word was her bond. A model of
kindness, whatever she said she would do, she always did. Before my return
to the Missions to Seamen, an organization was founded in England to
develop support groups at parish level throughout the country. It was called
the Flying Angel League. Dorothy liked the idea and with the permission of
my predecessor formed a central group in the City of Belfast encompassing
people from several parishes. In terms of a fundraiser it was an immediate
success.

When I arrived on the scene and having reviewed all of our fundraising
efforts, I could not help but feel that the original concept of local groups in
parishes throughout the country had a much greater potential than that of a
central group. I discussed this idea with Dorothy, suggesting that the
members in the existing central group would make excellent leaders in the
former connection. I had in mind that as Secretary she should have overall
responsibility for the League's growth and development within this new
framework. She promised to think about this suggestion and report back to
me. Subsequently she agreed that this was the route to go. In her capable

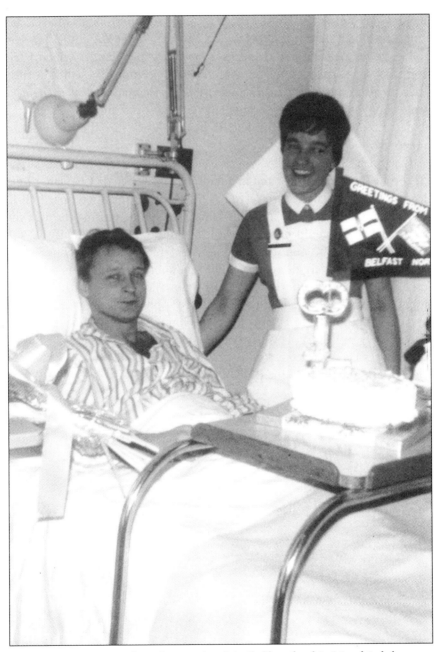

An East German seafarer hospitalized in Belfast for his 21st birthday was not forgotten by the late Dorothy Gunning who made the cake, which was accompanied by other gifts.

hands I was convinced that the League would go from strength which it did and contributed substantially towards the welfare of the Society.

I have related in some detail as a new boy the changes which I felt confident to make in my approach to this new position. These had as their base my prior experience in administration. Apart from one other change I was happy to go along with whatever had been introduced by my experienced predecessor until I could be absolutely sure that I should do otherwise.

One other change I wished to make and did. My predecessor was a man of considerable experience and in addition to being Senior Chaplain of the Missions to Seamen, he also served as the RNR Chaplain on board HMS *Caroline* in Belfast. Knowing the volume of shipping passing through the port I felt that I could not cope with this additional duty. I felt that my primary duty was to minister to full time seafarers in the Merchant Service and sea going military personnel. While no doubt RNR members fulfilled a useful role, they were nevertheless part-time sailors who went home most nights. The RN Chaplain of the Fleet fully appreciated my point of view and arranged for me to be appointed an Hon. Officiating Minister for the Royal Navy in Belfast. This gave me clearance to minister on board to all military vessels visiting the port. It also opened the door for one of the local clergy to be appointed to the RNR.

DOWN TO BUSINESS

One thing will become evident as the reader progresses through this book – the essence of our Ministry is to care, to be where the seafarer is in need and to do all we can to help, using the resources at our disposal. It is folly to think we can help in every circumstance for that would be impossible but we have need to become good stewards of the resources at our disposal.

The work varies from one country to another. In Northern Ireland in addition to the daily volume of deep sea ships using the port we had a large volume of coastal traffic (small ships trading between European ports), Royal Navy and other military vessels, major shipyards engaged in building and repair programmes, with crews living on board ships from time to time, and a Ministry to the families of seafarers residing throughout the province. Essentially we were the link between those ashore and those at sea. This section of *On the Waterfront* reflects life as I encountered it in the port of Belfast, Northern Ireland. The stories and incidents are authentic.

We met John, a first tripper on board ship, a small coaster. He had only been away from home three days. It takes a little time for these boys to settle down to a whole new way of life and frequently they are very lonely though one is not suppose to notice the signs. I invited John to visit the club when he was free to go ashore. I was not on duty myself but next day there was a report awaiting me. John did visit the club and the lady-hostess on duty soon took him under her wing and he did enjoy himself. John was only fifteen years of age and I understand he drank eight cups of coffee during the evening, on each occasion putting three pence in the Mission donation box.

I have said earlier that the Chapel in the Belfast Mission in those days was simply magnificent to look upon and had a very powerful atmosphere; here one felt oneself to be in the house of God. On one wall there was a memorial plaque which commemorated the lives of a number of lady volunteers of the Mission who lost their lives when their car plunged into the Pollock Dock during the second world war. They were part of a team from the Mission who ran a canteen for seafarers engaged on the infamous North Atlantic convoy. On Remembrance Sunday as we placed a wreath at this plaque it always brought to mind the immeasurable contribution ladies have given to seafarers over many years. The story which follows illustrates this great gift as it has been handed down from generation to generation.

The West German frigate *Scharnhorst* arrived for dry-docking. This was highly unusual as we did not normally have German military vessels dry-docking in Belfast. I remember asking why at the time but for the life of me I cannot now remember the reason. I believe it was something to do with the NATO alliance. It was estimated the ship would be with us for three months.

One officer made a translation from English into German of our brochure, a copy for each mess. Alan Jones, our Lay Worker, upon learning that they would have a prolonged stay in port booked a football pitch for their use one day weekly and arranged in advance a number of challenge games with local clubs.

There's an old Irish saying very apt in these circumstances: 'It never rains but it pours.' Within five days of their arrival the *Scharnhorst* was joined in the port by the tenders *Lahn* and *Nectar* who were paying a courtesy visit to the City of Belfast.

Worldwide I feel sure the Royal Navy has few equals when it comes to arranging hospitality programmes for visiting foreign naval vessels. A Liaison Officer usually contacts all shore based organizations whom he considers likely to offer hospitality and drafts a programme. This is no last minute face saver but usually takes place in advance of the arrival of the ship or ships in question. Organizations like the Missions to Seamen are thus given plenty of time to plan a programme in advance which can be infinitely more successful.

The Flying Angel Club in Belfast, thanks to the vision of my predecessor, was fully equipped to offer hospitality on a grand scale. We had a magnificent recreation hall with a fully equipped stage and a maple floor for dancing. Given advance notice of the arrival of these vessels by the Royal Navy Liaison Officer we had plenty of time for advance planning and could pull out many stops which would otherwise have remained closed. We invited the German Lutheran Pastor in Belfast to participate and he managed to bring with him many German speaking people from his congregation including a number of young ladies to join with our hostesses for dancing. One hundred and eighty six ships' personnel joined us for the occasion.

We had an age old custom whereby we always closed the day with a brief service in Church (family prayers). All may, but none must attend. The Pastor spoke both English and German. Together we drafted a brief service for the occasion in English and German. We sang two hymns. It was altogether a memorable occasion.

Of course all the other facilities in the club were also made available to our guests during their stay.

Here follows a brief extract from a letter thanking us for our hospitality.

> I wish to express my cordial thanks for your kind invitation into your home. My comrades and I enjoyed this evening in the Missions to Seamen and as spokesman for my comrades I say many thanks for your hospitality.

The memorial in our Chapel to which I have already referred spoke of a tragic past; the hospitality extended to these young German seafarers quietly spoke of forgiveness and continuity in service.

The weekend following the departure of *Lahn* and *Nectar*, three British submarines arrived in port: HMS *Orpheus*, HMS *Otter* and HMS *Walrus*. They had interrupted their exercise programme at sea for a very special reason. Sir Winston Churchill, Britain's wartime leader, had died during the week. Their Commander requested that I took their service of morning prayer on the quay-side to include a special thanksgiving for the life and witness of this great historic figure. Two hundred and one persons from the three submarines participated. Within one week my life had touched upon those who had gone before and after this terrible worldwide conflict. Pray God it may never happen again and that all of us will prove worthy of peace bought at such cost in human life to both sides.

In a sense every day is Christmas Day at the Flying Angel Club

Round the Christmas season most people spare a thought for the other fellow, though not all as this story illustrates.

It was Christmas Eve when a tiny coaster quietly entered the port of Belfast. The crew were famished as they had no food on board, only drinking water to keep body and soul alive. Over the Christmas season and for the next three months our place became their home away from home and many of our volunteers quietly helped others to keep their larder replenished.

These men had not received any wages for over three months. When their case had been fully documented the shipping authorities through the courts had the vessel arrested for the non payment of wages. The longshoremen's union weighed in with moral support and appealed to the general public to assist these men: victims of such terrible injustice. There was a tremendous response to this appeal from the public at large. Eventually the vessel was sold and the crew compensated; some of them were permitted to return home immediately while others had to stand by for the hand over to the new owners.

When I was a young boy, like many of my peers I kept an autograph book. The conclusion of this story has always reminded me of one entry in this book, 'The poor at giving have always won for giving is what they have always done.' One of the first things those who remained on board did was to throw a party to say thanks to their friends at the Mission amongst others.

In the forefront

The enormous bulk carriers and tankers which in time would become a familiar sight in the major ports of the world were at this time being designed, constructed and launched in the Harland and Wolff shipyards in the midst of fierce competition from the growing ship building industry in Japan. One such vessel of over 90,000 tons, a first of her kind, remains firmly fixed in my mind as we had such a lot to do with her crew as they took up residence on board and completed sea trials in and out of port to return about one year later for guarantee dry-docking. After their departure we received one of the most beautiful letters to say thanks for hospitality that I have ever received. Another followed in the wake of their second visit.

The Captain, Chief Officer and Chief Engineer were the first to arrive and as the building programme progressed they were joined by others until eventually the full complement took up residence on board. Our club became the place to relax ashore, a sort of home away from home, also providing entertainment and hospitality with no strings attached. All on board came from Italy and were openly appreciative of the club and everything our volunteers tried to do to make their stay both happy and enjoyable.

Following is a copy of that most beautiful letter about which I've already written.

> As you know it is not easy for me to express myself as I want, but as I can and how can I say to you our emotion, this deep ineffable sensation of gratitude to you, to all the staff, to all the hostesses that succeed to give us the best serene entertainment in Belfast. How can we forget lights, music, smiles, colours, here when in the night the wheelhouse is in darkness and only the Quartermaster's face is lighted by the reflection of the gyro's lamp

and the sky is all shining of stars dust. It is a magic harmony, all it is a touching souvenir of Belfast. The Church, your prayers, your songs for us seafarers, your voices, the mural painting that touched me to the bottom of my soul and I can't forget, for ever, all, all of you. We thank you, all the Mission, with all of our heart, God bless you.

Yours sincerely.

A year or so later they were to return again when the ship entered dry-dock for its guarantee services.

A local parish, supporters of the Missions to Seamen, decided to donate a mini bus to us which had been in service overseas but had hardly been used. I heard about the offer through the Society's head office in London and mentioned it to the Rector of this parish. The parish responded and we received this generous gift. I decided our Italian friends must be the first to have a tour in this vehicle. We would take the Antrim Coast Road including the Giant's Causeway, one of the most scenic tours in Northern Ireland, and I would do the driving myself. The tour was an unqualified success but when I returned home my wife enquired, 'What have you done with your voice, you sound strange, a kind of husky but quite different from ever before?' I won't go into the medical details of what followed; it suffices here for me to say that I was diagnosed as suffering from a haemorrhage in my vocal cords and it was prescribed that I should not use my voice for three weeks. Otherwise I was in perfect health.

I did not feel like sitting around and doing nothing for three weeks. It was not virtue but a feeling that I might get depressed hanging around so I purchased a slate and a packet of chalk and thus equipped decided to get on with my job.

Our Italian friends decided to throw a party on board ship for all of their friends at the Mission before sailing and I was invited. Italians are very excitable people. Every time they wished to communicate with me they would grab my slate to write everything down as if I was also deaf and could not hear. They had a bit of a scrum down between themselves for the slate, each feeling that what he had to say was more important than the other fellow. Soon I did not know whether it was them or me who needed the slate most. I resisted the temptation to shout, 'I can hear.' It took quite a time for my companions to convince them it was only my throat that was affected and that I could hear. This was their way of ensuring that I would not feel left out of the party.

Nobody's children but God's

One evening I had a long conversation with the Captain's steward on a South African Marine ship about the political situation in his homeland which he concluded by saying, 'Padre, in my country we coloured people are nobody's children but God's.' He left me to dance for a time and then came back when he addressed me very seriously. 'Padre when you were aboard today, you did not visit the Captain.' I explained that I had run out of time and had had to return to the club. 'Well,' he said, 'the Captain is in and he enquired if you had been on board.'

I was not going to let the grass grow under my feet upon receipt of a message of this nature so I drove to the ship immediately. The Captain was suffering from a very heavy cold but this was not the problem. He smiled when I told him the source of my information and remarked something to the effect, 'Well, that figures.' A devout member of the Roman Catholic Church, he went on to explain about our young friend. The youth in question and his pals who had accompanied him to the Mission, before going to sea had attended a marine training establishment in South Africa. The Captain had promised the Anglican Chaplain that he would keep an eye on these boys and see that they went to the various Seafarers' Missions when in port. With a broad grin on his face he remarked, 'They wanted to make sure that I knew where they were spending the evening.' I thanked him for this kindly gesture on his part especially in that none of the boys were members of his own Church. His reply I am unlikely to forget. 'Sure, Padre, aren't we all going in the same direction, only in different coaches.'

SEPARATION AND ITS EFFECTS

When I commenced my ministry with the Missions to Seamen I had a natural empathy with the seafarer who was destined to spend so much of life away from home. Some say absence makes the heart grow fonder perhaps, but sometimes separation can place a heavy strain on a relationship. In the seafarers' case time and distance add greatly to the load.

When I served in the port of Belfast, apart from those serving on coastal vessels we rarely set eyes upon local deep sea seafarers as most preferred to spend their precious leave with family and friends, which is understandable. Overseas it was different, when the club became home away from home in a strange port offering hospitality and recreation: a link with the family at a time of crisis through the international telephone service; an opportunity to worship with people living ashore and a Padre to talk to as the need arose.

Our contact with local seafarers usually came in one of three ways. Some of our most loyal and dedicated volunteer workers came from seafaring families. Again some of our most generous supporters financially were seafaring families. The third level of contact was not infrequently touched with sadness; this was when we would form a link between the seafarer and his family at a time of crisis or tragedy.

During my early years with the Missions to Seamen time and again I found myself full of admiration for the Marine Superintendents in most British shipping companies for the kind and sympathetic manner in which they always tried to deal with welfare cases. Rather than resort to an unfeeling telephone call or telegram to the next-of-kin, news would be channelled through the Missions to Seamen or a kindred Society to be relayed to the family. A large number of men in Northern Ireland chose to make their career as seafarers and this was reflected in my ministry. Again and again my role was to form the link between the overseas seafarer and his family.

It was 7.30 p.m. when I received a call from the Marine Superintendent of a British coastal shipping company. A local seafarer had been involved in an accident on board one of their vessels that day. The news he had received was that while it was not life threatening it was nevertheless serious and the man had been taken ashore to hospital. They would prefer that I called at the home and informed his wife rather than use a telephone for this purpose.

Experience had taught me never visit a home to convey news of this nature if humanly possible without having first gathered together all the information for the family as to how they could get an updated medical report upon request. Frequently for a variety of reasons (economics amongst them) we've had to remain the link but not always.

On this occasion I immediately consulted my Missions to Seamen guide book and while there was no club in this small port the Society did have an Honorary Chaplain. I telephoned him and having given him the information, we agreed that he would contact the hospital, ascertain the nature of the injuries and call me back at 11.00 p.m. In the meantime I would call to the home and break the news.

When I called to the home Mum was out visiting her mother who lived close by and her two boys were house sitting on their own. They directed me to their Gran's house where I found the wife and broke the news to her. Naturally she was upset and very anxious. I promised to return after 11.00 p.m. with an update following my telephone call. My colleague telephoned as agreed and soon I was back at the home again. It was bad news but could have been a lot worse. One foot had had to be amputated and he had withstood the operation very well and his general condition was very good. Distressing news but with a little counselling everyone realized that it could have been a lot worse and for this all were grateful.

A day or two later my Secretary was able to arrange for the wife to visit her husband in hospital. Our Honorary Chaplain booked accommodation locally with a parishioner as he was the Vicar of the local parish.

One day a lady sought our help. Her husband had had a nervous breakdown some years earlier, made a good recovery and never exhibited any signs of a recurrence. Now she was extremely worried about him and as a last resort had turned to us in the hope that we would be able to help.

He had left home three weeks earlier to join the crew of a small British registered coaster. She had spoken to him on the telephone since leaving home, when he sounded in good spirits. During their telephone conversation he informed her that he had made arrangements with the ship's Master for her allotment (allowance) to be forwarded on a regular basis by the shipping company. This was of course normal practice but no money ever arrived. She had been in touch with the shipping company and they had no record of him having joined the crew of this ship. She contacted the police and to date they were unable to trace him.

I took down all of the information in writing, making a particular point of asking her to spell her husband's name and the name of the ship he was supposed to have joined. I then decided to retrace some of the ground that had been gone over before in case some aspect might have been overlooked. Of one thing this lady seemed absolutely certain: unless her husband had had a recurrence of his earlier illness he was behaving completely out of character.

When I telephoned the shipping company I insisted upon spelling out the man's name and the name of the ship. In that moment the mystery was solved. The person receiving the previous telephone enquiries had made a serious blunder by not requesting the caller to spell out the name of the ship. Unfamiliar with the Northern Ireland accent this person had repeatedly taken down the name of the ship incorrectly. Compounding the problem, the company had recently introduced a new accounting system which initially had delayed the payment of allotments.

One very relieved lady left my office to return home.

It's been said the sea helps bring people together

This is certainly true when you're in the midst of a storm and all in the one boat. You depend upon each other for survival. Something of this quality of life rubs off onto others.

Having completed my round of ship visiting for the day and on my way back to the club I was hailed by a Customs Officer. He wanted to let me know that the second engineer from a British registered fishing trawler had been taken ashore to the local fever hospital where he had been detained. The Customs Officer felt that I would like to be informed and perhaps visit him.

When I arrived at the hospital about 7.30 p.m. this man gave an immediate impression of being glad to see me. Soon I was to know why. He was very worried about his wife as she did not have any ready cash and with him in his present condition she would not know what to do. He gave me full instructions to relay to his wife when I also promised to give her an update on his medical condition.

When my lay colleague visited him a few days later he had heard from his wife and she was coping magnificently according to his relayed instructions for which he was grateful. When he was discharged from hospital he made a point of calling in to thank us for the concern shown for his wife and family. All made possible because a Customs Officer cared.

A young German seafarer came into the club one afternoon asking for assistance to return home to Germany which was unusual as most foreign nationals would have their tickets, documents, etc. prepared by the local agent.

Upon making enquiries I found that this boy and the Master of his ship had got locked into a dispute and the Master had paid him off in the port of Cork in the Republic of Ireland to return under his own steam to West Germany. By putting him ashore without any arrangements having been made for repatriation was a serious omission on the part of the Master, whatever the circumstances which had given rise to him taking this course of action.

The youth got scared when he found himself in a strange place on his own and did not know how to set about the task of planning his journey. Some months earlier he had been to the Flying Angel Club in Belfast and had made friends but he did not know anybody in Cork to turn to for help so he decided to seek out his friends in Belfast by travelling north for this purpose. What he did not realize was that Belfast was located in Northern Ireland which is part of the United Kingdom so he was now an illegal immigrant.

The immediate concern was to regularize his presence in Northern Ireland which we did with a visit to the immigration authorities, who in turn referred us to the German Consul. The Consul could not have been more helpful and took care of all the arrangements for his return to Germany.

Here follows an extract from a letter received from the boy after he arrived home.

> Immediately after my arrival home in Bremen I wish to express my thanks which I owe you, for without your help I never would have found the right way. I learned by you that one is never alone on one's way if there is trust in God. Otherwise I would never have come home. In addition to this I wish to return thanks for the hospitality which I was granted by you. I never will forget this. When I arrived home I had to report all about Belfast and for many it was unbelievable that there are still good people on earth, people who want to help and assist in such helpful manner.

A PLACE APART

I have heard it said that Missions to Seamen Chaplains are by and large a bunch of individualists and so long as they are left to do their own thing most of them are happy enough. I could more or less subscribe to this opinion from my experience of long time Chaplains: by this I mean those who have made this ministry their life's work. Thankfully when the Almighty created mankind he went in for variety. In this sense, were another Chaplain writing this book the chances are that emphasis might be placed on different aspects of the same job. As I said earlier quoting St. Paul, 'One plants, another waters, but it is God who gives the increase.'

While our approach to the job may have differed from one person to another our basic faith was the same. One thing we had in common. We would all have loved to see our little Church well used but its use must be by free consent.

While our club door was open to all men, at the same time we had a specially responsibility to minister to the spiritual needs of those of whom it could be said 'were of the household of faith' or were freely seeking entry. Throughout the world of seafarers are countless people with a Christian background who look to the Missions to Seamen to provide them with spiritual nourishment, pastoral care, an opportunity to worship and a decent environment in which to relax when they step ashore in a strange land. Our ministry was addressed to people in every stage of Christian development.

Many ships were engaged in what was called tramping, that is picking up a cargo and bringing it from one port to another. Sometimes it might be a charter which required them to return again and again. Other ships provided a regular line service between ports of the world. It was always something of a reunion for us when old friends returned to port. In this connection one little vessel readily comes to mind. Annually they would return for about two months on charter to the Air Ministry to carry out some work on the local coast. During this time our club became home away from home. A common sight on Sunday afternoons was to see the Mate sitting down at the organ in the Chapel surrounded by his shipmates while they practised the hymns they had chosen for the evening service. Incidentally the Mate played the organ with two fingers.

Seafarers decorating the Church.

A couple of years running their visit coincided with our Harvest Thanksgiving and both occasions found them participating in the decoration of our Chapel for the occasion. The first occasion was a spontaneous effort as they happened to blow into the club when this work was in progress and lent a hand, but the second occasion was by no means so.

Knowing they would be in port on the second occasion they prepared in advance. A labour of love, they polished a pair of oars from a life raft, painted life buoys and prepared a host of other bits and pieces from their vessel to incorporate into the decoration scheme. In addition they brought along fruit and flowers which they had purchased.

These seafarers had a decided artistic bent and the two married together produced a nautical flavour like never before. Incorporated into their scheme was a huge fishing net suspended from the ceiling which drew grasps of admiration from everyone present as the work progressed. Two other symbols not to be missed were also included in the scheme: two forms of saving life, Man is body as well as soul, a large white rope cross and alongside, a life jacket. On this occasion two old and loyal volunteers, members of the Ladies Harbour Lights Guild and our student helper also assisted. The end product is best described in the Harvest hymn, 'Lord of all, to Thee we raise this our grateful psalm of praise.'

The Chapel was so designed that one could see into it from the adjoining recreation hall through glass doors at the rear. Raymond Piper's mural painted on the wall behind the altar was so symbolic that at night we invariably lighted it for everyone to see. On this occasion we left all the lights lighting in the chapel as we felt that most seafarers would appreciate seeing these symbols so artistically portrayed.

HMS *Russell* was in port for the weekend. My practice as Hon. Officiating Chaplain for the Royal Navy was to offer to conduct their worship services on board at a time to be mutually agreed. On this occasion the Captain, on learning that it was our Harvest Thanksgiving at the Mission, cancelled services on board in favour of attendance at the Harvest Thanksgiving at the Mission. In the morning twenty-six persons from HMS *Russell* attended out of a total congregation of thirty-six. One officer brought his wife along and she was so impressed with the harvest decorations that I had to promise to send her a photograph.

We had a congregation of one hundred and fifty six at our evening service which overflowed from the Chapel into the adjoining hall. Of those present forty three were seafarers and our staff, volunteer workers, some with their husbands.

Sea Parish is a title sometimes used to describe the relationship between members of the Anglican Church and the Missions to Seamen. All Anglican seafarers are members of Sea Parish which extends from one end of the earth to the other, for which Chaplains of the Missions to Seamen have special responsibility.

Whenever a seafarer was being instructed for confirmation we provided him with a card bearing his name and the name of his ship. Set out on the card were a series of classes (or lessons) on which the candidate was to be instructed. As the seafarer moved from port to port he would receive instruction from each port Chaplain in turn who would sign his name opposite the particular lessons he had given. Candidates were usually provided with a little reading which they were encouraged to do during the voyage between classes. It was the responsibility of the Chaplain who gave the final class to make the necessary arrangements for the candidate to be confirmed by a Bishop in his port, time permitting, or in the next port of call. These record cards always reminded me of the universality of the church as the seafarer moved from port to port all over the world.

I had the privilege on one occasion of presenting two candidates for confirmation. Invariably these services were held in the Mission Chapel or the Bishop's private Chapel and occasionally in a Parish Church. On this occasion my Diocesan Bishop already had a confirmation service arranged in a local Parish Church and our candidates were invited to join the parochial group rather than be confirmed alone somewhat in isolation.

One was an Engineering Officer and the other a Mess Boy from different ships. Their background leading up to confirmation is interesting.

The Engineering Officer I first met when he attended a dance in the club. We got into conversation which led to my taking him on a tour of the club. Standing by the baptismal font in the Chapel he remarked, 'My mother was confirmed about eighteen months ago when she was fifty seven years old. This is something I must do myself the next time I go ashore on leave as I felt very bad last time we went to Church together and I was not able to receive Holy Communion.' (In those days it was customary not to receive Holy Communion until after confirmation.) His ship was scheduled to remain in dry-dock for a considerable time. When I informed him that he could be confirmed in Northern Ireland and that there would be ample time for me to prepare him before sailing, he was delighted.

The Mess Boy arrived in Belfast with two classes to complete before he was presented for confirmation. He approached our lay worker to make arrangements to complete these while in port. On discovering that he had only two classes to complete and that his ship would be in port for some time Alan enquired if it would be possible for the two to be confirmed together, which was possible.

I asked the boy what led him to decide to be confirmed. 'It's like this, Padre. My father and my mother were divorced when I was three months old and I was brought up by my grandparents. When Grandmother died three years ago a little bit of my heart died too. Last year when Grandfather died my heart almost died with him. I loved them both very much especially Grandfather who taught me all I know. My mother remarried last year and now has no time at all for me. My father's pastime is chasing girls. I do not wish to make the same mistakes in my life. When at Sharpness [a British Merchant Navy Training Establishment] I listened to Mr Beamish [a Missions to Seamen Appointee] talking as a representative of the Church. I soon recognized that he was giving me the same advice as my grandfather, so I thought if this is what Christianity is all about I will be confirmed, because this is exactly how my grandfather kept telling me how to live. I trusted my grandfather as he was the only man who cared for me.' Mr Beamish had given the boy most of his instruction before he left Sharpness building upon the solid foundation laid by his grandparents and it was my great privilege to see him confirmed.

There were many ways in which Sea Parish fulfilled a need. One evening about 7.30 p.m. I was standing in the entrance hall of the club when in came the Chief Engineer from a ship in port whom I had met earlier in the day while ship visiting. We talked for a while when he turned to me and enquired, 'Where is the Church Padre?' and left me to say his prayers.

At 9.30 p.m. I was approached by a young seafarer whom I had also met earlier in the day. 'My father died last week, Padre, do you think you could say a prayer for him during the service this evening? I was away for the funeral and would like to feel that I had paid my respects. He was a good father to me.' We talked a little and later at our evening service we commended his father to God's gracious keeping.

At 11.00 p.m. 'That's the first time I've been in Church in four years, Padre, I don't know why I went but now I know that I should go more often,' a young seafarer remarked as he left the Church. In Church one boy in particular caught my attention. He had a beautiful singing voice and sang the seafarers' hymn 'Eternal Father' with complete abandon, totally absorbed in this act of worship. When I remarked on his singing as he left the Church he replied, 'I love to sing in Church and next time I'm here with your permission I'd like to sing a solo.'

I always stood at the door of the Church to say goodnight to the congregation as they filed past. The next seafarer with whom I spoke came straight to the point. 'What do you think of illegitimate children, Padre?' 'No less than any other child but why do you ask?' I replied. 'Because I've got one, that's why.' One word led to another and later we talked together.

In my experience there are not too many atheists at sea. When you talk in depth with a majority of seafarers you find that most have a healthy respect for the power that controls the elements, having experienced the raging of the sea. Most belong to one faith or another and do not get too excited about orthodoxy. They have one thing in common which ought to be the envy of the world: respect and tolerance for the faith of others. Indeed were it not for this tolerance our many blunders in the Missions to Seamen would have come to light a long time ago.

The following set of prayers I came across on the bulletin board of a ship registered in Hong Kong with a crew of mixed nationality. Nobody knew how or when it got there. I understand it survived every clean up and all were agreed: 'Very Good Prayers.'

'Great Spirit help me to remember never to judge another till I have walked in his shoes for at least two weeks.'

'O Lord let me not live to be useless.'

'Lord we pray not for tranquillity. We pray that Thou grant us strength and grace to overcome adversity.'

'O Lord reform the world beginning with me.'

'Let us have faith that might is right.'

'O Lord help us to be masters of ourselves that we may be the servants of others.'

'Let not that happen which I wish, but that which is right.'

'O Lord help us not to despise or oppose what we do not understand.'

'O Lord never suffer us to think that we can understand by ourselves and not need thee.'

'This is the day which God has made, Let us rejoice and be glad in it.'

'CAUTION: Do not open mouth until brain is engaged.'

VARIETY

'All in a day's work.' I've heard this phrase used many times to describe the variety of one's work. I doubt there could be another form of work or ministry which offered such variety as my position of a Senior Chaplain with the Missions to Seamen. Daily responsibility for the operation of the Flying Angel club, ship visiting and organizing programmes for others to undertake, welfare cases relating to seafarers serving on ships in port and ministering to the families of seafarers serving overseas. One never quite knew what one might be doing from one moment to the next as the following stories illustrate.

Worried

In every industry there are good and compassionate people employed in welfare departments and there are others, but generally speaking, in the final analysis it is the company that dictates policy.

A lady telephoned one evening to seek our help because she was worried sick. The shipping company which employed her husband had informed her several days earlier that he had been admitted to hospital in England. Since then his allotment had ceased and there had been no further news whatsoever of him from his employers. To add to her concern, now she had run out of money.

We immediately telephoned our Hon. Chaplain in the small port where her husband had been put ashore and within the hour we were able to put her mind at rest about his medical condition. We provided her with temporary financial assistance to meet the immediate needs of her family. Next day we contacted her husband's employers and informed them fully about her concern for her husband's welfare which had obviously been overlooked and of her financial predicament. Their response was immediate and compassionate.

It's a big world out there

While our dance was in progress one night I spotted a very young lad sitting alone at a table. I thought he should not be in the club as he looked too young to be serving at sea so I decided to do a little probing by engaging him in conversation. It soon transpired that he was a first tripper and was very home-sick. As the tears rolled down his cheeks he informed me that he would give anything to leave the ship, which was outward bound from Liverpool, to return home.

The lights in our dance hall were always dimmed for dancing so nobody would have noticed the tears but rather than risk exposure I suggested we adjourn to my office where we could continue our conversation.

After a little probing I discovered that his family had a telephone at his home and eventually I managed to get their telephone number. So armed I immediately booked a call to his home and put him on the line. This did the trick and he settled down immediately. When he had finished on the telephone I gave him one of our directories listing all of the Flying Angel clubs world wide. We now returned to the dance hall where I introduced him to a number of our hostesses, leaving him in their care. At the conclusion of the evening he left the club looking like a veteran.

Life has its joys and its sorrows

In Northern Ireland we were very fortunate in our seafaring families, many of whom gave back to the Mission much more than they would have derived from us. Some made a strong bond with the Mission and especially so when the husband upon retirement joined his wife as a volunteer.

One afternoon I was privileged to officiate at the wedding of the daughter of one such family in our Chapel. The bride's father, a former ship's Master now deceased, had been a dedicated volunteer during his retirement, as his wife still is. I had just ushered the bride and groom out of the vestry following the marriage service when I found awaiting me an urgent message from an international oil company which required my immediate attention.

A member of the crew from one of their ships had died in hospital at 12.12 p.m. and they wished me to break the news to his widow.

Priorities dictate a clergyman's agenda as in this instance, so I had to excuse myself from the wedding banquet to fulfil this sad task. I had difficulty locating the widow to whom I was the bearer of this sad news.

Eventually I managed to rejoin the wedding party just five minutes before the bride and groom left for their honeymoon.

'We've lost our boy'

These were the first words to greet me when a very worried father arrived in my office one afternoon. His son had chosen to make his career at sea. The parents had scrimped and saved to ensure that he received a good education and when the son decided to make his career at sea they had him apprenticed as a Cadet with a highly reputable shipping company.

Life got a bit out of hand for the boy when he was about to sit a navigation examination which if he passed would have enabled him to sail as a junior officer. He met a lovely girl who swept him off his feet. As many a man has learned, when Cupid strikes, sometimes there's no knowing where this may lead. In this instance the victim arrived home completely broke and was unable to keep himself any longer at navigation school to prepare for his examination or raise the cash to pay the fee required to sit the examination.

When the boy returned home his parents were very upset and in this delicate situation made no secret of their feelings but made one terrible mistake. They jumped to the conclusion that the young lady concerned was a bad type and asked their son to break off the relationship which he refused to do and walked out of the house. Later he telephoned to say that he had joined a ship and was serving on the lower deck and gave them the name of the ship. This was the last news they had received from him in four months. Eventually they contacted the owners of this ship in an attempt to trace their son and hopefully sort everything out. Alas, he had paid off the ship two months earlier and this company had no idea of his present whereabouts. Could we help?

Knowing the power of Cupid I had a feeling we were most likely to find a trail to follow from this source so I asked the father if he knew the girl's address? 'Yes, I do, but I have no intention of getting in touch with her as she has caused us enough problems as it is.' I replied that at this stage he might not wish to get in touch with the girl but if he needed my help then I must have this address. He conceded at once and gave it to me.

Situations of this nature are always very difficult to handle. There is the question of the invasion of privacy which has to be respected so one is required to be very careful in any attempt to bring about a reconciliation. Again, as a third party one must be very careful not to appear to be acting as judge and jury.

Bogged down and unable to make any progress at my end and after much careful thought I decided to seek in absolute confidence the help of a colleague in the port city where the girl lived. An experienced pastor, after very careful consideration he decided to visit the girl in her own home. What he discovered was a revelation in itself and put an entirely different complexion on the whole problem. She turned out to be a girl of genuine integrity with an excellent home background. Her parents had provided the boy with food and accommodation for one week but when she found out about the attitude of his parents she insisted that he stay no longer. He left her home two weeks earlier to join a ship and since then there had been no further news of him. My colleague drew a blank from this point onwards and having reported back to me we were agreed to tactfully try and locate the boy through whatever channels opened up to us.

My colleague was the Senior Chaplain in a large terminal port in England where men signed on and off ships on a daily basis. The Mission operated a hostel or hotel where seafarers could stay for a reasonable tariff when they paid off ship or while waiting to join one. Hopefully our young friend would put up here at some point and my colleague would be able to speak to him and advise him of his parents' concern.

A very worried father was once more facing me across the desk in my office. We were his last resort for news of his son, having explored all other avenues open to him. What was I to say in the circumstances? Suddenly the telephone rang and it was my colleague from England. The boy had paid off a ship and booked in for the night. My colleague had just spoken to him and explained how distressed his parents were by the breakdown in their relationship. He promised to return home immediately but his parents must understand that his feelings for the girl had not changed. Furthermore, he wanted them to know that he felt they were behaving in a very possessive and unfair manner by condemning this girl without having even met her. I thanked my colleague for a job well done and promised to deliver the son's message in full to his father.

The father quickly acknowledged that as parents both he and his wife had made grave mistakes in their relationship with their son for which they were truly sorry and would apologize the moment they saw him. 'We'll be grateful to have him home again and will tell him in person.'

Throughout this misunderstanding I was merely the contact person at family level while my colleague did all of the work, underlining the value of this great worldwide chain of service.

Keeping a weather eye out
It's often been said that the seafarer is more at sea on dry land than if he were sailing. Many years ago when the Irish Free State (now the Republic of Ireland) came into being the six north-eastern counties of Ireland chose to remain within the United Kingdom of Great Britain and were given the name Northern Ireland. The majority population in Northern Ireland is very sensitive about protecting its British heritage and for anyone to display

before them any symbols of Irish republicanism has the same effect as waving a red flag in front of a bull. You could get hurt.

The reader will appreciate my feelings when three innocents walked through the dock gate, each one sporting the Republic of Ireland flag stiffly out of his breast pocket. I turned my car on two wheels and went after them for it has been known in somewhat similar circumstances for fervent Loyalists to act first and ask questions afterwards. I have never seen anything disappear so quickly as these flags did when I explained the significance.

These poor fellows had thought they were in the Republic of Ireland and wanted to please the natives. Weren't they lucky!

My God, the chickens

A British ship was strike bound in port and a complement of officers had to remain on board to look after the ship when they had to do their own cooking. In the evenings most of them were to be found in the Flying Angel club. One evening an advertisement came on the TV for chickens. Suddenly a voice cried out 'My God, the chickens,' and this guy dashed across the room to grab his coat.

He spotted me in the background with a puzzled look on my face and hastily explained that he was cook for the next day and had put the birds in the oven to give them a bit of a do before he left the ship but had forgotten all about them.

I came to the rescue with the car and within minutes we went through the dock gate on our way to his ship.

American Coast Guard to the rescue came

There are usually a lot of birds on the ground near the grain elevators into which ships discharge their cargoes when they arrive in port. These birds usually congregate at the outlet where the imported grain is being loaded from the elevator for transportation inland. Whenever a human approaches there is usually a great flutter of wings as the birds leave the droppings and fly away to what they conceive to be a place of safety.

Conscious of the birds in flight as I was about to visit on board a United States Coast Guard vessel, my attention was drawn to a faint flutter where the birds had been. There was a pigeon stuck in a sticky mess of tar (soft or melted pitch) and it could not get away however hard it tried. It was very frightened. I tried to free it but soon realized that I would pluck it alive if I persisted.

There was only one thing to do in the circumstances and that was to appeal for help amongst the crew on this US Coast Guard vessel. I went on board and there were a number of men in a mess room to whom I appealed for help. Two volunteers immediately came forward while others equally concerned discussed with them what to use to free the bird which would not cause pain.

I led the rescue party to where the bird was trapped. They had brought with them the appropriate spirit, clean cloths and a pail of water and set to work painstakingly and gently to ensure the bird did not suffer. When cleaned and freed the bird was reluctant to depart as if a bond had been forged between her and her rescuers. She was probably weak and cramped from being trapped in the one position for a long time.

'We might as well finish the job properly,' said one of the two rescuers, 'so we'll take her on board where it's warm until she recovers her full strength.'

Seeing red

Our lay worker wrote: the Fire Brigade were playing football today against a Soviet freighter. The Fire Brigade team's colour is red and the Soviets too use red. Everybody's face was red when the two teams turned out to play. To cap it all we transported the Soviets in our red mini bus.

The right place at the right time

When I stepped on board an Italian freighter this morning the Chief Officer and the Chief Engineer were standing on deck in deep conversation. Alluding to the Chief Engineer, the Chief Officer said to me, 'My friend is very sad and disappointed as he has not seen his son for over eight months. His son's ship was due in Liverpool yesterday and he had written to say that he would travel over to see him in Liverpool on the Sunday evening ferry from Belfast only to find out too late that there was no Sunday evening sailing. His son has written to say that he would travel over to Belfast to see him. Now he does not know what to do. If he travels to Liverpool on this evening's ferry, his son may be on his way here. What to do?'

I counselled, 'Leave the matter with me and I will telephone our Chaplain in Liverpool and no doubt he'll contact the son and soon we'll know what to do.' Within a couple of hours I had a message for Dad to stand by as his son would be visiting next morning in Belfast.

There are times when there's no disguising

'I'm in need of spiritual comfort Padre.' The volunteer on duty ushered this seafarer into my office one evening as she felt that he should talk to me and these were the first words with which he greeted me. He was very drunk and my first impulse was to say that he'd already had more spirit for comfort than he was capable of holding. However I realized that I'd heard a cry for help. When this man left home to commence his present voyage his father had been diagnosed as terminally ill and he did not expect to see him again. Daily he awaited news of his passing, but it never came. This afternoon when his ship arrived in port a letter awaited him from his wife. The end was expected at any moment as his father was now lapsing into periods of unconsciousness. Having carried this burden throughout the voyage there was more to come, which his wife felt should not be kept from him. His mother had just been diagnosed as suffering from a brain tumour.

Altogether this was more than he could take so he'd gone out and got drunk to ease the pain. Pious platitudes are not much comfort to one in these circumstances. The mystery of suffering I have always found inexplicable; it can either make or break most of us. Yet in all humility I could say to our friend that while I could not explain the reason why, given the chance there is a power that can help us on our way and for the sake of those we love save us from self destruction. There was little more one could say.

The mystery of suffering is something most have to learn to live with at some stage in life but when shared it seems easier to bear. In this instance and in countless other situations our ministry would be a pale shadow were it not for the help of dedicated female volunteers like the lady who ushered this man into my office. They are always first to note a cry for help.

FUNNY INCIDENTS

The echo

Saturday was my getting in a plug day. By this I mean that whatever activity in which I was engaged I would somehow find a way to put in a plug or a reminder about our worship services on Sunday. On this Saturday evening as two young fellows whom I knew to be Anglicans were leaving the club I said to them, 'I'll see you fellows in the choir tomorrow morning.'

Our practice was to go ship visiting on Sunday mornings after Church service. I was always accompanied by my sons, Roger and Stephen. Seafarers are very generous people and spoil kids something rotten so for this reason I always had company. We would visit all ships that had arrived in port overnight and a few more if time permitted before lunch.

On this occasion as we made our way across an area of the dock, a voice rang out, 'Hello there, Padre!' and echoed all over the place. I could see nobody in sight, it certainly hadn't come from the ship we had just visited, perhaps the next, but no, not from there either. Again, much to the amusement of the boys, there was a repeat performance. 'Hello there, Padre,' once more echoing all over the place. There was one more ship that we were scheduled to visit but I didn't think it had come from there. By now I had arrived at the conclusion that someone was having me on and enjoying himself by doing so. Amidst their laughter I told the boys we'll pretend not to notice as we made our way to the last ship we had to visit.

Surprise, surprise, as we stepped on board a voice rang out from the crow's nest, high up on the mast head. 'Sorry we didn't make it to Church this morning, Padre, but we think you will have to agree we got fairly close to headquarters just the same, a lot closer than most folks at any rate.' I reckoned that physically speaking he had a point.

All steamed up

Young people who wished to make a contribution to help their fellow man or were contemplating taking Holy Orders and wished to test their vocation availed themselves of the student helper scheme operated by our society. Indeed many Bishops used this scheme to provide exposure for theological students who came from a sheltered background. Some student helpers would spend a year with the Society, others the long summer vacation period to work with the Chaplaincy staff. The monetary reward was minimal: twenty years ago it consisted of free board and lodging plus the vast sum of one pound sterling for pocket money. This job was a serious undertaking totally unrelated to monetary gain. It was surprising how many former student helpers later returned to the Society as Chaplains.

Our new student arrived one afternoon. He was enthusiastic to go ship visiting and as I had a couple of visits to make, I decided to take him with me. When we arrived at the first ship the Chief Officer greeted me over the side from the third deck up. 'I have the wife on board and I would like you to meet her.'

This ship had an all Indian crew so I thought this provided an excellent opportunity for our student to get his feet wet without having me breathing down his neck, while I paid my respects to the Chief Officer and his wife. After a few brief instructions I sent him on his way while I set about my task. When I returned to the car following my visit the student was already awaiting my return with a face as red as a turkey cock. Concerned, I enquired how he had made out? 'Very good,' he answered in a whisper and then went on to say, 'Perhaps not so good.' 'What do you mean?' I enquired. 'Well, they asked me if I would like some curry and when I said I would like to try some, they gave me a big plateful. I ate the lot, not wishing to cause offence, and they asked me, "Did you like it?" "Very nice," I said and with that they grabbed my plate again and filled it. Now I'm so hot I think I'll go on fire.'

The reader will recall how I was initiated into the service of the Flying Angel via the knacker's yard in the port of Dublin. It seems this student's destiny was to go by the curry route. Indian seafarers are noted for their generous hospitality.

Somewhat embarrassing to say the least

Sometimes I used to find that 'Petticoat Government' could be a hard task master if the ladies took charge of a situation. The members of the Ladies Harbour Lights Guild were always on the look out for new ideas to spruce up our entertainment programme. When these ladies decided to do something, they did it with a vengeance and there were no half measures. A decision was made to turn our New Year's Eve dance into a fancy dress. No male, myself included, was permitted to put in an appearance unless fully costumed.

The ladies gathered together a wide variety of costumes for the men to

Dorothy Parker on the right in fancy dress at Belfast Flying Angel Club.

wear. (After the ball was over, these were cleaned, folded and put away for the following year, the collection growing in size from year to year.) On the first occasion I went as a one eyed pirate with a black patch over the other eye. My costume was a hit and I even managed to get my picture in one of the papers. The following year became somewhat embarrassing for me to say the least. I got carried away by my enthusiasm.

The port was full of ships and at one stage we wondered whether we would have enough costumes to go around, so we had to encourage anyone who could dress in fancy dress on board ship to do so and come along to the party. A Norwegian passenger ferry with mixed crew, both male and female, arrived in port at the last moment. (They were due to relieve a local ferry due to enter dry-dock in a day or two.) Our lay-worker visiting on board extended an invitation to the party and explained about a possible shortage of costumes and encouraged everyone to do their best to attend in costume. I even dressed a Portuguese seafarer in my clerical outfit. He looked a bit shook as the evening progressed which caused me to wonder what people were saying to him. A learning experience, he could vouch for some of the tensions a Padre has to operate under! Myself, I'd decided to surprise the members of the Ladies Harbour Lights Guild on this occasion by going as one of them. The moment I made my appearance to take a bow I was conscious of a problem which took away a lot from my dignity: my bust would keep on slipping down around my waist.

This became a real problem as I made the rounds of the dance hall. Soon I spotted a gang of fellows from the ferry mentioned earlier and amongst them a guy who was literally poured into a pair of very tight slacks. He was busting out all over but had a very professional hair-do. By now my bust was down around my waist again, so I decided to confide in this seafarer. The lights had been dimmed for dancing as I approached him and said, 'Do you have trouble with these, too?' and lifted my bust into position. Everyone at the table went into convulsions with laughter. I thought I had been very funny.

We had a long standing tradition at this Mission, whereby we ushered in the New Year during a brief Watch Night service in Church. Always a memorable occasion when the thoughts of many are focused on absent loved ones. On this occasion I had to go chasing my Portuguese friend to recover some of my clerical wear to take the service. Actually I thought he looked relieved, probably thinking he might be expected to oblige.

When the party from the Norwegian ferry saw me dressed up in clerical robes and conducting the service, one by one they began to giggle and continued throughout the brief service. Recalling my joke to that guy in the slacks I resolved never to get myself into a situation like that again. While the service was of brief duration it felt like an age to me.

I had nobody else but myself to blame for this embarrassing situation in Church. Next day, feeling guilty, I got to thinking that perhaps these fellows would be embarrassed to visit the Mission on account of what had happened. I'd better call on board when they would know that I was not offended. The moment I began to walk towards the ship's gangway I noticed every crew member on deck was running towards the accommodation section. By the time I reached the deck there wasn't a member of the crew in sight so I followed them into the accommodation section, a sort of open foyer with a large stairway leading up onto the deck above. On top of the stairway stood what looked like the whole crew and they were grinning broadly. In the centre front row in her stewardess's uniform was the girl whom I took to be a man the night before and had posed that awful question, 'Do you have trouble with these too?' Imagine my embarrassment!

Boys will be boys

Most seafarers love children and within seconds can descend to their level. A visit to the Mission for our children was their most popular outing and one of which they never tired. During vacation times our sons Roger and Stephen were permitted to remain over at the Club for the after Church film on Sunday evenings. I noticed over a few Sundays that when the film had been under way a little time suddenly the door would burst open and a group of men would come rushing out babbling away in some foreign language.

I was puzzled and decided to quietly investigate. To my surprise there was my son Stephen sitting between two seafarers near the back of the hall. When the lights had gone out and the film was under way he began to manipulate a piece of black thread to which he had fixed a mouse. As the mouse began to move, his accomplices, one on either side of him, would draw it to the attention of the nearest group of seafarers. Male or female, few people can stand being close to a mouse, so there was an instant reaction. Up and out. Boys will be boys.

UPGRADING

A Chaplain with the Missions to Seamen occupies a unique role. He is to all intents and purposes a business manager, being responsible for the daily operation of the Club, a welfare officer, a programme director being responsible for the development and maintenance of an entertainment programme, Priest and Pastor. Though many Bishops will not like me saying so, apart from the theological aspects of ministry, few have knowledge of what is required of a Chaplain to function in this Ministry. Yet when it comes to the appointment of Chaplains, it's the Bishop who has the most say.

Theoretically speaking it is supposed to be the Committee members or Board members who apart from ministry hold executive responsibilities for the affairs of the Society. While this may be so it is the Chaplain who is called upon to offer leadership. It can be very frustrating for either party when an impasse is reached and devastating for the work of the Society.

Coming from a business background I have always felt that Missions to Seamen clubs should generate a fair proportion of income from services available through the club instead of attempting to provide everything for nothing. In holding this philosophy I have never met a seafarer who disagreed with me. This is not to say that as a charitable objective the work of the Missions to Seamen is not worthy of support but rather to underline that we have an obligation to make the best possible use of the resources at our disposal. Any surplus in the charitable pool can then be designated to help those who cannot help themselves. It is leadership of this quality which is demanded of every Chaplain in this twentieth century.

My predecessor in Belfast was a man of considerable experience which was reflected throughout the club. Anyone familiar with the history of the period when construction took place would have found that these facilities were state of the art at the time of construction. In those days society was very segregated but by the time I arrived on the scene many people were questioning the morality of the Christian Church being party to this lifestyle, with separate accommodation, e.g. lounges, billiard rooms and toilet facilities, for officers and crew respectively in a building operated by the Christian Church.

Again there was a remarkable difference between the quality and comfort in the furnishings in the officers' accommodation and that being provided for those serving on the lower deck. Yet some entertainment programmes and facilities were shared by all. Ironically we had one Chapel where as children of a common Father for the purpose of worship our equality was recognized.

I was very fortunate in that the overwhelming majority of our management committee shared these modern criticisms and were anxious to update. The Missions to Seamen in Belfast had earned a reputation for being a leader in its class and before any updating programme was contemplated it was felt that the overall situation should be reviewed to see what improvements and additions could be made.

Again about this time there was a noticeable and continuing improvement in the accommodation and working conditions on board British and Scandinavian ships in particular. Wages too had improved and overall the lot of the seafarer was much better. All of these changes underlined the need for us to review our operation in depth with a view to updating and keeping abreast of change. Another principle which had to be incorporated into our thinking was that wherever possible we should seek to derive an income from any additional services we hoped to introduce. While this might not be possible in every case there were some being considered which could generate income.

It is interesting to note that many of the services in seafarers clubs today which are now taken for granted were first initiated around this time. Just as we the Chaplains of this period had inherited much in the way of facilities, lifestyle, vision and quality of leadership from our predecessors, so it was hoped that future generations would learn from us. One notable introduction of the period was the development of the International Telephone Service. Its growth and development was slow at the beginning but this was not because Chaplains did not recognize its potential to bring families together but because the cost to avail themselves of the service was too much for the average seafarer. Few European homes could afford to install an instrument of this nature at that time. The pace was set by Greek seafarers, many of whom would be away from home on contract from two to three years. These long periods of separation caused men to think very deeply and they came up with an answer which met the need until such time as they could afford to have a telephone installed at home. By arrangement families would congregate at the local store near home to await the pre-arranged telephone call from the member serving at sea. It was obvious to us that this traffic would grow as costs decreased and we planned accordingly.

A colleague home on vacation from Australia brought to our attention another service which we could provide and which would generate a lot of income. In his club they did a fair trade selling locally produced souvenirs to seafarers. This immediately registered with me as time and again I had noticed in seafarers' cabins, souvenirs from different parts of the world destined for families back home. Our entry into the commercial field until now had been limited to the sale of toiletries, boot laces, candy and light snacks.

The Master of a British deep sea ship came up with another idea. Seafarers have a lot of time on their hands between watches when at sea. They need a hobby to pass the time. He spoke very highly of the contribution being made by the Seafarers Education Service (later known as the Marine Society) in this connection but he felt that the development of hobbies ought to be along the line that families could share in the result. If we could develop a hobbies section in conjunction with our plans for a souvenir shop where seafarers could purchase kits for rug making, model ship building, etc. we would be doing not only the seafarer a favour but his wife and family too and generate a little income for the club. As it happened this idea fitted the description for a memorial to a former Royal Naval Chaplain for which we had already received a substantial donation.

Incidentally in passing I have just remembered that the ship's Master mentioned in the previous paragraph himself took up a hobby somewhat late in life at the insistence of his elderly mother. She had made one or two voyages with him and became concerned about his drinking and decided he should have a hobby to occupy his spare time at sea. He did not have a drinking problem but his mother decided to act before he developed one. When he arrived home on vacation, Mum met him when he went ashore and immediately ushered him into an establishment where she had enrolled him in a class to learn the art of tapestry (needlepoint). Under petticoat government he had to tow the line day by day while on leave. Mum made certain that when he returned to sea he had all the equipment to pursue his hobby. She knew her man for within a brief space he got to like his hobby and discovered that he was something of an artist. My opposite number in the port of Durban, South Africa recognized these qualities and immediately commissioned the Master to make frontals for the Altar in the Mission Chapel there. These he completed in the seasonal liturgical colours.

I first met this Master when he was working on one of these frontals. His creations were original works of art and would probably command a high price on any market for this reason alone.

In the previous paragraph we touched upon the subject of alcohol and seafarers: a very touchy subject in some circles. We did not have a licence to dispense alcohol in our club though in most overseas clubs it was commonplace to serve beer. A majority of ships at this time had a bond on board and seafarers were able to purchase a case of beer for consumption there. I have never heard of a case where drunkenness became a problem. Questioning why in the Flying Angel club in Belfast he could not purchase a beer, one seafarer said to me, 'We're not interested in getting drunk, Padre, but most seafarers enjoy a beer or two in the evenings as we relax and watch TV.'

One point which escaped attention over the years was that there was a high proportion of seafarers who did not use our Club on a daily basis during a prolonged stay in port. Instead of them being able to drink a beer in the decent environment of the Flying Angel Club we were responsible for sending them pub crawling in a strange city because we were not licensed to dispense beer. This issue had been shelved over a number of years every time it came up for discussion at management committee level. Personally I was in favour of the Club being licensed to dispense beer and the overwhelming number of committee members were agreed. Together with those other additional services mentioned in this chapter we were agreed that our updating programme should include provision for dispensing beer.

Though having made this decision we were conscious that when the time came to make application for a licence we might run into opposition from a group who liked to regard themselves as a temperance lobby, which was incorrect as they were a total abstinence lobby. The majority of people in Northern Ireland, it was felt, were not total abstainers and took a drink from time to time; on this basis we could not refuse this right to visiting seafarers.

We were all set to go ahead with our updating programme, plans having been drawn up and agreed upon when the Corporation of the City of Belfast dropped a bombshell. A new ring road was to be built around the city which would go right through our building. Needless to say this announcement dampened our ardour for a time. Eventually, when we were unable to ascertain from the City exactly when the ring road would be built, our management committee decided to proceed as planned. It was felt that by the time the ring road was constructed in our area, if ever, we would have recouped the financial cost.

When the work was duly completed the privilege of inaugurating this new phase in the life of the Club went to the Rev. Prebendary Cyril Browne OBE, General Secretary of the Missions to Seamen, London, England.

GETTING DOWN TO BUSINESS

The trouble we had anticipated might come from the total abstinence lobby when we submitted our application for a licence to serve beer in the Club did not materialize as we had envisaged. Trouble there was but it came from different and unexpected sources.

The first hurdle we had to overcome was to persuade our Bishop that it was time our Club was licensed. Obviously our timing was right as he did not hesitate to give his permission even though he was shortly to retire.

Our plan was to apply for a club licence under existing law only to discover that we could not do so without infringing our constitution which was not possible under any circumstances. While our problem was unique within the United Kingdom at this time it appeared as if a similar difficulty may have prevailed throughout the UK as a whole at one time, but was overcome by the introduction of the Seamen's Canteen Clubs Act (or a somewhat similar title) whereby establishments similar to ours were licensed. Our Club being the only one of its kind in Northern Ireland at that time, this bill had never been processed through the Parliament of Northern Ireland. Yet as a province of the United Kingdom we were entitled to equality under the law.

It was felt that there might be considerable delay before the local parliament addressed our problem. Our solicitor was optimistic that there would not be undue delay provided we set about the task in the correct way. He was aware that a bill was in the process of preparation for a revision of licensing laws and that we must find a way to communicate our needs to the Minister in the hope that these could be addressed in the legislation being prepared. He suggested, 'As your solicitor, if I were to write to the Minister, my letter would probably find its way to the bottom of the pile.' Then turning to me he remarked, 'If this letter were written in your name as a clergyman making a request of this nature there would be an immediate response. It would be such an unusual request coming from a clergyman in Northern Ireland that when the Minister recovered from the shock he would respond immediately.' He agreed to draft the letter which I would sign. It worked and soon we received a letter of acknowledgement promising to take care of our problem in the revision of licensing laws currently in progress.

The political climate in Northern Ireland began to heat up about this time with a lot of in-fighting in the government party. The Minister in question, following a dispute with the Prime Minister, resigned from office. I kept in touch with his successor and monitored the Bill's progress until it became law.

By now I began to feel that I could earn a place in the *Guinness Book of Records* for my part as a clergyman in helping to liberalize the licensing laws for seafarers in Northern Ireland, even though many would disagree with my principles in this connection. A feature of the new Bill required that we signify by advertising in the press our intention to apply for a licence to dispense alcohol. Thus those who felt that they could sustain an objection would be provided with an opportunity to do so. By this time our Diocesan Bishop had retired and his successor, a former military Chaplain, agreed that we could proceed before going away on vacation.

The Archdeacon of the Diocese who was acting as Commissary for the Bishop during his absence on vacation now joined in the fray. 'Our advertisements were bringing the Church into disrepute. Did I know what I was doing?' I informed him that world wide and throughout the United Kingdom similar establishments were licensed but that one way or another the Bishop had given his permission for us to proceed. He then expressed the opinion that the Bishop being new to the Diocese would not have realized the adverse affect of the whole process when he gave his permission. I could not agree and said so. I became convinced in my own mind that the Archdeacon sounded as if he were reacting to a lobby or pressure group whose views he shared. If this group were to succeed the Club would never be licensed. It was like walking on red hot coals at this time.

The new legislation stipulated that applications for a licence could choose one of two options when making a submission. (1) In the name of the property owner. (2) In the name of the manager or person daily responsible for the administration of the business. Almost all applicants chose number 1 as did we. (Our property was owned by a trust corporation in London.) The Judge would not accept these applications as the owners lived outside the immediate jurisdiction. In the event of an infringement of the licensing laws this could present a problem and delay the serving of a summons. In the circumstances he gave permission for those applicants affected to chose the second option, having completed certain formalities, and agreed to hear their applications next day.

Now I found myself in unenviable position. I was the person responsible for the daily operation of the Club but would the Bishop agree for me to have the licence issued in my name? Not too many Clergy occupied this role.

The Bishop was away on vacation so I would have to answer this question for myself. I already knew the Archdeacon's feelings and even though he might be standing in for the Bishop, in the circumstances I just did not want to give him the opportunity to place a hold on proceedings. I was grasping any straw to procure the licence without having to take responsibility for doing so. First I decided to telephone the General Secretary of the Missions to Seamen in London and seek his guidance. 'It's outside my jurisdiction and I would counsel you to consult with your Diocesan Bishop before going ahead.' Now I was on my own. I felt that from what I knew of seafarers and their relationships with the Flying Angel Club an infringement at some future date was highly unlikely. Civic disturbances throughout Northern Ireland were becoming a growing threat and seafarers would be a hang sight safer drinking a beer at the Flying Angel Club than pub crawling throughout the city. 'Johnny on the Spot', I decided to go ahead and accept this responsibility.

The final hurdle and possibly a first in Northern Ireland was when as an Anglican Priest I stood before the Judge while he examined my qualifications to hold a licence.

It was an unusual situation but I kept my cool and must have acquitted myself well for we were granted a licence.

I never said a word to the Bishop or the General Secretary but in time history vindicated my decision when during Northern Ireland's civil war pubs became the main target of the terrorist bomber. Though I would hasten to add that like the seafarer, I too like a beer.

SHAPING UP TO NEW RESPONSIBILITIES

I have never been much of an accountant in the sense that every time I have attempted bookkeeping, catastrophe would follow as sure as night followed day. I could understand what I was supposed to do and what the result should look like but somehow I could never get there; my effort always ended in chaos. Anyone who has ever worked with me will confirm that I have always had a healthy respect for bookkeepers and rarely interfered with their work for this very reason. On the other hand my name is Parker and some would say 'nosy by name and nature' excluding bookkeeping. Now having the added responsibility of operating a licensed club I was determined to become acquainted as quickly as possible with every aspect of the business. I always found it difficult to be the boss unless I fully understood how things worked for myself, book-keeping excluded.

There's a wise saying, 'Fools step in where angels fear to tread.' It's surprising how frequently we hear sayings of this nature and let them in one ear and out the other until catastrophe happens.

On this occasion there was a call from the lady volunteer in the canteen. 'This beer keg is empty, the top needs to be disconnected and re-attached to a full one and I've no idea how it's done.' No problem, I thought to myself, I know the theory and proceeded to do the job. Did I get a shock?

Whatever I did to the valve on the full keg in the process of making the changeover, the beer gushed out. My mind went blank as I was re-baptized, only this time in beer. Were it not for a seafarer who came to my rescue and stopped the flow there is a good possibility I might have been drowned, too! 'It's only fools who step in where angels fear to tread.' I resolved this was one job I would never tackle again until I had practical training in how it was done.

We now had all these new services to offer at the Flying Angel Club and we needed a new brochure capable of communicating across the many language barriers which confronted us on a daily basis to people from Norway, Sweden, Denmark, Greece, Netherlands, Germany, Spain, Soviet Union, amongst others. When we went on board ship our practice was to try and make contact with as many people as possible. We visited the mess rooms, recreation rooms, galley, ship's office and occasionally by invitation the engine room, individual cabins and wherever seafarers were likely to congregate. During the course of our rounds we would distribute our brochure which listed the facilities available at the Club and also incorporated a map which pinpointed our location in relation to the port.

Until now our brochure had only been printed in English and year by year the number of non English speaking seafarers using the port continued to rise. Until now we had to depend upon those who spoke English to inform others on board, which they did not always do. This was by no means a satisfactory arrangement and updating had been put on hold until such time as our major upgrading programme had been completed.

A new brochure had to indicate in some form the facilities we offered at the Flying Angel Club. We could not afford the cost of printing in the variety of languages spoken by our patrons. Yet it was vital that we find a means to communicate, especially now, as in the future we would be looking to the newly introduced services to provide some revenue to cover the cost of operating. We discussed the problem again and again at Committee meetings but protracted discussion failed to come up with a solution. Eventually our Hon. Secretary came up with an idea which we all felt was worth exploring. He was acquainted with a gentleman who had retired recently from the advertising field and who had a reputation of being something of a wizard for solving communication problems. 'If his reputation is anything to go by and he cannot help us then nobody else can. He would probably enjoy the challenge and might even donate his time to the Society free of charge.'

I got the privilege of making contact with this gentleman. His suggestion was quite original: our brochure should incorporate a series of cartoon figures to illustrate the various services we provided on our programme. He sketched and prepared all of the cartoons for our printer, free of charge, and did not make any charge for consultation. Since then I have noted that a number of signs in airports and buildings used on an international basis are produced like this.

Some years after I had immigrated to Canada I found myself having to deal with a somewhat similar problem on a temporary basis in the port of Vancouver when I used these cartoons again. A few months later on the bulletin board in a ship visiting the port I came across actual copies taken of them and incorporated into the brochure of a seafarers' club in the United States of America. 'Imitation is the best form of flattery.'

This gentleman's contribution proved invaluable to foreign seafarers visiting the port. They now had a clearer understanding than ever before of what we had to offer at the Flying Angel Club. Attendance increased accordingly.

The following letter which came from a British seafarer, received a little time after our upgrading programme had been completed, illustrates very clearly how all of our volunteers adapted to these changes and took them in their stride.

Dear Padre,

We have been particularly busy on board since we left Belfast, so please forgive me for not writing immediately to thank you and all your very fine and willing members at the Mission for the welcome, help and unstinted friendliness.

The whole atmosphere of the Mission, the execution of its purpose was indeed a revelation to me. All this can only be put down to the overwhelming openness of mind (so prevalent with the people of Northern Ireland I found) and the happiness of the volunteers to act with human kindness. I cannot write my appreciation adequately perhaps, but may I say that the happiness and the work that goes into providing it at your establishment promotes many reflections.

May I be allowed through this short letter to thank you and everyone also associated at the Flying Angel for your benevolence, and assure you that you will be meeting me again on our return to Belfast.

THERE IS MORE TO REAL LIFE THAN JOY, IT'S ALSO GOT PAIN AND SORROW TOO FROM WHICH FEW OF US CAN ESCAPE

I believe there is a song in 'Oklahoma' which has words which go something like this, 'Everything's going my way.'

Of recent years whenever we had a party for a visiting naval ship everything went our way but it was largely because of the contribution made by two Royal Navy Liaison Officers, Lieut. Commander Barry Knowles and Lieut. Ian Shaw.

While parties would no doubt continue, sadly it would be without the contribution of our two friends. They had been attached to the Fleet Air Arm and served in the Royal Naval Aircraft Yard at Sydenham, Belfast. Both were lost during a test flight of a Sea Vixen aircraft. An extensive search followed in an effort to locate the two who were presumed to have bailed out of the aircraft but it was without success.

Eventually when the search was officially called off it was with a very heavy heart that I tried to comfort Ian's young widow and his parents. Only two years earlier this young widow had lost her brother in similar circumstances. Of one thing I could be certain from what I had known of Ian: whatever the circumstances he would have died doing his duty, as we found so often through our association with him.

As Honorary Chaplain for the Royal Navy in Belfast with responsibility for conducting their memorial service I would have found little difficulty changing places with one of my shore based colleagues as these men were my friends but this would not have been right. They had died fulfilling their duty and I must fulfil mine. There are times when words are cheap and one is tempted to place the Christian message of hope in the same category; this was one of those moments for me. Yet, upon reflection, quietly these words of Christ's came to mind and I was enabled to elaborate upon them. 'Set your troubled hearts at rest. Trust in God always; trust also in me. There are many dwelling places in my Father's house; if it were not so I should have told you; for I am going there on purpose to prepare a place for you . . . ' Like I'm sure most people present I found myself praying hard that the full significance of these words would become a reality for the bereaved. I would like to end this story with a Missions to Seamen prayer which I have used on similar occasions. It offers hope and comfort to the bereaved.

> O God of Love we thank and praise Your Holy name for all seafarers who have witnessed a good profession and passed through the waters into the heavenly kingdom. Grant that we may ever keep them in holy remembrance and bring us at last to share with them the eternal joy of Your presence through Jesus Christ Our Lord.
>
> Amen

In for a disappointment

A French naval ship paid a courtesy call on the City of Belfast. True to form the Royal Naval Liaison Officer did a splendid job arranging a very full entertainment programme for them which included a special dance at the Flying Angel Club and an extended invitation to make full use of all the facilities we had to offer during their stay. Our dance was an unqualified success.

About one week later this ship had to put into the port of Londonderry on a Sunday afternoon to land a crew member for hospitalization following which the ship's company were granted shore leave until the following morning. Londonderry is located about eighty miles from Belfast.

We had just entered the main lounge in the club following evening service in the Chapel when in walked this French Petty Officer in full uniform to a great welcome from a number of hostesses who had met him during his visit a few days earlier. It was about 8.30 p.m. and I immediately began to wonder where he had come from. When he had explained about his shipmate having been hospitalized ashore and about having been given leave until morning he went on to inform me that he had enjoyed himself so much during their last visit that he took the first train to Belfast to meet his friends again and hoped to return to Londonderry tonight.

'Here is my ticket,' he concluded in absolute silence for we knew there were no further trains to Londonderry tonight. When the seriousness of his plight sank in he looked distinctly uncomfortable. There was no bus service either and it would cost an arm and a leg to hire a car to drive him eighty miles. He had to be back on board by morning otherwise he might find himself on a charge for being absent without leave in a foreign country. We had to do something to relieve his agony.

I telephoned our Hon. Chaplain in the small port of Coleraine about fifty-five miles from Belfast. Unfortunately he was away from home. I explained the man's predicament to the Chaplain's wife, stating that I'd hoped to be able to persuade her husband to drive him from Coleraine to Londonderry if I brought him to Coleraine myself, but that was out now and I would have to go the whole way myself. 'That would be a long journey at this time of night,' she said and then asked me to hold on for a moment or two. Within seconds she was back on the line. 'I'm entertaining two guests, a husband and wife. When they heard of this man's plight he immediately volunteered to drive him from here to his ship in Londonderry.' I was astonished by such generosity freely extended to a stranger.

It goes without saying one very relieved Petty Officer soon joined me in the car for the first stage of his return journey to Londonderry.

You do what you can

I received a telephone call one afternoon from our headquarters in London asking me to call to a seafarer's home and break the tragic news of his sudden death to his widow. He had been found dead at the bottom of a dry-dock in London where his ship was undergoing repairs. It was presumed that death was the result of an accident.

Believe me, it's not easy to be the bearer of such tidings and one is anxious to do everything possible to ease the burden. In these circumstances one has to be extremely careful to ensure that the news reaches the next of kin before others, though there may be circumstances where of necessity one has to enlist outside support but this calls for caution in the type of person in whom one should confide.

When I called to this home, the widow was out shopping, her next door neighbour informed me. We got talking when I was able to discover this neighbour enjoyed a very close relationship with the family. She knew many of their relatives intimately so I decided to confide in her. Thanks to this neighbour a close family member was present to offer comfort and support to the widow within minutes of my breaking this tragic news to her.

A perfect example of how sudden and tragic news can be overwhelming and absorbing now came to light. I was totally unaware that the widow's mother was bedridden upstairs until called upon to inform her too.

Those who have been through a bereavement following the sudden death of a loved one will recall how when the initial shock has abated the mind begins to think. Could I have done more? It's infinitely more difficult for the widow of a seafarer separated by time and distance. In this case the deceased had been ill before rejoining his ship. Yet, two nights earlier he had spoken to his wife by telephone and he sounded in great form. Nevertheless the widow turned to me and said that she would welcome an assurance about the circumstances of her husband's death. I promised to do what I could and as quickly as possible.

Thank God I've always found that Marine Superintendents are not heartless men and unapproachable. Within hours I was back at the home and was able to inform the widow that since my first call preliminary investigations had already been carried out as to the cause of death. It was a tragic accident and her husband had met his death while performing his duties. He was considered one of the most reliable men employed by this company. I left hoping this news would help to set her troubled mind at rest.

'It's the brother, Padre, he was drowned . . . '

The first words uttered by a man upon entering my office one morning. He went on to say, 'I was at sea myself a few years ago and yesterday when the police arrived with the news the parents were devastated and had no idea what to do so I decided to get in touch with the Padre at the Flying Angel and see if he could help.'

The family had been in touch with the shipping company and as the deceased had only been in their employment for a few days they could not pay the cost of having the body brought home for burial. Burial would have to take place overseas unless the family decided otherwise but they could not afford to finance the cost of bringing the body home.

I offered to make arrangements through our London headquarters for a clergyman known to them to conduct the funeral service and have some photographs taken. In addition I suggested that we held a memorial service in our Chapel at the same time and if it could be arranged perhaps their family Pastor might be agreeable to preach. 'Thank you Padre, go ahead and make the arrangements, I knew the Mission would understand,' said my caller.

Though separated from the deceased mortal remains, yet in spirit family and friends were one. It was an ecumenical occasion too for their family Pastor was a Presbyterian Minister. In his brief address he spoke of having prepared the deceased for his brief journey through life from boyhood into manhood.

A touching expression of the brotherhood of the sea was also evident. In the congregation were five young boys from the Liverpool ferry. They had come into the club to play billiards but when they had learned of the tragedy they asked to be present.

A comfortable lounge was set at the disposal of the family immediately following the service where light refreshments were served.

We could not afford to take no for an answer

A seafarer because of his chosen career must endure periods of separation from his wife and children. The majority are great family men and grasp every opportunity to be together, dry-docking being one of them. The problem usually arose when the kids had to return to school.

Every possible avenue was investigated if Dad thought that by one means or another he could have the family along with him for another week or two. We knew from experience that when these men approached us to pursue a particular line of enquiry every avenue had to be explored. Neither could we afford to take no for an answer.

Our Lay Worker, Alan Jones, scoured the Belfast School District without success in an attempt to find a school that would enrol a bunch of kids for three weeks while they remained on board ship with Dad.

While everywhere the answer was no, nevertheless Alan did not stop trying. He bugged everyone he knew in the hope of success at some point and his perseverance eventually paid off. One of our hostesses happened to be a school teacher so Alan set his sights on her to find a solution. She came up with a satisfactory solution by providing the necessary books and lessons for parents to teach their own children until such time as they returned home to go to school. The moral, 'Never take no for an answer.'

Sharing the faith

One Sunday evening Alan Jones picked up a number of seafarers who required transport to the club. One, a practising Christian, decided he would attend the worship service in the Chapel before the entertainment programme began.

He informed Alan that he sang in his Parish Church as a boy before going to sea and now regretted that he had not been confirmed before leaving home. He appreciated his faith and hoped to be prepared for confirmation when next on leave. Alan immediately informed him that he could be confirmed through the Missions to Seamen and begin his instruction right here in Belfast. He was enthusiastic and wanted to begin right away. I had time to give him two classes myself before developing a throat problem and under medical advice I was forbidden to use my voice.

A former student helper with the Society and now a Priest serving in a local parish had time to give him two more lessons before his ship sailed. He also had time to visit our home during his stay and as usual with most seafarers was a real hit with the children.

The following letter arrived a couple of weeks after he sailed from the port of Belfast.

> I thank God you were there at the Missions to Seamen in Belfast, where I shall always remember the welcome I received. Through your work and understanding I find I am so much nearer to God, and what a wonderful difference it makes. Please give my regards and thanks to your wife for the wonderful lunch, and to the children, also to Mr Jones and Mr Craig for their help. I sincerely hope that your throat will heal quickly so you may carry on your great work. Thank you.

Our privilege to share in his joy

Christmas Day is a time of joy and celebration for all Christians when we meet in worship to celebrate the birth of the King of Kings. We had an additional reason to celebrate at this service for present in the congregation was a Nigerian ship's officer who was celebrating the birth of his first son in Liverpool.

One thing I will always remember about the members of the Ladies Harbour Lights Guild in the port of Belfast, they never treated their presence in the Mission Chapel as an afterthought.

On this occasion that presence was memorable. We adjourned for coffee immediately following the service of Holy Communion when the new Dad was presented with gifts to mark this never to be forgotten occasion. A ceramic dish featuring a Celtic cross to mark Dad's association with the Irish Church when his son was born. A pottery mug featuring the Red Hand of Ulster to signify his presence in Northern Ireland when his son was born. A boy doll in Irish national costume riding a donkey with pannier bags, a typical feature of the Irish countryside. While Dad waited for his telephone call to be processed to his parents in Lagos to announce the good news we gathered around him for a photograph. My son Stephen was particularly pleased when he found the new baby, like himself, was to be called Stephen.

The father later wrote:

> It is my hearty wish to express the fabulous hospitality of the 'Flying Angel' at Belfast. I have called at the various branches of the 'Flying Angel' in different ports and it is my candid opinion that the organizers are making

great sacrifices to the seafarers all over the world. Personally, I cannot forget the 'greatest honour' and happy feelings I have with the Belfast branch of the Flying Angel. My wife, my son and I will ever live to remember the Seamen Mission in Belfast. It is a great pleasure to express my appreciation and thanks to the group of girls who presented the 'surprise' gifts to me, and also to every member of the Christian folk of the Mission!

IN SOME RESPECTS THE CALLS MADE UPON CHAPLAINS VARY FROM LOCATION TO LOCATION

Northern Ireland in particular and the United Kingdom in general have a large contingent of the population who make their career at sea. In this respect, unlike an overseas posting, Chaplains are daily brought into direct contact with seafarers' families through welfare cases. Whenever I look through my notes relating to the years I served as Senior Chaplain in the port of Vancouver as compared with the port of Belfast this point is underlined for me.

One Saturday evening when I arrived for duty at the club in Belfast one of our female volunteer workers awaited my arrival accompanied by a lady whose face seemed somewhat familiar. This lady who was very drunk had asked to see me stating that we had met some months earlier when she had accompanied her husband to the club when his ship was in port. They had both visited the club on several occasions, I now recalled. At the time he had enquired of me the address of the local branch of Alcoholics Anonymous which I was happy to provide. I recalled thinking to myself at that time that this man must have had a problem which was now under control but good for him that he should keep in touch with AA and bring his wife along too.

Over the years I had become acquainted with several active members of AA, all of whom I came to respect and admire. They had a rare quality about their lives, a kind of serenity. They recognized that alcohol was a problem for them but had learned to control it. They were very frank in stating that unlike themselves alcohol was not necessarily a problem for everyone, but definitely for some. Very tolerant people, they could pass themselves in the company of others who were consuming alcohol on occasion without appearing to be resentful. Somehow to me these folk through this affliction had acquired an inner strength which placed them above the rest of us (common humanity) yet they are very humble folk ever ready to help a brother or sister in need.

It was obvious that this lady had a problem with alcohol as she openly carried a large bottle of gin which she guarded with her life and from which she took a sip from time to time. While I knew our volunteers would do their utmost to help, nevertheless I felt that we were out of our depth and should seek professional help. The obvious route to take was I felt through AA. A telephone call and within minutes a number of ladies from AA arrived. With their help we managed to have her admitted to hospital for treatment. By 10.00 p.m. she was bedded down for the night and I could return to the Club.

I came away from the hospital with a number of questions relating to this lady's background which needed to be answered. Knowing the name and date when her husband's ship was in port proved to be an advantage. Soon through AA I was able to establish contacts which led in her background. We were dealing with a pathetic case. Many people had gone out of their way to try and help her when she would show signs of responding only to lapse again. The local branch of AA, of which her husband was a member, had bent over backwards to help but it was all to no avail. Then a strange thing happened. She felt that she had let everyone down and did not have the heart to turn to them again for help so she borrowed the money for her air fare and boarded a plane to Belfast. In her confused state of mind she had decided to seek our help at the Flying Angel.

I visited her in hospital the day following her admission and over the next four days as did the ladies from AA. Regrettably, without a word with any one of us she decided to discharge herself from hospital which legally she was entitled to do. The hospital authorities were very compassionate and rather than discharge her onto the streets they telephoned me. We agreed to purchase an air ticket for her return journey to England and the hospital provided her with transport to the airport. I was able to have a few words with her before her flight departed but my visit was of no significance.

One week later I received a telephone call from the personnel officer in her husband's shipping company to enquire about her progress. He was astonished to learn that she had left Belfast for home almost one week earlier as she had not yet arrived home. On the other hand a telegram had been received by her husband on board ship requesting that he return home.

Soon we were to meet again. When I returned to the Club one day having been ship visiting, a message awaited me from the police at Belfast airport. They had been holding a lady who claimed to know me and had tried to contact me earlier but I was not available. This lady was intoxicated when she had arrived on a flight from Gatwick but in view of the long delay in my response the airport doctor had been called and she was admitted to the local hospital. It was already too late in the day for me to compile a full picture of this latest development for the personnel officer in her husband's company so I decided, following a visit to the hospital, to report back to him through their local branch of AA. They already knew about the telegram and were in daily touch with a member of the management staff in her husband's shipping company who was a member of AA.

Upon her return to England the first time from Belfast she had immediately fallen by the wayside to drift and drink for several days on the proceeds of her husband's allotment which she had collected on her return. Eventually she reached the end of the road and felt totally ashamed having let so many people down who had gone out of their way to help her. It was then that she decided to try once more and make a new start in Belfast. Somehow it seemed to be different on this occasion and she appeared to be more open and frank than she was on the previous time.

During the days which followed in the hospital she co-operated with the medical professionals, completing fully and willingly the programme they had set out for her. Local members of AA kept in touch with her. Eventually the day came when she was able to return home to England, now a much wiser person, into the fellowship of her local branch of AA where she was assured of the support and encouragement of her husband's friends who had never lost faith in her.

Throughout her second stay in Belfast, at the request of the AA member on the management staff of her husband's company, he was kept fully informed about her progress.

This story is by way of a personal tribute to Alcoholics Anonymous without whose assistance I could not have coped on this occasion and others. I have never known them not to respond to a cry for help whatever the circumstances.

A mother's appreciation

It is our job to try and ease the pain. A lady in some distress visited me one day. She had received a letter from the shipping company who had employed her son to inform her that he was being held in custody by the Australian police and would be deported at some future date. No further information was given. She was devastated and did not know to whom she should turn for advice. A friend told her to consult us.

When you could not solve a problem on your own there was always headquarters in London. Thanks to their effort, within hours I was able to inform her why the boy had been taken into police custody and where. A couple of days later further news arrived, enough to put her mind at rest and remove all cause for immediate concern. The following moving letter arrived to express her appreciation for what little we did.

> Just where to begin to sincerely thank you and all concerned with the Missions to Seamen regarding my one and only I do not know. Words fail me to express my gratitude. I cannot find words which would deeply express my very sincere appreciation. I feel less tense and being able to get a letter to my son has also relieved me so much. He is all I have, and it's only natural as a Mum, it's all very worrying for me. Perhaps when the Rev ... [our overseas Chaplain concerned] visits him he will make my son understand that his home coming will be a blessing to this home. I pray my son will soon be home, that will be a wonderful day for me.
>
> Once again sir, I warmly thank you for your wonderful help. It's something I won't ever forget. When I get over all this strain and anxiety, I shall personally call and pay tribute to the Missions. I owe them so much, but at the moment I am under Drs. orders and my financial side is not as it should be, but I can honestly assure you once I return to work I will make a donation to the Mission which has done so much for me. My sincere thanks.

Our current Student Helper (A.M.H.) has written ...

This evening, just before Church Service, a seaman, the Steward on the MV — came into my office. He told me he would like to do something for seamen in hospital, but as with many people, did not want to come into personal contact so as to avoid embarrassment. He then produced from his pocket two large pouches of tobacco, with papers, and one pound (sterling) to be divided between them. He apologized for the small quantity, but said it was all the Customs would allow, and pay-day was a long time ago. Then before I had time to thank him properly he had vanished into the Church.

We often get spontaneous acts of charity towards ourselves in the form of packets of tobacco, drinks, etc. on ships, because most men who have been at sea for a short while seem to learn the joy of giving, and for all their down to earth approach, are really kind hearted.

However this particular seaman had found a way to express this by giving to the all too often forgotten sick, and had also used another of the seamen's good qualities, that of humility in not accepting praise.

It is also worth noting that the same seaman, with the help of a friend, collected seventy-five pounds (sterling) for the Durban Mission in two days, to buy a fridge, coffee machine, working surfaces, and other things to make life easy for the ladies there. His gift, as I have said, is typical of the basic generosity of seamen.

IT'S A DIFFERENT WORLD OUT THERE

Apart from the supervision of the daily operation of the Flying Angel club and the visitation of ships my lifestyle as a Chaplain with the Missions to Seamen in the port of Belfast was very unpredictable. One never quite knew what one would be called upon to do from one hour to the next.

This morning I learned that the Skipper of a Polish fishing vessel had been taken ashore to hospital soon after arrival in port. Emergency surgery was required, and when I got to the hospital he was already in the operating room. I spoke to the staff nurse on duty in the recovery ward and explained who I was and left her a visiting card with words to the effect that if there was anything we could do to help him or if he needed anything not to hesitate to telephone us.

Over the years I learned that if you can anticipate a need in advance it's wise to make preparations and not wait until the last moment. On this occasion I knew that this man when recovering from his operation would appreciate being visited by someone who spoke his native language. I began to make enquiries and I learned over the years a good place to begin with was the BBC Northern Ireland. If they could not help they would frequently suggest other leads. A member of their orchestra was from Poland but would not be available to contact until next day which suited admirably. I had made a start and could get on with other work until next day.

I was in the midst of my evening meal at my home when a telephone call came through from the staff nurse in the hospital. The Skipper had come through his operation very well but one aspect of his recovery was giving some cause for concern. It would be very helpful if we could provide someone to translate for the doctors to communicate with him. I promised to find someone as soon as possible and make our way direct to the hospital. Panic stations! I now realized that we had a serious gap in our advance welfare programme. Instead of having an updated list of people who could speak various languages to call upon in an emergency we had to go looking for people to do so at the last moment. This should not be and would have to be rectified in the future.

So much for the future but what of now? In panic I visited one ship after another to try and locate someone who could speak English and Polish, telephoned the Harbour and Provincial Police Forces and a number of other organizations but to no avail. My last resort was to try the student residence attached to Queen's University Belfast in the hope that a Polish student might have been enrolled at the University. I struck oil but unfortunately he had gone out for the evening with his girlfriend and the staff reckoned it would be difficult to locate him. When I explained the nature and urgency of my request they promised to do their utmost to try and locate him.

Now feeling something of a failure, I set out for the hospital accompanied by my last resort, a friend, a Russian Jew who had spoken a little Polish as a boy and was prepared to do the best he could under the circumstances. When we arrived at the ward an urgent message awaited me: 'Telephone home at once.' The warden of the student hostel had telephoned to say that they had located the Polish student and having explained about my visit he responded immediately by saying that he would be happy to help. He was now waiting for me to collect him and bring him to the hospital. You could say that the intervention of the warden and her colleagues at the student hostel was providential for neither the Skipper nor the Russian Jew understood one another.

We left the hospital about 10.00 p.m. with a great feeling of relief and satisfaction but somewhat humbled to realize the dangerous gap there was in our welfare programme of which we were totally unaware until the need arose. 'A stitch in time saves nine.' I resolved a list would be compiled forthwith and updated regularly. 'To be forewarned is to be fore-armed.'

It feels good when you're thanked

1) An anonymous donation of 50 pence sterling was handed into our reception desk from a seafarer with instructions to be used to put flowers in the Church.

2) The Chief Steward from a Swedish freighter handed me three pounds (sterling) as a donation towards our Christmas Party.

3) I hardly had time to thank the latter gentleman when the doors of the club suddenly burst open to make way for the Chief Baker of the Royal Fleet Auxiliary vessel, *Sir Percival*, carrying a large Christmas cake, beautifully iced and a perfect model of our club. He was escorted by twelve fellow-countrymen (Chinese) two of whom carried large trays with a variety of savouries. The cake we were to keep for our Christmas Day party while the other goodies we could eat immediately. Appreciation for hospitality received.

Contrast

When I arrived at the top of the gangway of a Soviet freighter I was greeted by a young seafarer in a most pleasant manner with a broad smile. 'Just wait a moment or two,' he said. He was a friendly young man and I complimented him on his spoken English by saying, 'Very good English.' 'Just a little,' he responded and then pushed the bell to summon an officer on deck as is customary on all Soviet ships.

When the officer came on deck I handed him our brochure and stated how all would be welcome to enjoy the facilities we had to offer. He glanced through this without comment until he observed a cross printed above the listed times of our Church services. Now somewhat annoyed and with his finger pointing at the cross he remarked, 'No that here, this Russian ship.' I tried to point to the other symbols representing billiards, dancing, table tennis, football, etc. as if to say we've got these too and nobody is going to force you into religion, but he was not having any and handed me back the brochure with the words, 'This Russian ship, we no come to your club.'

By contrast, in another area of the port was another Soviet ship from which the crew regularly visited the Flying Angel Club and obviously enjoyed themselves, returning again and again. Alas, as time progressed, until the break up of the Soviet Union most crew on these vessels were forbidden to visit our Club.

Frequently you do what you can in the hope that you are doing what is required in the circumstances

A Chaplain with the Missions to Seamen can find himself in many difficult situations and it is not always easy to know exactly what one should do in given circumstances. Our primary motivating force must be concern for the seafarer. Wherever possible we try to contact a Pastor or Priest of the seafarer's own religious denomination and encourage him to assist in a welfare case or seek his advice.

An inexplicable tragedy had occurred. The Chief Engineer committed suicide by hanging himself in his cabin on board ship. He was a wealthy man and had no financial concerns so far as anybody knew. Before taking his life he penned a note of apology for his action to the crew and his family, merely stating that he did not wish to live any longer.

I contacted the only Greek Orthodox Priest residing in Ireland and made him aware of the circumstances and of the need to minister to the other crew members, all of whom were Greek. He lived in Dublin and was at this time recovering from major surgery and was incapable of travelling. We had a long conversation and in the circumstances was happy that I should do what I could.

I then visited the ship's Master and offered to conduct a memorial service on board using the late Chief's cabin myself. He informed me that his Father was a Priest in the Greek Orthodox Church and he felt that he would approve. 'Seafarers are very superstitious people and it would relieve their minds to know that a Priest had come on board and in prayer asked Almighty God to receive the troubled soul of the Chief and grant him peace.' On hearing that I would give a brief address, the Master agreed to have someone translate the service from English into Greek.

The warm handshakes which followed the service from members of the crew indicated very clearly their gratitude and approval. It was new territory for me but entered into in the knowledge that whatever the imperfections of our holy things the Almighty would forgive and make good.

I'm your man

Would to God that those of us who seek ordination to Holy Orders in the Church were as dependable as we ought to be. Alas, our performance does not always match our profession save for a few.

I once knew a Chaplain with the Missions to Seamen who had pursued a career at sea before training for ordination. His forthright honesty and compassion throughout his ministry was refreshing. He had no ambitions other than to serve seafarers as a Priest within the framework of the Missions to Seamen. Most people would envy his reputation.

A local Rector contacted me about a young parishioner of his who had gone to sea and was about to spend his first Christmas on board ship. He was serving on a British coaster which would be tied up in a small port in the UK over the festive season. The boy had been in a spot of trouble earlier on and had mastered his difficulties like a man. The Rector was concerned about him having to spend his first Christmas away from home and would appreciate any hospitality that could be extended to him.

Without fear of contradiction I could assure this Rector that his parishioner had landed on his feet and could not be under the care of a more understanding or compassionate man, an opinion shared by all my colleagues who knew him. Acknowledging my letter of commendation he had written, 'I'll take care of him, Joe, and bring him everywhere with me. If he needs a chance, I'm your man. I'll give him one.'

All too often it's poor old Mum who bears the brunt, though she rarely complains

A seafarer was found dead in his bunk on board a small coaster in a UK port. His elderly mother was listed as his next of kin and she lived in Northern Ireland. My colleague in this port was contacted in the hope that he could arrange to have the news conveyed gently to his elderly mother and here is where we fit into this sad tale.

I had known the deceased who had many problems over a number of years and tried to help on several occasions but all to no avail.

The mother lived in a pensioner's bungalow on a housing estate not far from central Belfast. A new Minister had just commenced duty in her local Church. Being slightly deaf she automatically assumed that I was he when I called. Like most proud mothers she spoke in most glowing terms of her grown family living in the neighbourhood but made no mention whatsoever of the deceased. I could not get a word in and did not wish to interrupt until she had finished.

I began to wonder if I had come to the wrong house and if there had been a mistake. When she eventually stopped talking, gently I enquired if she had another son by the name . . . ? Her reply was pathetic, 'Yes, but he never bothers about me. He is wild and selfish, the black sheep I suppose. He was a lovely boy, but was destroyed from the moment he left home to go to sea. I often worry about him as he is in poor health and abuses himself greatly. The last time I saw him was two months ago in hospital, here in Belfast. He promised to come here afterwards but never did.'

With a very heavy heart I had to gradually get around to informing her that there would be no need for her to worry again as her son was now in safe keeping.

A sample of today's mail

I feel I must write and thank you for the comfort your kind words gave me on the telephone last night. My mind is eased to know that he is being so well cared for. Everyone has been very kind during this difficult time, nurses and staff at the hospital, and our friends and neighbours. I alone know just how my husband will appreciate you visiting him.

During the last seventeen years my husband has given me a lifetime of happiness, love and comfort. My son, daughter and myself should get on our knees and thank God for giving us such a wonderful husband and father. I pray God will give me back a little of my health and strength so that I can give him the help he now needs. If love and prayers will help him he will soon be well again. Thanking you once again.

This letter is evidence of a very strong bond. It helps contradict the all too frequently thoughtless image portrayed of seafarers and their families: out of sight out of mind. The husband informed me that his wife was crippled with acute arthritis and a heart condition. She lived on her own confined to two rooms and was looked after by neighbours and had to be assisted in and out of bed. He had been admitted to hospital with a suspected coronary attack and was deeply concerned about his wife when she received this news. They had spoken over the telephone from the hospital and he detected that she was still very worried. In the circumstances he found it very difficult to relax himself which he was supposed to do. I promised to telephone his wife and reassure her about his condition and inform her that he was making good progress. She was much relieved to hear from me and promised to telephone me if she felt any further cause for concern. She did too, about 10.00 p.m. the following evening. She had received a message from the hospital about her husband's condition which was very confusing. I promised to call back after I had visited the hospital and did so after 11.00 p.m. when I was able to explain the misunderstanding and assure her there was no cause for concern. Her letter was in response to this call.

Snippets from a Christmas programme

It was becoming an established tradition on Christmas Eve to go carol singing alongside ships in port. Year by year the number of participants increased with more and more members of the Ladies Harbour Lights turning up for the occasion. This year we had the best turn out ever and could really make ourselves heard.

One of the first ships we visited was a Norwegian bulk carrier. The Master and everyone on board, as was customary in their country, were just beginning their Christmas celebrations. The Master insisted that we join them which we agreed to do for a time having first explained the purpose of our visit to dockland in general. It was a memorable occasion, the crew danced around the Christmas tree singing carols in their own language. Our visit was something of a nostalgic one for the Master who informed me that the first couple to be married in our Chapel were members of the crew on a former ship of which he was Master. Though we were all enjoying the party nevertheless we had to leave as we were expected to call to many ships in port.

When we were almost alongside a Soviet Union freighter, suddenly the gangway was hoisted up out of reach. It was difficult to say whether an officer had given instructions to raise the gangway before we attempted to go on board or if the watchmen took fright when they saw such a large crowd approaching the ship singing merrily.

Anyway we sang them a carol and by the time we reached the end, the crew came out on deck to look and listen but the gangway was not lowered. On occasions like this one regretted the limitation of language as none of us could communicate with them in their own tongue. Though I doubt it would have made any difference had we been able to do so as by then all personnel on these ships were closely chaperoned to ensure they did not communicate with anybody ashore.

We were accompanied by two Greek seafarers who joined us for the occasion as we left the club. After a busy night it was agreed that theirs would be the last ship we would visit. It was well past our quitting time but we could not disappoint the Greeks and had to go on board for hospitality had been arranged. This was once again a memorable occasion when our carol party and the Greek seafarers took turns singing carols in their own language.

We don't always get our priorities right

I don't make any great claims to sainthood and have as much to be put right in my own life as the next guy. However, in this latter part of the twentieth century in which I write I'm absolutely convinced that most of us guys (humans who profess and call themselves Christians) need reminding on occasions where our true priorities as Christians should lie. I was brought up on the old Anglican prayer book. Christmas, remember, used to get a little out of hand in the form of celebrating towards the end of the day and it was difficult to apply the brakes. However next day on the Feast of St. Stephen, the first Christian martyr, we were reminded of the cost of following Jesus Christ when the liturgical colours changed to red. Regrettably, instead of labouring to emphasize this contrast, of latter years the Church transferred this Feast day to the holiday season in August when most people are on holidays. So much for putting the emphasis in the right place. On Christmas Day at our party, in the light of all of the festivities and full and plenty for everyone I could never get away from the message of St. Stephen's Day. We had a duty in the spirit of Christmas to share our blessing with those less fortunate than ourselves. I mentioned this to seafarers and it became our custom to pass around the hat and take up a collection from everyone present. Over two years running this collection was donated to War on Want.

On this occasion a few days before Christmas a Spanish seafarer had been killed in a tragic accident in Belfast leaving a widow and two small children. Once again the hat was passed around with this family in mind when a sum of thirty-one pounds sterling was donated for them. A few days later the Spanish Consul General wrote,

> I would ask you to thank in my name all the people the collection made on Christmas Day. I am very grateful for the thirty-one pounds received, which will be sent to his wife in Spain.

WHILST UNREST IN NORTHERN IRELAND WAS BECOMING A DAILY FEATURE ON THE WORLD STAGE VOLUNTARY SOCIETIES SUCH AS THE MISSIONS TO SEAMEN WITH MINOR ADJUSTMENTS TO THEIR PROGRAMMES SIMPLY CARRIED ON AS ALWAYS

Apart from the summer months, we usually held three weekly dances at the Flying Angel club. We could do this because we had a large and dedicated membership in our Hostesses Guild. The holiday months of July and August presented a bit of a problem. The number of hostesses decreased as some were away on holidays. We also had another problem: while our main recreation hall was magnificent and had a beautiful maple floor ideal for dancing there were no side windows. Daylight entered through panels in the ceiling or roof space which meant that it lacked the darkened atmosphere associated with a dance hall. It was very cumbersome to draw the roof blinds to eliminate daylight.

It seemed wrong to be indoors three times weekly on summer evenings, yet we had an obligation to make some provision for the entertainment of visiting seafarers. Following a little brain storming we came up with the idea of chartering a bus twice weekly during these months to do local tours. Our Hostesses Guild organized coffee parties and other events, and the proceeds were used to subsidize the cost of the tours and provide seats to seafarers at a reasonable cost. Much to the delight of seafarers many hostesses, if free, would join seafarers for the tours, each one paying her own fare.

The tours were an unqualified success but the programme eventually had to be cancelled with the spread of civil disturbances throughout the province. We were left with no alternative as rioters began to hijack and burn buses so for the safety of all concerned very reluctantly we had to cancel out.

It would be very difficult to find an equal to the Hostesses Guild in Belfast. These ladies knew what they were about and they were prepared to make personal sacrifices to attain the Mission's objectives. They knew that the seafarer ashore in a strange land appreciated the opportunity afforded him through the Mission for contact and fellowship with those who live ashore. Somehow a way had to be found to bridge this gap.

We did the best we could in the circumstances. A new simpler mechanism was installed to draw the blinds in our entertainment hall and dancing was restored on these two evenings, though on occasions we were short of hostesses owing to vacation times.

Do you believe in premonitions?

I remember on one occasion having a long conversation with a Presbyterian Minister about his role during wartime. He was in charge of a large congregation in an area which was predominantly inhabited by people who made their career at sea. Sea going was a tradition for almost every male in this community. I hardly need elaborate much further about what he had to do as ships in convoy after convoy were sunk. It suffices for me to quote, 'I don't know how I kept going as I came to feel like the angel of death on occasions.' I knew exactly how he felt for this was very much part of my work to be the bearer of sad tidings.

I received a request from a British shipping company early one morning to inform a young wife that her husband had died suddenly after being admitted to hospital in a European port. Within two weeks I found myself visiting the same neighbourhood to perform the same task. On the previous occasion it was to inform an old lady of her son's death and now this young wife with a family of three, the eldest being thirteen years old.

Having invited me into her home the widow immediately turned to me and said, 'It's my husband, he's dead.' I could only reply in amazement, 'I'm afraid so.' While we waited for a family member to arrive she informed me that throughout the night she had an overwhelming sense of an impending tragedy and the very moment she saw the Missions to Seamen badge in my coat lapel this seemed to confirm her feelings.

A decision was made not to bring the body home for burial and that cremation should take place overseas and the ashes be returned to me for burial in local waters.

With people living ashore the funeral usually provides an opportunity for family and friends to pay their last respects and commend the deceased to God's gracious keeping. It's therapeutic for the family, helping to bring to a conclusion the immediate sense of mourning by paving the way for their lives to continue. I always felt as a seafarer's Chaplain in circumstances of this nature that it was incumbent upon me to try and do the next best thing. We arranged with the family to hold a memorial service in our Chapel to which relatives and friends could be invited. Over sixty people attended and we provided light refreshments in a lounge following the service.

It's a small world. Immediately following the service a lady walked up to me and said, 'What has happened today and over the preceding days is typical of the Missions to Seamen.' She then went on to tell me her son was killed in an accident at sea some years earlier and she had experienced the same ministry from the Rev. Don Lewin in the port of Dublin. This was interesting as I had been trained by the Rev. Don Lewin there.

The widow had requested that donations be sent to the Missions to Seamen instead of flowers by those who wished to do so. A number of people present at the service had placed these in envelopes on a chair at the back of the Chapel as they left. When these envelopes were collected by my secretary to have official receipts mailed to donors she found in one envelope a sum of money accompanied by three small rose buds. A compassionate person, she immediately concluded the rose buds came from the children. She sought out the youngest of the three and asked him to accompany her to the Chapel. 'Now I want you to look around and tell me where we should place these rose buds in memory of your Dad.' He took time to look all around him before finally placing them at the foot of the cross on the altar with the words, 'I think everyone will see them here.' There they remained until they withered.

It's not always easy to reason why

I received news of a most terrible disaster at sea by telephone one evening. A small coaster on a regular run between a Belfast shipyard and a port in England had been lost with all hands. Most of the ship's company were well known to us at the Flying Angel club except for the Chief and Second Officers who both lived locally and normally went home when the ship arrived in port. Indeed only a day or two earlier the Master paid a visit to our library and selected for himself a pile of books which he took back to the ship to read.

Ironically the telephone call I received was from the company's Marine Superintendent asking me to inform the next of kin of the two local men involved in the tragedy, neither of whom I had ever met. I do not believe that I will ever forget this experience. I was completely unprepared for the circumstances to confront me in both homes.

When I called to the home of the Second Officer his wife greeted me and invited me into her home. She was a wonderful lady and insisted that I sit down and make myself comfortable before we talked. She then looked across the room at me and said, 'It's all right, I know, I've been watching television and saw it all.' How this broadcast was ever allowed to be made before the next of kin had been informed I will never know. It appeared that a TV camera crew had recorded the tragedy from the shore. Neither the Marine Superintendent nor I had delayed in calling to this home. I was devastated and again wholly unprepared for my next call.

It transpired that the Chief Officer was a widower, his young wife having died only two years earlier leaving two little girls, one aged six years and the other aged eleven years. Grandma, his wife's mother, now kept home and was helping raise the two little girls. Fortunately they had not seen the news broadcast but just the same I must confess that for the moment words simply failed me.

The people of the United Kingdom, a sea going nation, learned much from tragedies of this nature in their history and established a number of charitable bodies to render financial assistance to next of kin. Our society's Chaplains acted as agents for a number of these bodies which meant that we were in a position to channel immediate aid. The Sailors Children's Society of Hull and the Ship Wrecked Mariners Society amongst others never failed to render aid, both immediate and long term, in these and many other cases.

Some time later a badly decomposed body was washed up on the east coast of England, and enough facts came to light to make it reasonably certain that it was the body of the Chief Officer. An unusual watch strap on the arm, if it could be identified as his, would confirm other findings. Grandma telephoned me to say that the eldest daughter had been with her Dad when he had purchased a watch and if it was the same she could make a positive identification. Grandma had received a beautiful letter of sympathy from the Rev. Alan Coleman, Chaplain at the Tees Missions to Seamen, when the tragedy occurred. She now wondered if she were to let this little girl travel over from Belfast accompanied by her aunt and uncle to identify the strap, would Alan take care of them? I telephoned Alan at his home but he was not available so I spoke to his wife. Her immediate response, 'Just send them along and give them Alan's telephone number and we'll take care of everything.' The little girl identified the strap as being similar to her Dad's.

The remains were brought to Belfast for burial and rested overnight in our little Chapel in which the funeral service was held next day at the request of the family. It was conducted by their own Minister, a member of the Methodist Church, and I assisted. Over two hundred people attended when the congregation overflowed into the adjoining hall. Of this number at least half were seafarers who lived locally. I felt very sorry for the wife and two daughters of the Second Officer whose body had never been recovered.

Grandma, an unforgettable lady of character and courage, was eventually appointed the children's legal guardian. Though she carried an almost insurmountable burden yet she made others feel that they were doing all the work. The source of her strength I would have no hesitation in attributing to 'Amazing Grace'. She was later to write.

> Just a few lines to thank you for all your kindness to the children and myself. I never really knew people could be so kind. I was only getting over the death of my only daughter and this has knocked the courage out of me. I just can't understand how two such happy people as . . . . and . . . . had to be taken away from their little girls. But this I will understand, you helped a lot just by talking to us and we felt we should have been happier seeing they were together again. God bless you and again many thanks.

Separation and its consequences for the seafarer and his loved ones

Can you imagine what is must be like to receive a message that a loved one has been hospitalized overseas far from family and friends and you have no idea why? 'It's my son, Padre. I received a letter to inform me that he was admitted to hospital in Singapore and I'm very worried about him.'

With experience one could frequently reduce the immediate cause for concern in these circumstances. If the message was received by mail, generally speaking there was no immediate cause for concern. No doubt further news would follow in a day or two and it usually did. One could also provide them with the mailing address of our Chaplain in the port concerned. He would no doubt be visiting the patient and deliver any mail addressed to him.

The overwhelming majority of British shipping companies at this time were, I found, very considerate of families in these circumstances and one usually had little cause for concern where the family member was serving on a British or Scandinavian ship. However, we always tried to hold a watching brief and check back in a day or two to enquire if further news had been received. In this instance when I checked back a very worried Mum greeted me, 'There's been no further news.'

Her son was a Radio Officer with a reputable company who contracted this service to shipping companies. I informed the mother that neglect of this nature seemed out of character with both companies from my experience of them. However I would contact them and express her concern and get back to her with news later in the day. I contacted the welfare department in both companies and remonstrated about the insensitive manner in which this officer's hospitalization overseas was being handled which was causing distress to his mother. It transpired that a member of the staff in the former company had been negligent in her duty to follow up the first letter. A letter of apology would be mailed to the mother immediately.

Within an hour I was able to return to the home with an up to the moment medical bulletin reassuring a very worried mother. A couple of days later I was back again with a letter from our Chaplain in Singapore. Obviously he had been to see her son about the same time as she sought my help. This letter added to her reassurance.

Watching, waiting and far from home

One afternoon a British seafarer died in hospital without regaining consciousness, the result of an accident on board ship. Immediately following the accident his elderly mother and her sister travelled over from England to remain by her son's bedside where apart from a few breaks they had remained until then, a period in excess of three months.

We identified with this sad little group almost daily by making several trips to the hospital to fulfil one need or another for the ladies, although there was little we could do for the son save to pray. The only break these ladies permitted themselves was to visit our home twice weekly for a couple of hours and very reluctantly avail themselves of a couple of sight seeing trips with Alan Jones, our Lay Worker.

I was taking my day off duty when news of this man's death reached me. The daily flight to their home town had already departed so my wife invited them to spend the remainder of the day at our home where they had already established a relationship with our children. Quietly the shipping agents made arrangements for the deceased body to be returned home for burial.

After this long and distressing vigil by her son's bedside Mum still found time in the midst of coping with her bereavement to write and say thanks for what little we had tried to do.

Many thanks for your welcome letter and for all your kindness during my son's illness. It seems so hard to believe that he won't come home again, but as you say he would have been probably maimed for life and God knows what was best for him. We had a nice funeral service but I would have liked you to be here, but I know we were in your prayers. I must thank you also for getting in touch with his Union for me. There's been a chap down, named Mr Lynch from Manchester Seamen's Union and he was very kind and said I'll be all right on their part as all his union books were paid up and they have my name as next of kin, but they cannot do anything until after the inquest which will be in eight weeks.

Please thank Mrs Parker and the children for their kindness during our visit. Will write again.

Yours sincerely,

UNDER THE SHADOW OF THE BOMBER
AND THE GUNMAN

While the Missions to Seamen in Northern Ireland drew the bulk of its financial support from the non Roman Catholic community, nevertheless in keeping with the philosophy of the society world wide our objective was to serve all seafarers irrespective of race, creed or colour. At no time was I ever pressured to do otherwise. In view of the religious content associated with the disturbances in Northern Ireland over the past twenty years, I feel it is incumbent upon me to make this statement.

The Apostleship of the Sea, our sister society in the Roman Catholic Church, was a comparatively newcomer on the world scene compared with the Missions to Seamen. Seafarers are drawn from every race and creed and it's true to say that a majority would detest any hostility between our two bodies. We each went our separate way in tolerance and understanding. My predecessor, the Rev. Ted Matchette, gave a lot of assistance and advice when the new Stella Maris Club was constructed and opened in Belfast. Following in his footsteps, at no time did political or denominational considerations cloud our relationship.

My first actual experience of a riot situation occurred one Saturday just prior to taking my annual vacation. I had been visited earlier in the day by a young man whose father had just died. His brother was a seafarer and his ship was due at any moment in an Australian port. He wondered if we could get a message about the father's death with a request from his mother for him to come home if at all possible. I promised to do my utmost and report back at his home later in the day.

After a number of telephone calls and later in the day I was able to visit the home in a predominantly Roman Catholic area of the city with news. Our Chaplain in the port concerned had everything in hand. The ship had not yet arrived in port but he had been in touch with the local agents and arranged his return by air upon arrival. Our Chaplain would meet the ship himself and break the news. On my return journey to the club I ran into the tail end of a riot. Little did I realize that this was but the tip of an iceberg which would change the course of many of our lives.

Under normal circumstances my ministry occupied most of my time with the result that generally speaking my wife had to be father and mother to our children. She did not complain but now with civil disturbances on the increase throughout the province, community clashes and riots daily it did not bode well for the future. We realized that if this situation continued to get out of hand we would be taxed even more so we decided our holiday was essential: a change of environment for rest and refreshment when we would ignore all radio and TV news bulletins, as living in Northern Ireland at this time one tended to live from one news bulletin to the next.

We arranged to spend a couple of weeks in a beautiful rural setting in county Kerry in the Republic of Ireland where I had agreed to do holiday duty in a local parish. Being the tourist season I was required to officiate at additional services held in local Churches and we were accommodated free in a large well appointed trailer in the grounds of a local Church of Ireland Rectory (Anglican). We did our own catering. With a young family and an unhealthy bank account this was one way of providing a holiday for the children and for my wife at least a change of scenery away from the threat of violence.

Memory in Ireland goes back a long way with regard to political events. People remember what they want to remember. It is very selective.

When the troubles erupted in Northern Ireland many were shocked to learn that in the Republic there was a sizable undercurrent of religious intolerance and understandably, a degree of support for their Roman Catholic co-religionists in Northern Ireland and, even more frightening, support for the objectives of the Provisional IRA. It was against this background that we were to learn of the latest developments in Northern Ireland.

Stephen, our second son, was fooling around in the sea with other kids when a man close by, on hearing his accent, entered into a conversation with him. 'Are you from Belfast?' 'Yes.' Now came the inevitable question. 'Are you a Catholic or Protestant?' 'A Protestant.' 'So it's your crowd who are killing all the Catholics in Belfast.' Poor Stephen, scared by this unprovoked verbal assault, replied truthfully, 'My Dad only works there; I was born in Dublin,' and he immediately made his way over to where we were sitting on the beach and related the encounter to his Mum and me. His interrogator disappeared so quickly from the scene that we did not even get a look at him.

My wife and I were both born, raised and educated in the Republic of Ireland so this man's outburst did not come as a surprise to us. While we realized it was by no means representative of the thinking of many people in the Republic, it did represent the thinking of some. What percentage we could not say but certainly not a minority, it would seem at this time. What lay behind this verbal onslaught directed against an innocent boy? The answer was more tragic than we could ever have anticipated. Life in Northern Ireland would never be the same again. We'd observed a news blackout since we'd left home The events of the previous days had been dreadful and wholly unjustified and until now we knew nothing about them.

In Londonderry a group of Republican supporters had chosen to fly the Starry Plough flag (which was associated with the socialist side of Irish republican movement) from a prominent position in the Bogside, a neighbourhood inhabited almost exclusively by people of the Roman Catholic faith and of a republican tradition. To Loyalists this was like waving a red flag to a bull. It was interpreted as complete anarchy. Eventually the situation got out of hand and despite the use of CS gas to control the crowd and to ward off petrol bomb attacks and attacks from stones thrown at them the police gradually lost control, their numbers having been depleted by injuries and exhaustion. The Northern Ireland Government eventually decided to ask for the assistance of British troops, so a company of the Prince of Wales Own Regiment took over duty in the city.

The same day in Belfast, Roman Catholic and Protestant crowds faced each other in Divis and Dover streets. Protestants entered Roman Catholic areas and burned down many houses. In a confused situation four men and a young boy died by shooting in Belfast with sniping going on all night and next day. Eventually, as in Londonderry, units of the British Army arrived to take up duty in Belfast. Six hundred troops of the Third Battalion Light Infantry with fixed bayonets took up positions in the city. They succeeded in manning a line between Protestant and Roman Catholic crowds and this formed the basis of what was to become the established 'Peace Line'. Owing to difficulties in establishing protection quickly enough many more Roman Catholic houses were burned down. Many Roman Catholics as refugees fled to the Republic of Ireland for protection.

(I am indebted to *A Chronology of Events* Volume 2 1968-1971 published by Blackstaff Press Ltd. Belfast for much of the information contained in the latter summary.)

Needless to say these developments brought an immediate response from the Government and many people in the Republic of Ireland. A predominately Roman Catholic country (in some respects militantly so) and with its history and long unforgiving memory, at this time there was not much sympathy or even attempt to understand the Northern Ireland Unionist's point of view or Protestant fears. In these circumstances sympathy not unnaturally tended to gravitate towards the people of their own faith in Northern Ireland. In an emotional outpouring of public anger many windows were broken in the British Embassy in Dublin where the Union Jack was torn down from its flag pole and burned. The real tragedy of this uncontrolled public euphoria was to provide within the Republic in the years to follow an objective and a fertile recruiting ground for the Provisional IRA. The roots of the Northern Ireland problem were by no means as simple as they were being portrayed and few had the time nor the inclination to investigate and listen, to the delight of the Provisional IRA. At heart I was an Irish nationalist but of a rare breed, a more mature breed I liked to think. The Ireland of my dreams was a sovereign thirty two county state where being Protestant or Roman Catholic was of no account in one's relationship to the state.

My Ireland, if worthy of sovereignty, must be born of voluntary consent and not the product of the bomb or the bullet. 'Ireland is her people' and the love of Ireland insofar as I'm concerned is best demonstrated when Irish men learn to love their neighbour as themselves. In the meantime while still a Chaplain with the Missions to Seamen I would carry on as if I were a citizen of the world having a relationship with seafarers of every race, creed and colour.

Our work continued while the shadow extended

We returned from vacation to find Belfast a very changed city. People on both sides of the political divide were afraid for their personal safety and that of their families. Though troops had by now been dispersed and were on patrol throughout the city nevertheless many people in working class neighbourhoods where the conflict was more intense had little confidence in the ability of the troops to protect their neighbourhood. Their fear could be described as naked; they were almost incapable of trusting anybody but known members of their own community. Rumour and mistrust were rampant: a deadly force to contend with throughout the whole community and explosive too.

In this volatile situation various communities formed vigilante groups for defence purposes to patrol their own neighbourhood. I joined a patrol group in the dock area which in time was disbanded when the military earned the confidence of those residing in the area. It was a relief when this happened as it was not easy to function all day in relation to my work in the port and then with this group for part of the night. Alas, mistrust and suspicion spread when other vigilante groups eventually became recruiting grounds for terrorist organizations.

Unlike later years in Northern Ireland, at this time street riots were commonplace. Because of this threat public transport at night had to be suspended in many areas. The facilities we had to offer were now more valuable in the life of the seafarer than peace time. Our hostesses realized this and kept our dances going. They formed voluntary car pools to transport their colleagues who had no transport to and from the club. Canteen and fund raising volunteers did likewise. We never lacked volunteers to keep the club open and functioning during these very difficult times when fear and community anxiety was stretched to the limit.

The overseas press, radio and television were having a field day with every news bulletin reporting on the latest atrocity in Northern Ireland. The fall out from this was to reverberate in the form of concern by seafarers serving overseas about their families back home. The following is an extract from a telegram I received from a Chaplain in South Africa.

'Check safety' and there followed a detailed list of names and addresses of eight families living all over the city. None lived in a riot zone but as a result of media reports those away from home had become concerned. We had no alternative but to call to every house in these circumstances and report back as requested. This entailed a lot of extra work on occasions.

One morning about 2.00 a.m. the telephone by my bedside rang. It was the Master of a passenger ferry which sailed between the British mainland and Belfast. He had made his home in Belfast and his wife was one of our most dedicated volunteers. Listening to the late night news he learned that his home was in the centre of a volatile gathering that could erupt at any moment. His wife had informed him that the house was surrounded by troops and she appeared to be almost sick with anxiety. Could I help?

No time to ponder, mine had to be a knee jerk reaction: 'I will go to your home immediately and insist that she accompany me here where she can spend the remainder of the night.' When I arrived at the front door, having explained myself to the military, I could hear the telephone ringing in the hallway. It was the Master calling to inform his wife of our arrangement and he had difficulty believing that I had arrived already. In the meantime my wife prepared a bed to receive our guest for the night.

What I have mentioned in the lead up to this chapter and in the chapter itself about the expansion of civil disturbances in Northern Ireland was to get even worse, making it very difficult for our work to continue, but thanks to a body of marvellous people we never closed our doors even when tragedy struck in our very midst. Within months the situation deteriorated even more as the Provisional IRA emerged from amongst the rioters to bomb buildings and murder and maim people through their bombing campaign and eliminate others with their guns. The main target at this stage in their bombing campaign was the pubs.

I could not but help feel that it was providential we had secured a licence at the Flying Angel club before all of this began as it was to get even worse as time progressed when there was a Loyalist backlash.

He won't need this now

The personal safety of seafarers using the port became a matter of concern for all of us at the Flying Angel club at this tragic time. We made a visit to every ship to warn seafarers of the conditions prevailing ashore. We would acquaint them of the facilities we had to offer in the hope they would not go wandering about the city.

Security and safety precautions of one kind or another could not put on the long finger in relation to the club, for tomorrow might be too late. This morning I came in early to attend to one such matter up town before I went ship visiting. A local shipping agent stood awaiting me on my return to the club.

One hour earlier he had occasion to call on board a ship in port to transact business with the Master, an old friend. They had not met for some years so there was a lot of catching up to do in the way of family news. The Master was particularly proud of his twenty year old son who had followed his father in his choice of a career at sea. His son was serving with an international oil company and his ship was at this time in dry-dock in Japan. Father and son were both due leave shortly and the Master was counting the days until they would meet again. Before the agent left the ship to go ashore the Master handed him a letter to mail to his son.

When the agent returned to his office a tragic message awaited him to deliver to the Master. His son had been killed in an accident in dry-dock and he was to arrange for his passage home by the quickest possible route. The tragic news had already been relayed to the boy's mother.

The agent in the circumstances not unnaturally could not face the task of being the bearer of such tidings. He asked me to do so while he personally made the travel arrangements and would then follow me to the ship. When I informed the Master of this tragic news there was a look of blind unbelief on his face. It took a little time for the news to sink in, when his immediate concern was for his wife whom he said had been ill recently. 'I must go home at once,' he said. I was able to assure him that his wife had been informed and was coping. Likewise that the agent would be returning shortly to take him to the airport having booked him on the first available flight.

We had time for him to call into the Club and in the privacy of my office talk to his wife on the telephone. After his telephone call he turned to me and said, 'I just can't believe it, Padre.' It was even more ironic to hear his reply when the agent discreetly returned to him the letter addressed to his son. Looking at this he said, 'He won't need this now.'

Forging a link with families

The British being a seagoing nation, it was inevitable that over a period of time schools would be established where the basic skills of seamanship, pre-sea going training in efficiency, safety and manning would be given. One aspect of this programme enjoyed my admiration. Every encouragement, it seemed to me, was given to societies like the Missions to Seamen to become involved in the programme in the interest of promoting the welfare of the seafarer and his family. Though I'd never visited one of these establishments yet I got to know quite a bit about them from first-trippers who usually knew where to find us, having heard all about us at the pre-training establishment they had attended.

A number of the boys from our area in Northern Ireland usually went to an establishment at Gravesend in England. One Missions to Seamen Chaplain there tried seriously to forge a link between the student's family and the Missions to Seamen. Immediately a student graduated he would inform the Chaplain nearest to his home in the hope that at this point the Chaplain would follow up by establishing a link with the family. In turn I would write to the boy's parents or legal guardian enclosing a list of our Chaplains world-wide and inform them not to hesitate to contact anyone of us, myself included, if they had cause to be concerned about the boy. Some ignored my letter while others responded immediately by writing to say how comforted they were to hear from me.

One evening a very worried father called to see me. His son following his pre-sea training had left home five weeks earlier to join his first ship in a European port and since then he had heard nothing of him. There had been a postal strike since he'd left home but it was long since over. He wondered if I could provide him with the name of the local company who acted as agents for his son's shipping company and he would try and pursue enquiries through them. I was able to do better than this and within minutes by telephone I was through to the headquarters of the company who employed his son. I could assure the father that his son had joined the ship where he was still employed and was in excellent health so there was no need for further worry in this connection. I also told him that the Master of the ship would have a tactful word with the boy and make sure that he wrote home from time to time.

A seafarer's appreciation as expressed in a letter to members of the Ladies Harbour Lights Guild

I have chosen to include this letter primarily to illustrate how much seafarers appreciated the contribution these ladies made towards their welfare. It should be remembered that at this time Northern Ireland was enveloped in civil disturbance.

> I apologize for not being able to write you earlier because of the sudden change of sailing schedule. I promised to write and I did not mean to do so late. Time and tide wait for no one and nearly a month has gone by since we said good-bye to one another. I hope every one of you has been getting on well. Can you send my regards to . . . . and . . . . and tell them I will write to them as soon as possible.
>
> You all have been very friendly to me. I must admit I miss you very much. Never a day past I didn't think of you and the people I met in the 'Mission'. Your friendly reception is unforgettable in my memory.
>
> Monday – a dance night again. Clock hands pointed towards the enchanted hours which is what the French call 'le Petit à Sept' gloaming. This was the moment I used to be ready for going to the 'party' held in the 'Mission' when I was in Belfast. But now I had to lock myself up in my cabin dreaming. I am not a dreamer, nor a fantastic, but this is the only way to do now as the ship is on sea. Through the porthole, looking down at the dark blue sea water through which the ship is sliding her way forward, ripples of it widen and widen, and to my ear comes the 'whir' of it – a sound that is always touched with loneliness and a soft regret for something. You don't know what. This is what the life at sea is.
>
> Life on sea is quiet as one could imagine – as quiet as the snow or rain or the rustle of trees in midsummer. Everyone could feel the monotony of it. Nevertheless I am busy for preparing of the coming Nov. exam. I have to spare three hours a day to study. The hideous figures of the course of 'accountancy' I am going to deal with now. Pardon my ending the letter now. Excuse my rough hand writing and poor English. I've to be in a hurry.
>
> Regards to . . . . and . . . .
>
> With my fondest wishes.

IT'S NOT THEIR WAR, YET TRAGICALLY
AS IN ALL WARS THE INNOCENT SUFFER TOO

The calm of our lovely summer evenings during 1971 was disturbed by the not infrequent sound of gunfire or the boom of a bomb exploding followed by the sound of emergency vehicles: ambulances, fire trucks, and police making their way to the scene of the latest explosion. Life had changed so dramatically from what we had known a few years earlier and we all had to try and cope with this new situation which was so unpredictable and in many instances demonstrated a total disregard for the sacredness of human life. One had to admire the spirit of the people as establishment after establishment was bombed sometimes with loss of life and injuries when in a matter of hours a sign announced 'Business as usual'.

The terrorist, 'our ghostly enemy', remained unrestrained and one never knew where or when he would strike again, do his evil deed and disappear.

We always felt that the terrorists would respect the Flying Angel club as neutral ground and for this reason it was probably the safest place in the city for a seafarer to be found. Our concern was for the damage we might sustain were the terrorists to select an establishment in our immediate vicinity for bombing.

One night I dreamed a dream and kept waking up with one question on my mind. What if a bomb were to explode at the garage opposite the club, shattering the windows in the main lounge which at this time was usually full of people? Following a very restless night and knowing the reason my wife said to me, 'You should do something about this immediately to protect everyone inside from splintering glass in the event of an explosion opposite.'

I was frightened by the threat of danger so I got busy the very moment I arrived at the club. The proprietor of the garage was most helpful and detailed one of his staff to come to our assistance right away. He made frames covered with wire mesh (small holes) for the windows. As an added precaution we also covered the glass with clear contact paper. We worked on to finish the job before going home. I was not on duty in the club this evening but could leave for home with an easy mind.

About 9.00 p.m the Provisional IRA did as we had anticipated and placed a bomb at the garage across the road. When it exploded we did not have one piece of glass remaining in the windows in the front of the club but we had none inside either as the fragments of shattered glass lay strewn on the sidewalk. When the bomb exploded, standing beside the window in the main lounge was the wife of a German seafarer who had been travelling with him. Apart from the effect of shock otherwise she was not injured. It hardly bears contemplation how many casualties there would have been and the extent of their injuries had my wife not underlined the risk we were running and insisted that I act immediately.

The murder of an innocent person came very close on this occasion. A piece of metal shrapnel (probably from a petrol pump) went through a window in the office, then through a cupboard door one inch thick before imbedding itself in packets of cigarettes stored in this cupboard. A member of staff who should have been on duty but fortunately was absent would have been seated in the path taken by that piece of shrapnel. Following my retirement amongst my souvenirs was this piece of shrapnel which I had mounted and suitably inscribed and then presented to the Central Office of the Missions to Seamen in London where it is now displayed on a wall in the Chapel.

News travels fast, and soon after the explosion my telephone began to ring. It was not idle curiosity but one person after another volunteering to clean up the mess. 'The Mission is not going to close, these fellows have nowhere else to go and after all it's not their war.' Such was the calibre of the people who supported the Missions to Seamen in Belfast.

Some months later we got it again from a different angle. A bomb exploded, this time in an oil storage depot a little distance from the rear of the club, damaging many glass panels in the roof over our Chapel and recreation hall and sending me from one side of my office to the other with the force of the explosion. Fortunately the oil was of a consistency that did not ignite easily.

When you consider that annually somewhere in the region of 20,000 seafarers were using the club at this time it helps underline how valuable this service was in their lives.

As in every war it is the innocent who suffer most

I'm not a pacifist though as one attempting to follow Jesus Christ some would say that I ought to be. There is that constant choice we must all make about how to control violence and protect the innocent. By making the choice to use physical force, in a sense one chooses the lesser of two evils. The real tragedy of war, however, is that invariably it is the innocent who suffer most.

The Dutch motor vessel *Waardrecht* arrived in port one day. Pretty soon the crew became acquainted with our club which they visited daily. I was on duty this evening when two members of the crew called in to book telephone calls to their families in Holland to reassure them that they were all right. 'All right, what do you mean?' I asked. They looked as if they'd had a shock. Now it was my turn. René Heemskerk, a member of the crew, had been shot and killed while sitting in a dentist's waiting room in Belfast. It was 7.30 p.m. and this was the first I had heard of the tragedy.

My immediate reaction was one of horror and unbelief that this could happen to a stranger. I could identify the victim in my mind's eye and simply could not believe what I had heard. He was a very outgoing person and quickly made a lot of friends in the club, so very young, so full of life. What a totally unnecessary tragedy.

I decided that I must visit the ship immediately and offer my condolences to the Master and crew. This was an entirely new role for me as this innocent boy had been murdered by my fellow-countrymen. I had never had to do this before. All on board were in a complete state of shock yet they welcomed me without recrimination when they could so easily have done otherwise given the circumstances. I stayed for a while and promised to return again next day. The thought struck me before leaving that the body would most likely be returned to the Netherlands for burial and that the crew might welcome an opportunity to pay their last respects to their former shipmate. I spoke to the Master and offered to conduct a short memorial service in our Chapel if he and the crew would like me to do so.

The needless death of this young man was inexplicable as he had no connection with the troubles in Northern Ireland. The only possible explanation was that his assassin must have mistaken him for a British soldier. (His hair style, short back and sides, probably gave rise to this idea.) One way or another the cowardly pursuit by his attacker, never for one moment attempting to test his hunch before killing him, speaks for itself.

When I visited the ship next day the finality of this terrible tragedy had already struck home. The Master informed me that it was the wish of everyone on board that we hold a memorial service in the Mission Chapel. Many of the crew showed visible signs of distress, especially René's friends and close associates. We arranged for the memorial service to take place on Sunday evening which incidentally was Remembrance Sunday.

Not unnaturally the crew by now were very nervous about walking ashore so at their request we arranged for a fleet of taxis to transport them to and from the service which was a very sad occasion for all of us. In addition to the Master, officers and crew from René's ship and our volunteers, many of whom had come to know René during his brief time with us, the service was also attended by representatives from ships in port, Harbour police, shipping agents and other voluntary seafarers' societies. The congregation were asked to sign a list offering their condolences which we agreed to forward to René's parents.

When I tried to write and express our sympathy to René's parents, words failed me. I prepared draft after draft, each one to be rejected in turn. The death of a seafarer far from home is difficult at any time for the family, but in these circumstances and with one so young what could one say? Amidst my shame I decided to recount only happy memories.

> Prior to the tragic day René was a frequent visitor to our club. I can still picture him in my mind's eye, tall, fair and handsome as with unbounded energy and good humour he joined enthusiastically in our entertainment programme. He loved to dance. Then at the end of the evening's entertainment he would find time to attend family prayers in the Mission Chapel.

We enclosed a picture of the congregation in the Chapel for the memorial service and a picture of our entertainment hall where René liked to dance.

Copy of a letter received at the Missions to Seamen from the Master of the MV *Waardrecht* before sailing from Belfast

Belfast, November 16th, 1971

Dear Sir,

Herewith I want to express our thanks again for the very best your people of the Mission did to our crew when the MS *Waardrecht* was in port. And especially during the days when our wiper R.W.E.L. Heemskerk passed away during a very sad accident.

Special thanks for the Church service on November 15th, 1971 during which you remembered Heemskerk so very much.

We all know that sometimes we have to pass away, everyone of us. But to may know that one is waiting us and to tell people of this great knowledge we often forget, but you didn't.

A little we, a crew, can do. However to make sure you can go on with this honoured work, please receive our gift in this attitude.

Wishing you and all the people of the Mission GOD's very best Blessings, we remain,

'Your brethren in CHRIST',

W. SNOEK

Master *Waardrecht*.

Soon one of our greatest fears was to be realized. The beginning of the Loyalist backlash.

A bomb of about 50 pounds exploded in McGuirk's public house in North Queen's Street, Belfast [close to the docks], causing heavy casualties. The building was totally demolished and rescuers worked all night to extricate the trapped people. By Sunday morning the number killed was 15 with 8 injured. In a riot which followed the explosion at McGuirk's bar, 7 people were wounded by gunfire; 3 policemen, 1 soldier and 3 civilians.

(In Belfast, a group calling themselves the 'Empire Loyalists' claimed responsibility for the explosion.)

As the terrorist campaign escalated day by day there could have been few people who did not feel a sense of foreboding as the year 1971 drew to a close.

FORGIVE MY BEING PERSONAL

People never cease to amaze me. During the past week here in Western Canada we have had the good fortune to have been spared the devastating effect of the 'Ice Storm' which played havoc primarily on the provinces of Ontario and Quebec. I have listened to many sermons and preached a few about how as Christians we should take care of our fellow man. In the face of this need no sermon was necessary as we saw on television enacted before our very eyes what it means to care. People are great; despite our many shortcomings man has the potential for greatness in terms of human kindness. There were the few who did their gouging but the overwhelming majority demonstrated a concern for their fellow humans that was inspiring.

This storm and the reaction of ordinary people brought to mind a storm of another kind in Northern Ireland. You could call it a civil war where the stranger in our midst was taken care of by ordinary people concerned for his welfare. They had no idea who he was, what nationality he was or what religion he was. Though largely unacknowledged save by those whom they sought to help, it is people like these who shed light on our darkness.

One Chinese seafarer from Hong Kong wrote me,

> I just don't know how to express my gratitude for your care of us. No one is paying so much attention to seafarers as you are, except our own relations.

Our children grew up very largely within this environment and as a family from the time they were toddlers they were very much part of the Mission and especially at Christmas time. Though tragedy was to come our way in 1972 and this would be the last Christmas we would spend together as a family, nevertheless we have these beautiful memories. Readers will have to forgive me for not including the highlights of our ministry from here on leading up to that fateful day.

The day I will remember always

The spread of the campaign of injury, death and destruction initiated by the Provisional IRA in Northern Ireland had been compared to a form of creeping paralysis gradually enveloping more and more of our freedom. It was continuous agony for parents on both sides of the political divide lest their children become indoctrinated in the way of the terrorist: a distinct possibility which in time materialized for some.

21 July 1972 held out the promise of a beautiful day when the sun would shine high in the sky. It felt good to be alive and we thanked God that the terrorist could not stop the sun shining whatever else he would try to do. What we didn't bargain for was that while the terrorist could not stop the sun shining, he could block its rays from shining upon us, which is precisely what he did.

It was vacation time and the children had no school to attend so we usually had breakfast together. Roger, our eldest son, was always the first member of the family to rise as he had a paper route to complete before breakfast. Stephen, our second son, didn't have his own route yet but he relieved on occasions, though today was not one of them.

Ever conscious of the civil disturbances throughout the province, one of the first things I did upon arrival at the breakfast table was to glance through the morning paper for news of the latest atrocities, but there was no paper today.

Roger was here so I concluded our paper boy must have missed us out. Stephen, aware of my habit, sat there grinning at me like a cheshire cat which infuriated me at that hour. Knowing Roger had already been out and about I turned to Stephen and half jokingly said to him, 'You know how I like to glance through the paper when I arrive at the breakfast table, the least you could have done when you saw it had not arrived, was to slip up the road and get one.' Always a joker, his face lit up in a broad smile as he looked me straight in the eye and said, 'Dad, would this one do instead?' and promptly pulled out the paper he'd been sitting on. Charmer boy, that smile disarmed most people, myself included.

In strife torn Northern Ireland at this time many parents were reluctant to allow their young folk to wander too far afield for recreation purposes, especially at night. There was the threat to life and limb and the fear of them being inveigled in all innocence into an association with some terrorist organization. So of necessity, brothers were thrown together to become closer than best friends. Our two boys, Roger and Stephen, shared a bedroom and were indeed best friends. Stephen had a passion for music, and was, we believe, quite talented. He was a pupil at the Belfast School of Music and played third horn in the Belfast Youth Orchestra. He played the French horn and frequently said to his Mum that if he could not play his beloved horn he would not want to live. A complete extrovert and with his passion for music he seemed to attract a lot of attention to himself; indeed at this time it seemed more than either his brother or sister. Karen being very young did not notice, while Roger, who was older and could easily have shown resentment, never did, but instead was continually championing that Stephen be given every opportunity to upgrade his musical skills.

Money burnt a hole in Stephen's pockets: made round, he believed it had to go around. This morning he was in the money, having been paid for completing one job or another, so he persuaded brother Roger to accompany him to one of his favourite haunts, the trick shop in Smithfield Market. Though Roger had lined up some work for himself in the early afternoon which necessitated travelling a distance outside town, nevertheless, he did not want to disappoint Stephen, so he agreed to accompany him. This was to be the last time they would spend together.

My wife had some shopping to do downtown so she and the boys took a ride with me by car to the city. Karen went to play at the home of one of her friends. When we reached the Missions to Seamen car park we parted company, each to go our separate way, my wife to her shopping, Roger and Stephen to Smithfield Market and me to the Mission. Before leaving Stephen, with a broad smile on his face, turned to me and said, 'Be seeing you, Dad.' These were his final words to me and this was the last time I saw him alive.

The sun was high in a clear blue sky as we parted company and so it remained until early afternoon when suddenly, all hell broke loose as bomb after bomb exploded (twenty two in all) throughout the city causing a large cloud of smoke to ascend over the city obliterating completely the sun and that beautiful blue sky, God's gift to man, by man's inhumanity to man. The symbolism was not lost. Man must find another way to live.

I was inside the Flying Angel Club when the unbelievable began to occur and could not believe the sight of my own eyes when I went outdoors. Within minutes our volunteers, without a thought for their own safety, were busy trying to console girls from local offices who had barely escaped with their lives. A large pot of strong tea was made and a cup administered to each one as a cure for shock. We set up a telephone service for those who wished to call home and say they were alive. I got the job of regulating these calls, the essential message and no more.

All this time my wife was going through agony as bombs had exploded in our quiet residential neighbourhood too and both Stephen and Karen were missing. She examined two dead bodies, but there was no sign of either child. Eventually Karen was located, but there was no sign of

Stephen. This had Dorothy very worried as on a previous occasion following another terrible explosion in the neighbourhood he had put his head around the door and said, 'I'm all right, Mum, I'm going back to help.' His silence on this occasion was ominous.

Dorothy tried and tried to get through to inform me at the Mission, but of course I was keeping the lines busy with outgoing calls to families and totally absorbed in what I was doing. Eventually she managed to get a message through to me via a public telephone in the building to say that Stephen was missing. The seriousness of the situation went right over my head at first. I can still recall the look of unbelief on Dorothy Gunning's face when I replied, 'Never mind, he will show up, as he's probably helping somewhere else.' I continued to regulate the telephone calls all the time, wondering why Dorothy continued to look at me the way she did. Suddenly the penny dropped. I must get home quickly. The terrorists were still having their revenge as traffic was snarled up like never before. I pleaded my cause for mile after mile along the way and people believed me and let me through. Another side of human nature.

The end of a terrible day

It was close to midnight, 21 July 1972. A man in the middle facing the greatest crisis in my life, I had to be alone to sort myself out, to come to terms with the unbelievable. The neighbourhood was quiet now, so I could stand unobserved at the scene of the crime so to speak.

On this afternoon our dearly loved second son Stephen had been killed at this spot when a car bomb, planted by the Provisional IRA outside a small greengrocer's shop, had exploded.

In this quiet location, in a totally residential neighbourhood devoid of any strategic targets or valuable commercial property, another misguided blow had been struck by those who claimed to be our liberators. Ironically, their victims were totally innocent and Irish by birth: a young mother, an elderly spinster, and our dearly loved fourteen and a half year old son. We were later to discover that the casualty list would have been much larger were it not for the bravery of our beloved Stephen who died as he tried to warn others that a suspicious car had been parked in the area.

Here I have described but one scene in the total havoc and carnage the Provincial IRA wrought upon the City of Belfast and its people that day which has become infamously known as 'Bloody Friday'.

I will spare my readers by not describing here in detail the state of my son's mortal remains from which I later had to make a positive

The boy on the right side of this picture is my late son Stephen who was killed by a bomb in Belfast, 21 July 1972, 'Bloody Friday'.

identification. It suffices for me to say that I thought I recognized Stephen's hands which together with a box of trick matches found in a trouser pocket and a Scout belt, all helped to provide positive identification. The belt I recognized immediately as having been decorated by himself while only a day or two earlier he had fooled me with the trick matches.

Still ringing in my ears at this late hour as I stood where Stephen had died was the remark his Mum had made to our family physician, Dr Loughridge, who without being called, awaited our arrival home from the mortuary. 'He was only a little fellow, but thank God I was able to enjoy every moment of his short life.' Stephen adored his Mum and thought that she was the greatest. A dedicated mother, she could truthfully make this claim. Weighed down by the magnitude of this terrible happening, I could not prevent myself from thinking – Why Stephen of all people? The boy who only a few weeks before had pleaded for a better understanding of the plight of his peers whom he felt were being enveloped by the civil strife that surrounded them and which was in danger of becoming part of their daily lives.

When not on duty in the evenings in the Mission, I frequently took a brief walk around the neighbourhood before settling in for the night. Stephen loved to accompany me on these walks. Once he asked, 'Dad, why does this keep on happening in our country? Can nobody do anything about it? Can nobody stop it?'

This day Stephen had given his all and is no longer with us, but his questions remain. Despite the agony of losing our beloved son, we realized as he himself had previously indicated, it could so easily have been otherwise, had he been born elsewhere. Instead, he had died a hero.

We had named our son Stephen in simple admiration of the courage and integrity of the youthful St. Stephen, the first Christian martyr who died as he prayed for his murderers, 'Lord lay not this sin to their charge.' Very much aware of our inadequacy, my wife and I resolved that with the help of God we would try and follow this example.

The aftermath and public reaction

Altogether twenty two bombs exploded in Belfast city that Friday afternoon; the majority were, I believe, car bombs. It was reported initially that eleven persons had been killed and 130 had been injured. However, the total number who had been killed was later corrected to read nine persons when the security forces were able to identify dismembered bodies. Six people had been killed in an explosion at Oxford Street Bus Station (4 civilians, 2 soldiers). Two of the civilians were youths aged fifteen and seventeen years. On the Cavehill Road, three persons had been killed: our son Stephen, an elderly spinster and a young mother of seven.

That same day in Derry, three large bombs exploded in the centre of the city causing extensive damage to shops and business premises, but thankfully nobody was injured.

I also understand that rail services between Dublin and Belfast were cut off early on Bloody Friday by an explosion which derailed a freight train.

Telephone services between Northern Ireland and the Republic of Ireland were also disrupted by explosions. Our next of kin live in the Republic of Ireland, so we could not communicate to them immediately the tragic news of Stephen's death. Eventually, when we found that the service to London was not affected, we telephoned a message through the Missions to Seamen, London to one member of the family in Dublin explaining the circumstances and requesting that the tragic news be conveyed to other family members.

The Belfast Brigade of the Provisional IRA issued a statement accepting full responsibility for all the explosions in the Belfast area on Bloody Friday, with a face saving qualification to the effect that warnings had been issued at least thirty minutes to one hour before each explosion. We could have been spared the crocodile tears for as the later history of the activities of the Provisional IRA reveal, these warnings were something of a farce as they had no means whatsoever of ensuring that those whose lives were in danger would receive them; nevertheless the practice was to continue as a sop to the bereaved.

Our son earned pocket money every week by doing grocery shopping and washing her car for a local shopkeeper. It was at this time that he spotted the suspicious car which contained the bomb. His employer was very seriously injured when the bomb exploded, from which cause she died five years later.

A joker by nature, ironically before leaving the house, Stephen wrote the following message in his sister Karen's scrapbook – 'I was here.' Can we ever forget? Later his Mum had to explain to Karen about his death and of his new whereabouts, while I had to do likewise with brother Roger.

The following editorial was published in the Republic of Ireland by the *Sunday Independent* on 23 July 1972:

We are the cowards

These are the dark days for Ireland. We live in an age of cowardice, with the guilt spread evenly between the highest and the lowest in the land.

We foster the men who planned the murders of innocent men, women, boys, and girls in Belfast on Friday. We fed these people with propaganda. We took advantage, when we could, of their exploits. And because we are not a morally courageous people, we never seriously tried to stop their excesses.

Those among us who could have acted to halt the course of tragedy preferred to do nothing. Those who could have spoken out, when words might have meant something, chose to hold their tongues. And the rest of us were content to let matters slide.

Now all us must pay the price for this neglect. There is a black sin on the face of Irish Republicanism today that will never be erased. Murder now lies at the feet of the Irish nation and there is no gainsaying that fact.

We cannot change the past, however much we regret its record. But if we wish to restore the honour of our people, now is the time to act.

We must break the paralysis that leaves the good name of the Irish people in the hands of unscrupulous men. And we must find a way to make restitution for our failings.

Mr Lynch, as our elected leader, can give substance to his call for deeds rather than words at the present time. He has the power to declare a day of national mourning for all the murdered innocents of the North.

If he will do this, then let those who work on that day donate their earnings to a fund, administered by the heads of all the churches in Ireland, to be donated to the suffering relatives of the dead.

It is a paltry gesture, but at least it is a deed that will show the Irish people have compassion and a will to act at a time when their eyes are fixed northward and can see only terror and misery.

Heroes

As for our posturing patriots, they go from one military success to another. Have no doubt about it, in years to come, we shall be singing alcoholic ballads about their many deeds of heroism, and history classes will instruct our grandchildren how a selflessly dedicated group of men and women bravely resisted public opinion and pressed on with their sophisticated political objectives.

The gallantry of those who planted bombs in the middle of Belfast's shopping areas on Friday (and then ran like hell), will be sanctified by the Almighty God of Ireland republicanism and reverently embalmed in what we are pleased to call our national heritage. We won't have a ballad to commemorate the butchered fragments of a woman we saw on the telly being shovelled up by a fireman. Who said Dan Breen is dead? His spirit is alive and well and looking forward to a cosy corner in whatever parliamentary system we are going to have for the next 50 years. Is nobody going to shout stop?

The integrity of the writer of the foregoing article, his courage, compassion and generosity of spirit deeply impressed the author and his family.

The bombings in Belfast on 21 July 1972 were widely condemned throughout Northern Ireland and overseas.

On Saturday 22 July 1972 a loyalist paramilitary body issued a statement to the press. The Ulster Defence Association called for a day of mourning the following Tuesday in Northern Ireland to commemorate the innocent people murdered by the IRA including those slaughtered in Friday's explosions in Belfast. Of course, no mention was made of the many innocent Roman Catholics who had been judged and summarily executed earlier on by Loyalist terrorists in Northern Ireland, while over the border in the Republic at this time, many well known IRA activists enjoyed freedom to strut about in defiance of God and man.

NOW THERE WAS NO ESCAPE

Overnight I found myself in the forefront of the Northern Ireland problem. I cannot say reluctantly for the tragic circumstances of my son's death had electrified me and more than anything else, I was resolved to do my utmost to save others from sharing the same senseless tragedy. My wife shared my desire and we were in agreement to do everything we could to achieve this goal.

The statement issued by the Ulster Defence Association mentioned in the previous chapter presented me with my first opportunity. An old saying came to mind, 'The Devil makes work for idle hands.' I could not help but think that a day of mourning sponsored by the UDA with their reputation, could well result in death for some innocent person. We could learn to live with the tragedy of our son's death, but under no circumstances would we wish to provide others with a misguided opportunity to avenge on our behalf. Through media, we appealed for people to go to work as usual and by so doing, help to reduce tension in the community and thus avoid further bloodshed.

The BBC enquired if I would be agreeable to be interviewed concerning the circumstances of my son's death. I agreed to do so. It is an interview I am unlikely to forget – for it must have taken a very long time. The interviewer was sensitive, patient and kind. So soon after the experience of trying to identifying my son's mortal remains, a vivid picture of that scene with which I had not yet learned to cope, kept coming to mind. The interviewer would, I felt, gladly have brought the proceedings to a conclusion, but I persisted, to deliver what I considered to be a valid message for Ireland's so-called freedom fighters, who were responsible for my son's death.

While the foregoing interview was taking place at the BBC, my wife had a visit from a representative of the local community to enquire if I would be agreeable to take a memorial service for those killed on Bloody Friday at the Cavehill Road Shopping Centre. Dorothy agreed on my behalf and went on to state that I would probably be accompanied by Fr. Hilary Armstrong, two of whose parishioners had been killed in the explosion. Fr. Armstrong, a Roman Catholic priest, had visited the scene immediately following the explosion.

By now I was already beginning to clarify my thinking in relation to this terrible tragedy in which we found ourselves engulfed. The story of the Cavehill Cross which follows explains my thinking in this respect.

Note: The plate recording this gathering had already been made before we were aware that the number killed had been corrected to read nine persons. A further plate has been added to the cross explaining this correction.

THE
CAVEHILL CROSS

TO THE GLORY OF GOD
and in sacred memory of

MISS BRIDGETTA MURRAY
(65 years) Antrim Rd., Belfast 15

MRS. MARGARET O'HARE
(34 years) Balmoral Ave., Belfast 9 (Mother of seven)

MASTER STEPHEN PARKER
(14 years) Tokio Gdns., Belfast 15

Innocent victims of a terrorists' outrage who died
in a car bomb explosion at the shopping centre,
Cavehill Rd., Belfast, on Friday the 21st July, 1972.

'To live in the hearts of those you leave behind is not to die'

Of those responsible for their deaths you are asked to pray,
'Lord lay not this sin to their charge' (Acts 8 v 60)

Several hundred people of all religious denominations from the Cavehill Rd. area attended a Memorial Service on the 27th day of July at the spot where the explosion took place. This service, organized by the local residents was conducted by the Rev. J.D. Parker (Stephen's father) and the Rev. Hilary Armstrong.

During the service Mr Parker, taking two pieces of wood from the debris of the explosion, in reference to the tragic divisions of our community, held up one piece before him, saying 'In the centre of the word SIN is the letter I. Whatever one's religious or political views may be it is sinful if we continue to allow them to divide us from our fellow men. We all share to a degree in guilt for the tragedy of our time. We have all failed.' With the second piece of wood he formed the two into this cross. He then hammered a nail into

The Cavehill Cross.

the cross and invited Father Armstrong to hammer in the second; symbolizing for the future that we pledged ourselves as a community (and individually) to test our views in the light of Christ, trying to follow the example of St. Paul in crossing out the 'I', being able to say with him, 'I live and yet no longer I, but Christ liveth in me.' If we and future generations honestly try to do this then the tragedy of today will never be repeated.

A plea was made for the cross to be moved annually to each Church in the neighbourhood as an act of witness to future generations of the tragedy which follows when men continue to ignore the light of Christ and pursue instead their own selfish aims. The hope was expressed that there would be the type of procession and service held that all those who want to make Northern Ireland a place of which every citizen can be proud will attend.

(The cross was given into the care of the Rector of St. Peter's Parish, where Stephen was being prepared for Confirmation.)

'BLOODY FRIDAY'
In addition to the explosion at the Cavehill Rd. Shopping Centre, twenty-one terrorists' bombs exploded in Belfast City. On this day altogether 11 people were killed and 130 injured, so Friday the 21st July infamously became known as 'Bloody Friday'.

READER, the only fitting memorial to those who died is when you in all honestly are trying to say with St. Paul, 'I live and yet no longer I, but Christ Liveth in me.' HEREIN LIES OUR PEACE.

The road of no return
The purpose of this book is to present readers with a series of stories and incidents about seafarers and their families, the struggle and joy in fulfilling their needs under the auspices of the Flying Angel flag of the Missions to Seamen, and the involvement of a Padre and his family with them for over thirty years.

It is a record of the immeasurable contribution of the volunteer workers and others associated with the Missions to Seamen who helped care for the seafarer, a stranger in our midst. It's a story which at this point for me had been touched by the indescribable tragedy of the death of my son at the hands of his fellow countrymen.

However hard we tried, both my wife and I could not get away from the fact that through Stephen's death we had acquired a new priority in ministry which must take precedence above all others. This was very difficult for me as I'm an all or nothing sort of guy. I have a one track mind.

We had lived both North and South of the Irish border, members of the majority community in Northern Ireland and members of the minority in the Republic of Ireland. Our son had been murdered by fanatical Irish nationalists – sons of our Roman Catholic fellow citizens were being murdered by fanatical Northern Ireland Loyalists and whether the Churches were prepared to admit the fact or not, religion as practised in both Northern Ireland and the Republic of Ireland had done little to diffuse the difficulties arising out of the age old problem of a divided Ireland.

I suppose from the start we both had the feeling that eventually we would not be treated too kindly by those with vested interests. Whatever the consequences we were resolved to do whatever we believed we had to do. Following Stephen's death I continued for some months with my ministry in the port of Belfast, though I must confess, in a very half hearted fashion compared with my previous involvement. My priorities now lay elsewhere.

While I had always enjoyed an excellent relationship with the local committee of the Missions to Seamen nevertheless people could change and not everybody might agree with my course of action. I could not leave myself vulnerable. I had accumulated a lot of vacation time so I approached the General Secretary of the Missions to Seamen in London to know if I was free to promote peace initiatives locally using my accumulated leave. He willingly agreed. I took this precaution so that I could not be accused of using Missions to Seamen funds for my own purposes.

The creation of the Cavehill Cross represented our first attempt at community reconciliation. It was to be followed by a number of initiatives designed to achieve this goal: a hunger strike in Belfast; a hunger strike in Dublin; an Ecumenical Service of Penitence and Re-dedication to Peace, the last being preceded by A Time to Remember at Belfast City Hall when crosses were planted in the grounds for all who had died in the present troubles. I addressed public meetings promoting reconciliation and other gatherings but sadly few were sponsored by the Churches.

Many individuals gave wholehearted support to what we were doing and saying. We received request after request from people who wished to be identified with our philosophy and witness. In response we launched a Trust to promote this witness which we named Witness for Peace. The trustees would have to comprise both Protestant and Roman Catholic faiths on an equal basis.

The General Secretary of the Missions to Seamen in London, England, in consultation with my Diocesan Bishop, agreed that I be granted one year's sabbatical leave to lead this movement. Altogether about 40,000 people identified with the movement and purchased our badge. To wear our badge people were expected to make the following commitment.

1) BE HONEST. 'Open confession is good for the soul.' We have all shared in the creation of community fears, prejudices and hatreds, by what we have done and by what we have failed to do. We cannot escape our duty now to make it known by public witness to those who resort to violence that no cause justifies the deaths of [to be updated with number] people, injuries to thousands, the involvement of children and teenagers in violence, not to mention the destruction of property and the livelihood of all our people.

2) BE GENEROUS. It's expected of you. 'If you forgive men their trespasses, your Heavenly Father also will forgive you; but if you do not forgive men their trespasses, neither will your Father forgive you your trespasses.' (Jesus).

3) BE JUST. 'O man, what is good; and what does the Lord require of you, but to do justice and to love kindness and to walk humbly with your God.' (Micah)

4) BE CONFIDENT. 'I can all things in Him who strengthens me.' (Paul)

Our witness did not endear me to the supporters of the Provisional IRA or the Loyalists' cause. When eventually the British Government together with the Government of the Republic and at that time a majority of politicians in Northern Ireland agreed to set up a power sharing executive to govern the Province I openly supported this attempt to bridge the gap of centuries.

Soon in addition to the Loyalist paramilitary bodies and the Provisional IRA and their fellow travellers, others with vested interests came out in force to oppose the whole idea of power sharing. This development was going to overlap the conclusion of my twelve months sabbatical leave. I realized that I could find myself deserting a sinking ship if I returned to my ministry in the port immediately. There was no alternative open to me at this time save to trade in the hope that I could be free to lend my support to the beleaguered executive. Chaplains of the Missions to Seamen cannot function in any area without a licence from the Diocesan Bishop. I was informed by the Society's General Secretary that there was only one option open to me at this time: resign my position as Senior Chaplain in the port of Belfast when I would be granted a further six months sabbatical, after which I would be offered an overseas posting through headquarters in London. The Church of Ireland would not agree to my leave being extended from Belfast. Beggars can't be choosers and even though it nearly broke my heart I resigned to gain time. The rest is history: in time the power sharing executive fell.

My assistant was licensed in my place. It appeared I had grown completely out of favour with the Church of my birth for I did not get a single offer of employment, nor did anyone in authority even offer to help me in this connection. A man under authority, I had no alternative but to accept under protest the decision of my spiritual superiors and emigrate as many of my fellow countrymen had done before me in somewhat similar circumstances. Time will, I believe, vindicate our stand.

Indeed as I write in 1998 the Peace Agreement just signed in Northern Ireland is very little different from the Sunningdale Agreement which brought the power sharing executive into being. The only significant difference is that approximately 2,500 people have died since then and the majority of people are war weary.

The following two letters published in newspapers at the time were supportive. There were many others addressed to my home but space does not permit their inclusion.

'A Witness for Peace', in references to the Rev. J.D. Parker.

I would endorse your final paragraph, particularly the words that 'the Belfast community has been the richer for his presence among us.'

However, in the knowledge, as I understand it, that he will be posted overseas in a few months, I would like to thank the Rev. J. Parker most sincerely for his untiring efforts, spiritually and materially, on behalf of seamen who live or visit Northern Ireland, irrespective of creed or colour.

There are many seamen's widows, injured seamen, sick and retired seamen, who know his full Christian charity and who I know will join me in paying tribute to this fine, forthright man. Our prayers for his future well-being go with him.

Having known Mr Parker for a number of years, he epitomizes for me the renaissance period of history, as the rational, conscious forward moving Christian, and strangely enough, often reminded me of the message contained in that extract of Dante's 'the Divine Comedy'. 'Deny not to that little span of life the brief allotment of your waking hours that yet remain to you – experience of that un-peopled world behind the sunset. Consider from what noble seed you spring: you were created, not to live like beasts, but for the pursuit of virtue and knowledge.'

May the Prince of Peace bless you and your family Rev. J. Parker, and thank you again.

Yours etc. . . . .

'Dedicated'

'I am sure I am only one of many people in the Province that were deeply touched by the recent appearance of the Rev. Parker on television. . . . I have had the advantage of experiencing the benefits of his pastoral ministry during the fruitful period when he was an energetic curate in east Belfast. In those days, his influence among the young people in particular was deep and penetrating and his fearless stand for Christian principles earned him the profound respect of those people to whom he ministered to such good effect. . . . This East Belfast parish parted with him in sadness at their great loss and many of the parishioners maintained contact by sharing with him in his new work as Chaplain to the Missions to Seamen. In this new sphere of activity I was again brought into close contact with the Rev. Parker in my capacity as Denmark's Honorary Consul, and on many occasions had reason to be grateful to him for the care and compassion which he showed to Danish seafarers, especially to those in hospital far from family and friends.

'Cruel Blow'

'The outbreak of terrorism in the Province and the loss of his dear son on Bloody Friday was a cruel blow to a man who had befriended the sons of so many others . . . His reaction and that of his devoted wife in launching the campaign 'Witness for Peace' was typical and his passion for reconciliation was a measure of the loss he had sustained. . . . Many of us lesser Christians have marvelled at his forgiving spirit and in many he has rekindled a fire of hope in the ashes of despair. It is a commentary on the Christianity of the Province that a man of this calibre appears to have few clerical friends and in the midst of a shortage in the ministry has been rendered redundant.'

EMIGRATION TO CANADA

One apologist for the Church of Ireland (Anglican) felt that the term 'emigrate' used to describe our departure from Ireland conveyed an entirely misleading impression. Had he taken the trouble to contact me personally he would have found the use of this word correct.

We were limited in the amount of furniture and other effects we could afford to take with us. Sentiment had to be cast aside again and again in the face of pure economics, and what we could not take with us we had to sell.

The affairs of Witness for Peace had to be gradually handed over to others and personal commitments fulfilled until the end of the year such as 'A Time to Remember' which by now had become an annual event. The movement's accounts had to be audited and an orderly transfer of all affairs made to the Society's Trustees.

Goodbye to countless friends and supporters verbally and by letter occupied a lot of time.

The Irish doctor who performed our medical examinations for the Canadian emigration authority handed my wife a gift of a beautiful piece of Tyrone Crystal with these words, 'You will notice there is a rough side and a smooth; life is like that, we have got to learn to take the rough with the smooth.' That piece of glass enjoys pride of place in our home today. Its symbolism has not been lost.

One final and emotional duty my wife had to perform was to present a trophy on behalf of our family to the Belfast Youth Orchestra in connection with our son's Memorial Trust Fund when she was given the honour of presenting the first Award made by the Trust. This ceremony took place during a recital given by the Youth Orchestra in St. Anne's Cathedral, Belfast.

Day by day we carried out the multitude of tasks demanded of people in our situation until the final day when we departed from the province. Emotionally we were in turmoil but such was life.

Before concluding this part of the narrative I want to refer briefly to a conversation I had with our beloved Stephen which was later to have a profound effect upon my life. 'Dad,' he asked, 'Why does this keep happening in our country? Can nobody do anything about it? Can nobody stop it?' He then went on to say, 'I wonder what it will be like when I'm seventeen?' The irony of the conclusion of this portion of the narrative is that we sailed out of Southampton, bound for our new home in Canada, on Stephen's seventeenth birthday.

Journey to Canada

Written by my daughter Karen with help from her Mum.

We left 5 Tokio Gardens, Belfast, Northern Ireland on my birthday, 28 January 1975. This house had been our home for eleven years.

Our journey began by travelling to Dublin by train. There we spent two days visiting our relatives and in particular my grandmother, who was sad to see us leave, knowing we were going such a long distance away. On 31 January, we flew to London where my father was commissioned at a Service in the Chapel of the Headquarters of the Missions to Seamen. It was a Service of Commendation for his future work as Senior Chaplain in the Port of Vancouver, British Columbia. While in London we managed to see a little of this wonderful city. St. Paul's Cathedral is very near the Missions to Seamen building so we did see round it and went right up into the famous 'Whispering Gallery'.

While awaiting the departure of the container ship on which we were to travel from Southampton to Halifax, we stayed at a lovely country cottage near Axminster in Devon. The weather was very good and I was delighted to have a very lovable golden retriever named Cassa to look after for a week while her owners were away. Soon we heard the date of our sailing, 13 February, so early on that morning we drove to Southampton, called at the Missions to Seamen Club there, and were brought by their Chaplain, the Rev. Roberts, to see the MV *Dart America* on which we were to travel to Halifax on the east coast of Canada. She seemed enormous and climbing the gangway was quite a feat. My Mum didn't care to look down, she doesn't like heights very much! We then heard that she would not set sail until 11.00 a.m. next morning, the 14th, so we managed to see a little of Southampton before spending our first night on board.

11.00 a.m. next morning we left Southampton, watching the land disappear slowly and feeling excited but yet a little sad too, realizing that we were about to begin a new life in a strange country. The crew were very pleasant and we had a lot of fun playing snooker, table tennis and darts. Mum and I even rode the fixed bicycle to keep in trim. The food was very good, and with so little exercise we sometimes felt we'd perhaps eaten too much, so we had a run round the deck. Space is limited on deck on a container vessel as there is so much room taken up by the cargo, but we managed quite well. Sometimes it was so windy that we had to remain on one of the lower decks as it was so difficult to keep upright. As we got further out into the Atlantic the colder it became and one felt the loneliness of the sea, nothing in sight but huge waves as the ship dipped her nose down and then rose again.

We had the great thrill of seeing two fin whales one morning from the bridge of the ship; I was sorry I had not got my camera at the time. Often as the sea became more rough, we were thrown from side to side; we experienced a Gale Force 9 which is quite a gale and at night in your bunk it became difficult not to roll out on the floor. However, we were all reasonably good sailors, none of us was sea-sick, but my Dad and brother felt a little queer for a couple of days. Mum and I tried to play table tennis during a gale, but we played more often on the floor than on the table and one evening when a seaman was showing a film in the recreation room I fell right off the chair as the ship lurched!

21 February at 11.30 p.m. we docked in Halifax. I was asleep, but Mummy said it looked like fairyland with all the lights twinkling and the tug boats lit up going by the ship in the harbour. Next morning in daylight we saw this vast country which was to be our new homeland. There was a lot of snow and it was cold but bright and sunny. The Chaplain of the Missions to Seamen in Halifax, the Rev. Lee, came on board the night we docked and again in the morning to take us to the Flying Angel Club in the dock to have a cup of coffee. He and his wife together with a member of the committee of the Mission in Halifax took us in two cars to the railway station (we had quite a large number of cases as we knew we should have to live out of these for some time, until the container carrying the pieces of furniture and personal belongings we had chosen to bring with us to our new home eventually arrived).

We boarded the train for our first stop, Montreal. We were now beginning the next step of our journey; we had already come 3,000 miles and had to travel a further 3,000 right across Canada to Vancouver on the west coast. This journey was quite an experience. We gazed at the accommodation and wondered just how four bunks to sleep in at night could possibly be made up in the small section allotted to us. However, we soon found out when we returned from our evening meal in the dining car and saw that our porter had already made up our beds. They are very comfortable and roomy if you stay inside behind the curtains which run along the corridor. However, you are liable to do a nose dive into your bunk if you happen to be standing in the corridor if someone passes by and the train gives a lurch. Also you have to scramble underneath to find your various belongings. My Mum did a lot of scrambling one night on all fours looking for her book and she got rather cross when she could not find it. I'm afraid I was the culprit as I found it next morning amongst my belongings!!

The snow was feet upon feet high in places and enormous icicles hung from the roofs of the typical wooden Canadian houses. They were so often isolated buildings miles from the next house, with white snow covering everything. The sun reflecting on the snow was almost blinding in brightness.

Montreal is a huge city, also a very interesting one, but unfortunately we only had three hours here and did not see a great deal. My Mum fell in love with the little imitation seals that you see in the souvenir shops and has promised herself a gift of one for our new home. The ice cream shops are super, you can get about twelve different flavours and it's so hard to choose!

We once again boarded the train to complete our rail journey and the next big city we were to come to was Ottawa. We had only a ten minute stop here. It was perhaps a little early to see Canada at its best. We have been told spring or the autumn (the fall! it is called here) are the most beautiful times of the year. We certainly saw snow as we have never seen before and pine trees. We were often amazed how people could live in such remote and isolated surroundings. As we came across the flat prairies the snow began to diminish and we were excited knowing that soon we should be coming through the Rockies.

We rose early on the morning of the 25th to see as much as possible, having come through Jasper during the night. A dome car had been attached to the train at Edmonton and we went up into this where we could really see the scenery from a vantage position. It was quite breath-taking, the sun glinting on the snow beside the lakes, the deer tracks visible as they had come down during the night to the water's edge; the majesty of the mountains high above us, the train going slowly round the edge of the lakes. It was sometimes a sheer drop to the water on our left and high above us sheer towering mountains on our right. The train travels slowly for two reasons, the most important one being that any great vibration could start a snow or land slide depending on the time of the year. Often we could see tiny stones tumbling down onto the track and one could just imagine how it would be if this was a great fall. Indeed we passed a part of the land where this had actually happened many years ago. The landslide had buried a whole Indian village and everybody had been killed; you could see the small humps in the ground, the only evidence that there had ever been any buildings there. We passed several Indian reservations and the small brown eyed Indian children in their colourful parkas (fur hooded anoraks) smiled and waved to us as we passed by.

We were now coming into a small place called Chilliwack and were about one hour's journey from Vancouver. Here when we stopped we had a very pleasant surprise: the Assistant Chaplain of the Mission in Vancouver had come all the way by bus to meet the train and ride to Vancouver with us. What a kind and thoughtful welcome. This was the Rev. Spilman. We gazed at the Fraser River, shining in the sunlight; the fishermen could be seen from time to time – we were very excited. We had our eyes glued to the windows looking for the first sign that said 'Vancouver' – there it was, we were here!

You would have to see the snow capped mountains that surround the city of Vancouver to understand when I say that they are really beautiful. They tower above the city on the north shore making the harbour one of the most beautiful in the world. We had arrived, we stood for a moment each with our own private thoughts as we started a new life in a new country knowing God would be with us to help us in the days ahead.

VANCOUVER,

BRITISH COLUMBIA,

CANADA

NEW EMIGRANTS

As a young man when I first joined the Missions to Seamen I had to give an undertaking (unless particular considerations dictated otherwise) that I would be prepared to serve anywhere in the world, which did not concern me, the reason being that I knew it would be but a temporary measure following which I would return to my native land. While for some far off hills are green, for me there was no place like the land of my birth. In having to emigrate for keeps in our circumstances with two of a family to support, my wife and I felt that we had been dealt a cruel blow. The Church had exercised its judgement and we had no alternative but to obey. However, we were resolved to give this new life our best shot. It could well become a blessing in disguise. Thankfully, whatever else we might have lost we had not lost faith and while it would take us a little time to make adjustments and adapt to living in a new country we would survive.

Looking back upon those early days in Canada, even though we spoke English, words did not always mean the same thing as in Ireland. Some incidents could be funny but could also gave rise to a lot of distress. On one occasion my wife asked for a rubber and shocked all the ladies within earshot – until a kind lady took her aside and explained what this word meant in Canada! She should have asked for an eraser. Again, in Ireland we drove an automobile on the left hand side of the road; in Canada you drive on the right hand side. One had to become familiar with a whole new set of laws before qualifying for a Canadian driving licence.

However I did know my job and though I say so myself was probably more qualified than anybody else in this Ministry in Canada. In this respect I was very confident.

One very unsettling discovery we were to make soon after our arrival. It had been agreed that the Mission to Seamen in the Diocese of New Westminster would provide living accommodation according to Diocesan regulations. Before we left Ireland we were given to understand that the intention was to purchase suitable accommodation. My wife and I, mulling over this proposition, felt that it would be preferable no purchase were made until after we arrived as we both felt consideration would have to be given to location. Our son wished to attend University and our daughter, a secondary school. I wished to be near the port. Excessive travelling costs we had to avoid. We suggested that an apartment be rented for the minimum period and thus give us a chance to assess the situation ourselves. We were assured in writing before we left Ireland that this presented no problem and that they would do as we had requested.

When we arrived in Vancouver no apartment had been rented and we were immediately housed in the home of a board member and his wife who were on vacation. This was the month of February and our son and daughter could not sign up for school as we had no idea where we would be living next and for how long. Within a couple of weeks we were transferred to another house in another area of the city, once more on a temporary basis, and still we had no idea in what area we would finally be located. So far as I was concerned enough was enough; this promise had to be fulfilled. Eventually it was fulfilled, but not without having undermined our confidence in those who were in charge of the affairs of the Society.

The Missions to Seamen in the Diocese of New Westminster had recently come through a very difficult period in its history. The three major societies operating locally who catered for the welfare of seafarers, the Apostleship of the Sea, the British Sailors Society and the Missions to Seamen, had amalgamated to form one society which had not worked out and was dissolved with each one reverting back to operating its own separate club. This exercise had been at some cost to all three. Prior to the amalgamation the Missions to Seamen operated out of its own premises, a purpose built club, and it now operated out of a heritage building on the Vancouver waterfront leased from the National Harbours Board of Canada. Our total capital consisted of somewhere in the region of $350,000 following the dissolution of the Ecumenical Society, out of which we were later to discover had to come the cost of providing us with accommodation. When I accepted this appointment I had been promised full information relating to the dissolution but this was never provided. About 14,000 seafarers annually were making use of this new Flying Angel Club which had been partially and poorly adapted to our use.

Almost from day one I found myself in open conflict with the executive committee of the society. In previous appointments I had held with the society the Senior Chaplain was credited with having a degree of experience and the qualifications befitting his position which entitled him to occupy a leadership role. It soon got under my skin to have to try and work with a Board of Directors, the majority of whom were totally unqualified to direct me in my ministry and ordering of the affairs of the society. The crunch came when they managed to win ecclesiastical support on an issue which in all conscience I could not support, the acceptance of which would have had the effect of changing the character of my ministry for all time.

Having endured daily confrontation in Northern Ireland, the scars of which had not yet healed, my wife and I both felt it would be better for me to resign and hopefully find secular employment rather than have to endure this all over again. When I offered my resignation to the Bishop he asked me to remain in office while the whole situation was investigated and accessed. Months elapsed during which time I carried on with my ministry in the port while at the same time the Board continued to meet unconstitutionally without my presence.

Eventually, a few weeks before Christmas, the General Secretary of the Society in London came to an agreement with the Bishop for the newly appointed Assistant General Secretary in London to carry out an investigation and report his findings to the Bishop.

The Rev. W.J.D. Down carried out an investigation consulting all concerned. A meeting of the Board was convened at the Diocesan office, also attended by a few supporters who identified with the feelings of a majority of the board who wanted me to go. When the Rev. W.J.D. Down reported in my favour he then turned to the Bishop and said that it remained for him to signify whether or not he wished me to stay, as no Chaplain could function without the approval of the Diocesan Bishop. The Bishop turned to me and asked me to remain in office which I agreed to do. My reply was followed by the resignation of a majority of the board and their supporters. A tiny minority did not resign which included a Master Mariner who later became our Hon. Secretary.

Christmas was almost upon us and still reeling from the effect of so many resignations, as I looked to the future it seemed so blank until my wife said, 'Never mind, you've still got us and we'll manage somehow, we will build again.' She promised our Christmas Day banquet would be as good as she could make it and that seafarers would not suffer because of what had happened. It was, too, and as we later learned, was the first Christmas Day banquet to be held for many years.

Such was our initiation to the Canadian scene. I'm not going to say it was not painful, for it was following in the wake of what we had been through prior to our arrival in Canada. On the other hand I can say with hindsight that the experience was therapeutic as we were forced to leave the past behind in order to survive. The society too benefited in the long term. Cases of this nature would in the future no longer fall between two stools – an overseas Diocese and a Head Office in London, England. Soon after the

Rev. W.J.D. Down took over as General Secretary, head office in London became Central Office, signifying that authority within the society in this respect lay with Diocesan Bishops as after all it was under their licence that Chaplains function. No future Chaplains would be caught between two stools.

Some two years later I was handed a copy of a letter addressed to the Rev. W.J.D. Down who had by now become General Secretary of the society which fully vindicated my stand on these issues and which I was grateful to receive.

COPY

Dear Bill:

You will perhaps remember me as one of the directors who met with you in Vancouver when you were out on special visit in December, 1975. At that time you made a decision with respect to the Rev. Joe Parker, our senior chaplain, which was not generally accepted by the board and which subsequently was followed by a mass resignation of all but a handful of directors.

As Hon. Treasurer I chose to continue on the board at what was a difficult time for Joe Parker and I am happy to say that I made the correct decision, just as you did.

I have found Joe a delight to work with and I can tell you that in my opinion he is doing a first class job, a feeling that is shared by other members of the board. The Mission is operating very well, attendance is increasing month by month and steps are being made to put the whole operation on a sound financial footing. The move by Rev. Parker and his family to our Mission premises is proving to be a popular one and, in addition to assisting in the financial picture, is making for a more homey atmosphere and efficient operation.

I thought that you might appreciate receiving this unsolicited note from one member of the former board who chose to continue.

I trust this letter finds you in the best of health and spirits.

A NEW START

I had considered glossing over the facts contained in the previous chapter but upon reflection felt it would be inappropriate for me to do so as after all the future course of my ministry and the history of the society in the Diocese of New Westminster which I had been privileged to lead for over eighteen years was dictated by this troubled past.

Before we proceed to the future and with the benefit of hindsight I would like to make the following comments about the past. Some are tempted to apportion blame for the failure of Ecumenical Collaboration. It's easy to be wise following an event and especially so for armchair critics far removed from the scene. It should be acknowledged that there was external pressure being brought to bear to conserve funds and avoid duplication. The solution in the form of Ecumenical Collaboration seemed to be the answer. I hate to say this but my reading of the situation was that such collaboration was the 'in thing' at that time. These were early days in terms of ecumenical collaboration and there was an awful lot to learn. It should be acknowledged that this coming together was a visionary and courageous move on the part of all concerned and especially the clergy and through head office in London was commended to the world as such. Though it failed for one reason or another and there was a separation at local level, nevertheless both locally and internationally in the long term we have all benefited from this experience. Today both locally and at international level, all three societies are to be found working together from under one roof.

Looking to the future the reader will note a distinct difference between the narrative in this section of the book and earlier. Visit any two ports in the world and you will note there is a difference as the ministry adapts to local conditions. In my ministry up to now I was fortunate in that I inherited from those who preceded me a structure upon which I could build without conflict, but here in the Diocese of New Westminster my ability to do so was challenged from the start. I met this challenge for what it was and in the end it was decided that my destiny was to remain and lead the society into the future. What was achieved could never have been realized were it not for the dedication and contribution of many people, some of whom are named in this section of the book.

The work of caring for the welfare of foreign seafarers visiting the port of Vancouver began in St. James Church about the year 1897 when the Rector, the Rev. Fr. H.E Clinton, set up a Seamen's Institute adjoining the Church. Within a few years it had become obvious that responsibility for such work was more than parochial so in 1906 it was decided by Diocesan Council that the Institute link up with the world wide Flying Angel Missions to Seamen. Apart from the brief period 1969-1972 when the Missions to Seamen was involved in the ecumenical venture already mentioned, the ministry continued within this framework as an outreach programme of the Diocese of New Westminster though even within the latter framework the link with the Diocese was maintained. So it could rightly be claimed that the Diocese has an unbroken record of caring for seafarers dating back to 1897.

On that fateful day when I was called upon a second time to accept responsibility for the future leadership of the society, these facts did not go unnoticed with me. Unlike many other branches of the society which in their initial stage were promoted from London the Missions to Seamen in the Diocese of New Westminster had its birth and early beginning within the local community. While it was essential that we retain our place within the great world wide chain of service being provided under the Flying Angel flag of the Missions to Seamen our future existence depended upon the local community. In other words we had to become what our name implied, an outreach programme of the Diocese of New Westminster. We had to get back to basics by strengthening and building upon our original foundation, with the degree of flexibility that would be required of us in future for ecumenical collaboration.

One of the first lessons I learned in life is that those who pay the piper eventually seek to call the tune. Again, when economic pressure is applied in order to survive, many compromise and sometimes lay aside the lofty ideals which brought them into being in the first place. Over time this can lead to confusion.

Our society and its sister organizations over a number of years had come to depend upon the community chest for the bulk of their financial support. To retain this support an amalgamation was called for which did not work out and now we were back where we began with our future in jeopardy. I resolved from the moment that I was asked to lead the society never to be a part of any fund-raising agreement which would again permit the future of our work to be placed in the hands of an outside body. We would set up our own fund-raising organizing. It seemed to me that this was necessary not only as a protective measure against external pressure but as a necessary discipline against excessive spending on our own part.

We live in an age when most people are literate. We can communicate far and wide and control our own publicity. One of the first major decisions we made in our reorganization programme was to launch the *Flying Angel Review* to be published twice annually in the spring and the fall. Its aim as clearly stated was not to expand my profile as Senior Chaplain or to instruct readers in the Christian faith but to help provide an opportunity for people who supported our work to be able to review what was being achieved on a regular basis and hopefully also to stimulate and solicit further support. A promise was made to try and avoid a personality cult with regard to staff, reporting only on their involvement in the work of the Mission and not upon their private lives. In other words the *Review* would deal specifically with activity which concerned the affairs of the society.

Now with the benefit of hindsight I can say without fear of contradiction that the *Review* over time came to be one of the most valuable instruments in the life of the society, fulfilling its objectives beyond our wildest dreams. We made a point of ensuring that it would always arrive on time. The spring edition would report on our annual general meeting, and include a financial statement or a copy of the current budget, details of forthcoming events to which supporters were invited giving them due notice to plan accordingly, reports, actual photographs and stories about our work. The fall edition always incorporated the various appeals we made at this time of year, e.g. 'Operation Renewal', the Christmas Appeal for food, volunteer helpers throughout the year and for Christmas Day and for banquet nights over the festive season and for people who could entertain. Through the *Review* my wife was able to recruit sufficient volunteers to serve several hundred seafarers at banquets over the festive season; in addition all the food was donated free. It is no exaggeration to say that in time the *Review* came to be worth its weight in gold. The *Review* was our mouthpiece, and even in this book I depend on former issues for facts and information.

It's a sad reflection upon mankind world wide that deserving causes such as Cancer Research, Red Cross Relief, Diabetic Association, Aids, Heart and Stroke Foundation, Save the Children Fund and the Missions to Seamen amongst countless others are all dependent upon voluntary donations for survival. In addition to seeking Royal Patronage in some countries or the patronage of those with wealth, all too frequently the staff from these organizations have to learn how to beg too. It certainly does not make for easy living.

We aimed to provide a home away from home for visiting seafarers within this beautiful old heritage building. Unfortunately, there was much that needed doing before we could achieve this goal. Battleship linoleum covered most floors. We had a few comfortable chairs, but the majority were tubular steel stacking chairs with wood seats. We could only get two channels on our television set. All the walls were painted either lavatory green or cream. The seafarer could not see into the Club when he arrived, but was greeted by a solid wood door. Our first project had to be a major transformation in this area to replace the institutional atmosphere with that of a home away from home. The very first issue of the *Flying Angel Review* contained an appeal for the money to complete this transformation; we called it 'The Operation Renewal Appeal'.

Until now the society had been promoting an appeal of a different kind. As a kindly and thoughtful gesture, supporters were asked to fill a shoe-box with small gifts and a Christmas card. These were put on board ships scheduled to spend Christmas at sea for distribution amongst the crew on Christmas Day. It was called Operation Shoe-box and these gifts were much appreciated by the recipients. On the other hand I was to discover that a similar project was being duplicated in the port by a Chaplain of the Christian Reformed Church. There was little point in our duplicating this effort with so many other needs of our own waiting to be fulfilled. Instead we decided to suspend Operation Shoe-box and let our Christian Reformed colleague fulfil this need as he did not have to find the money to operate a club.

The very first issue of the *Flying Angel Review* carried an article announcing the suspension of Operation Shoe-box in favour of Operation Renewal. In support of this change we quoted an extract from a speech made by the Southampton Chaplain at a recent conference in the United Kingdom. Describing the new look Mission in Southampton, Mr Roberts said, 'The plan had been to set very high standards of decoration and facilities. The result was that club usage had exceeded all forecasts,' and he believed the society's future lay in the provision of smaller, carefully designed clubs which would attract men by the excellence of their facilities. 'Seamen today are not paupers,' said Mr Roberts. 'It is not part of the mission of the Church to offer seafarers charity. They want service, they want somewhere to go where they won't be a stranger, but if they find low standards, they won't be back.'

We went on to say that it would be wonderful if all those who in the past had generously contributed to Operation Shoe-box would be agreeable instead to make an annual contribution to the society at this time of year. We would call it 'Operation Renewal'. The response was magnificent and we received sufficient funds to pay for the cost of carpeting the main lounge reception area of the club (a very large area). One seafarer was to comment immediately, 'The institutional look has gone, Padre, it's more like home now.' Thanks to our generous friends this was exactly what we wanted to hear.

Like the *Flying Angel Review* 'Operation Renewal' went from strength to strength over the years and this annual injection was used to transform many aspects of our work. Our directors would choose a project annually that needed doing and this would become the basis of each appeal. In this sense we were constantly updating and renewing.

GETTING DOWN TO BUSINESS

Our Christmas banquet went off without a hitch and Dorothy was able to see for herself how much it was appreciated by seafarers. The *Flying Angel Review* was launched and appeared to be well received. The Operation Renewal Appeal had been well subscribed. This was about as far as we could go until such time as we got a new board.

Whenever I reflect upon this period, the agony and drama which preceded it, the loneliness of this struggle apart from the fellowship of my family and those few stalwarts who identified with us, one prayer always comes to mind.

> O Lord God, when you entrust any great matter to your servants, grant us also to know that it is not the beginning but the continuing to the end until it is thoroughly finished which yields the true glory; through Him who for the finishing of your work laid down His life, our Redeemer, Jesus Christ.

We had a long road ahead and nothing must be allowed to detract from our goal to try and establish this work on a firm footing. There were times when it got very scary along this road but thankfully in my wife I had someone who was prepared to go all the way.

A date was selected for our annual general meeting and an invitation extended to all those entitled to attend. The next item which demanded our immediate attention was to draw up a slate of people to be nominated for election to the new board. This would probably be one of the most important elections in the history of the society as those elected would be responsible for drafting and implementing future plans and these we had to get right. The new board turned out to be a well balanced team. Thankfully the Hon. Treasurer from the former board agreed to stand and was elected. A total of four master mariners were elected bringing to the board valuable sea-going experience when they made use of Flying Angel Clubs world wide. There was the vice president of a shipbuilding company, a former sea-going Chief Engineer, an authority on current building designs, projections for the future, types of vessels, capacity, number of crew, etc., essential information as we planned for the future; Mr Norman Hacking, Marine Correspondent of the Vancouver Province, a recognized authority on the shipping industry who likewise during his career spent some time serving at sea; Mrs Carol Lowe, President of the Anglican Church Women of the Diocese of New Westminster. The President was The Rt. Rev. David Somerville, our Diocesan Bishop whose support and co-operation we valued enormously, and the Vice President the Rev. Fr. J.G. Gardiner, Rector of St. James' Parish where our work had its birth. The present club was located about ten minutes walking distance from St. James within the Parish and it was fitting that this link should be restored.

The presentation of the annual financial statement and Hon. Treasurer's report is a vital component of any annual general meeting. On this occasion the Treasurer anticipated a shortfall in excess of $30,000 in the current year merely to keep going as we were. 'Because of the fairly substantial income producing assets which the Mission has in the form of investments totalling approximately $225,000 our single largest item of revenue is our interest income. However at the current annual cost of carrying out the most important work of operating the Mission and caring for the welfare of our visiting seamen, it can readily be seen that it will be necessary to draw on our cash reserves and, as a consequence, decrease our interest earnings.' There was an awful lot yet to be done in the way of capital expenditure to upgrade and adapt the building for current use.

My wife and I, now having full access to the Mission's financial standing, realized that a substantial portion of the society's capital had been liquidated to purchase the house in which we resided. While we bore no responsibility for this state of affairs nevertheless we were anxious to assist the new board to ease the society's financial burden and at the same time improve the services we had to offer.

The board set up a special committee to evaluate the society's work, evaluate future needs and come up with ideas and suggestions for the future. My wife and I had a good look at the second floor of the building to see if it could be adapted for us to live there, but before putting this suggestion to the special committee we had an architect friend from Ireland (now living in Vancouver) look the place over and confirm whether or not the alterations we envisaged could be carried out. His verdict was yes.

We spoke to the special committee and agreed to live above the club leaving it for them to decide whether or not to recommend the acceptance of this offer to the board.

The advantages:
1) Living above the club in more or less the same environment as seafarers, the Chaplain and his family could identify closely with them. Just as

Our Lord Jesus Christ entered our world so as his representatives we would enter the world of the seafarer.

2) The club would be transformed from a lock up institution to that of a home away from home under the constant care and supervision of my wife and myself.

3) Many people were afraid and reluctant to work as volunteers in this area. By living in the area we would be sending a message to everybody that there was no need to be afraid. We could not afford to employ a large staff and would have to depend upon an endless supply of volunteers to meet current and future needs.

4) It was the intention of my wife to act as coordinator of volunteers. Living upstairs she could build a close relationship with them.

5) The newly acquired Chaplain's residence could be sold and part of the proceeds used to pay for the cost of creating this apartment and the balance returned to invested capital to generate income. All the separate charges associated with another property would be saved: property tax, repairs and maintenance costs, gas, water and electricity; telephone and travelling costs for Chaplain.

Negative arguments we considered and rejected

A) The club was located in an industrial area on the waterfront. It was a much maligned and deprived area of the city. Response: If the Clergy of St. James Anglican Church, The Clergy of St. Paul's Roman Catholic Church and the Sisters of the Atonement could live on busy Powell Street in this neighbourhood, why couldn't we in our own grounds?

B) Living over the club we would have no front door and would always have to pass through the club to enter or leave our apartment. This would be like living in a glass bowl. Response: A very definite disadvantage but this was a sacrifice we were prepared to accept in the interest of the Mission.

Though not designed for this purpose, on occasions when privacy really mattered we could use the fire escape.

My wife and I put forward two conditions which our offer was subject to:

1) There was no school in the district for our daughter to attend. The society would have to pay her school fees wherever she was admitted. While still young she would have to be driven to and fetched from school which my wife was agreeable to do.

2) Knowing my wife I had visions of her spending a lot of time in the club

for one reason or another as a volunteer. An automatic dishwasher must be installed in our apartment.

The special committee in their evaluation of our current programme felt we should be catering for a greater number of seafarers. Our operation should be expanded with a view to increasing income from these services and attracting more seafarers to the club. In the long term, while it was realized that the number of personnel serving at sea would decrease with the ever increasing change-over to container ships and large bulk carriers with smaller crews, this would have little effect upon us in Vancouver as trade would continue to expand into the distant future as the country was developed.

Mr Ted Jones and his company, the Burrard Dry Dock Co. Ltd., initiated our expansion programme by manufacturing a magnificent wood and glass display counter together with two display and storage units to stand alongside to enable us to enter the souvenir trade.

The special committee recommended the acceptance of our offer to live above the club in a new apartment to be created for this purpose. There would be adequate accommodation left over for future expansion. Nobody could see any reason why this development should not take place as it would both enhance the club and save money. Mr Fred Spoke, Port Manager, not only gave permission for this development, but agreed to have the work carried out by the port maintenance department at cost.

Long time friends of the Missions to Seamen, the Company of Master Mariners of Canada, had the use of the second floor of our building for meetings and office accommodation. Now that we had decided to convert this space into living accommodation, alternative space had to be found. We did not wish to sever our connection with the company which contributed generously in support of our work and individual members of which were numbered amongst our most dedicated supporters, both financially and as volunteers.

Captain Alan Cabot a member of the company, also chairman of our executive committee, soon took the situation in hand. With assistance from his colleagues in the company he constructed an office and lounge area for meeting in the basement area of our club at no cost to the Mission. A temporary measure, it met the immediate need and with paneled walls and pipes overhead it would have put one in mind of old time ships' accommodation.

When I saw what could be achieved now, acting as Captain Cabot's journeyman or assistant, we went on to construct a temporary apartment in the basement hopefully to house a student helper. It consisted of one bedroom, a living room, kitchen, shower and toilet. We had to call in professional help with the plumbing, otherwise we could take credit for the remainder of the work.

In the port of New Westminster the ministry to seafarers was shared between our society and the Apostleship of the Sea, working together in partnership. We had club premises at Fraser Surrey dock and the Apostleship of the Sea had their club in the basement of a Roman Catholic Church in the City of New Westminster. The work was substantially financed by an annual grant from the United Good Neighbours Campaign but this grant was insufficient to cover our outlay and we had to subsidize the cost of our involvement. This work being in the Diocese of New Westminster was under our jurisdiction.

Once again our special committee made a study of this operation. In the first place it was discovered that as long as we accepted funding from the United Good Neighbours we were not permitted to organize a fund-raising drive in this area. Secondly, the latter body continued to reduce our annual grant and we were being forced to continually increase our subsidy to make good this loss. Thirdly, it also transpired that the majority of seafarers preferred to visit the club in the City of New Westminster to the one by Fraser Surrey dock. Our staff person in the area transported seafarers to the city club where he assisted at all social functions. In other words there was no justification in maintaining two clubs.

It was decided that the club close by Fraser Surrey dock be converted into residential accommodation where our staff person would live. We also entered into an agreement with the Diocese of New Westminster for our staff person to assist part-time in a local Parish for which we were paid. Altogether these changes did result in a financial saving but regrettably in the long term it foundered when the United Good Neighbours cut off all financial support for our work in this area, forcing us to service the area from Vancouver.

These years were of necessity mean and lean and they had to be if the work of the mission was to survive. It's easy to spend and get into debt but it's a great deal more difficult to get out of debt and it can be very painful for those who are left to carry the can.

Year one from the proceeds of Operation Renewal we laid the carpets chosen with an eye on the age and architecture of the building. Year two with the proceeds of Operation Renewal it was a paint job. We took great care not to behave like Philistines and slap on any old colour which quickly came to mind; instead we sought guidance in the selection of colours which would enhance this beautiful old heritage structure, be pleasing to the eye and practical. In this many felt that we had been successful. We still had a long way to go before our work was established on a more firm foundation but we were beginning to get there.

By April 1977, our Hon. Treasurer was sounding more optimistic, 'an improvement of approximately $6,000 over the preceding year and more than $10,000 below the budgeted deficit.' He was hoping it would be possible during the current year to restrict the deficit to approximately $13,000. The benefits to be gained from the reorganizations mentioned in this chapter had not yet come into effect.

WHAT IT'S ALL ABOUT

We've spent much time these last few chapters discussing our departure from Northern Ireland, arrival in Canada, misunderstanding and conflict, during which time the work of the Mission still carried on.

Burning the midnight oil

When did you last write home? A familiar question which was frequently displayed on bulletin boards many years ago in Flying Angel Clubs around the world. It was meant to act as a conscience jerker for seafarers who were causing anxiety to their families by not writing home. These people invariably fell into two categories. Firstly, those who were neglectful about such things and continually put off until tomorrow what they should do today; it was too much bother. The second category was both sad and embarrassing for the man concerned: he could not write and would have to wait until he found someone whom he could trust absolutely to pen his news for him. Old timers amongst our Chaplains would speak of the latter group with great reverence relating how in confidence they had fulfilled this need from time to time. I never had this experience during my ministry though I knew it was a fairly common occurrence at one time.

On the other hand I'm of a generation who experienced the growth of another method of communication until it became almost commonplace world wide. I speak of the International Telephone Service. In an earlier chapter I mentioned how for some years in Ireland, the UK and European countries generally few households could afford to install a telephone. I can remember how Greek seafarers would telephone their family who would assemble at a local store near their home. One call after another we would process to the same number. By arrangement each family would assemble there to receive their call.

When we emigrated to Canada in 1975 almost every household had a telephone and unlike Ireland or the UK, here there was no charge for local calls. However, it came as quite a shock to discover in this progressive land that the only way we could book an overseas telephone call and recover the cost was to book time and charges. When a call concluded we then had two options: suspend all further bookings until time and charges were received or continue booking calls on our second line. Alas, at busy times operators were very slow to call back with time and charge. Indeed sometimes we had to suspend all operations until we received the time and charge for previous calls. Frequently, when we complained, we were told the operator had tried to call back when a particular call was completed but our telephone was engaged. Soon night after night we were burning the midnight oil as we had to receive payment for every call before the seafarer left the club.

In Belfast, that city of terrorist outrage, this was a problem which of necessity we had to overcome. Whenever a bomb exploded near any area in dockland it was instant news on radio and television. Many seafarers, out of concern for their families, would use the telephone to get a message through to their home that they were safe. In this environment and these circumstances, delay could be crucial on occasions so we made representation to the telephone authorities who arrived at a solution to the problem. We were provided with a list of the charges to the countries we called most frequently. They then installed on each telephone a buzzer which would ring the moment the telephone receiver was replaced on its cradle at the conclusion of the call. Our operator activated a stop watch at the commencement and conclusion of each call, thus procuring details of the duration of the call. We would charge accordingly.

Now, thousands of miles from Belfast, I found myself once more making representation to the telephone authority to help alleviate a similar problem. The use of a public call-box with language difficulties and requiring the correct change in Canadian currency ruled this out for 99 per cent of our patrons. Nobody was interested in providing such a service in those days as there was not much money in it, only work and problems, so we had to be the pioneers. Eventually the telephone company in Vancouver came up with a similar solution to that in Belfast.

'Time waits for no man.' When I retired in 1993, annually at the Flying Angel Club we were processing somewhere in the region of 13,000 calls for visiting seafarers, though by now the system was highly sophisticated by comparison with those pioneering days. During my lifetime we have come a long way from the day when one of the principal notices on the bulletin board in most Flying Angel clubs asked the question, 'When did you last write home?' The telephone has now become affordable and there is one in most homes. Instead Chaplains might well ask of today's seafarer, 'When did you last phone home?'

All have a contribution to make *(by Dorothy Parker)*
First published *The Flying Angel Review*, Series I, Volume I, Fall Edition,
1975

I need your help, Dorothy. Can you get somebody else to take over in the
Canteen?' A few minutes later I was being introduced to a young Japanese
seafarer. My husband explained, 'He can read English, but finds difficulty
with pronunciation and has been discussing the problem with Jim White,
our student helper. He now wants to record the spoken word and has
brought along a text book and recorder. If you can read the lessons for him
while he records, then he hopes to be able to practise during the next
voyage.' Concluding, my husband remarked, 'Unfortunately we don't have
a lot of time, as his ship is due to sail at noon tomorrow.' It was now 10.15
p.m. and the Club was due to close at 11.00 p.m. Taking my seat I glanced
at the content of the textbook and resolved to do my best. Our young
friend, having adjusted the recorder, picked up a chair and sat down close
by me. When I began to read in my 'best' English, he pointed to every word
nodding his head in approval.

When it came to closing time and Joe reappeared I was gasping for
breath, having read continually for three quarters of an hour. There was
such a look of disappointment on the young man's face, that it was obvious
that he had hoped to record a lot more. Turning to me for approval, my
husband suggested we continue on board ship. He understood and his face
lit up, as we set off, bringing Karen, our fourteen year old daughter, with
us, she having accompanied us to the Mission.

We arrived at the ship at 11.40 p.m. It was fun to see the look of
unbelievable surprise on the face of the watchman as we all trooped on
board and made our way to the officers' lounge. There wasn't another soul
in sight; obviously everybody had turned in for the night. I recognized a
picture of Fujiama on the wall and Karen was intrigued with a model
geisha girl in a glass case nearby.

Now it was study time again, only on this occasion we had observers to
keep us company, my husband and Karen. I read on and on about ships
procedures and international maritime law. Occasionally as I came across
words which were literally 'jaw-breakers', I would steal a glance at my
husband's face which registered unspoken relief: 'Thank God you are
reading and not me, for I don't know how I would have got around that
one.' Finally we reached the book marker just as I was beginning to wonder
if my voice would hold out. Our young friend was ever so gracious in

thanking me and insisted on having our names, address and telephone number. We left the ship at 12.30 a.m. while this solitary figure waved from the quay-side until our car disappeared from sight. Before the ship sailed, in very broken English, he telephoned to thank us once again. So another link was formed in that great chain of fellowship which the Church through the Flying Angel is initiating daily throughout the world.

Full marks to the Captain

The quay-side was deserted, the harbour ever so peaceful and quiet apart from the noise of the seagulls and water lapping against the quay; a familiar scene in most harbours on Sunday when cargo is not being worked. Suddenly the silence was broken by the clatter of feet as a Chinese seafarer in the distance came pounding down the gangway of a ship I was about to visit. Everybody else on board appeared to be asleep, but being the watchman he saw me coming. Running towards me with a broad friendly smile, he greeted: 'You Angel man, you Angel man, I take you to the Captain.' He was so persuasive that there was nothing I could do but follow him. When we arrived at the Captain's day room, our friend turned to me and said, 'Moment', then disappeared into the Captain's bedroom. Seconds later he emerged with the Captain who was still in his pyjamas and bleary eyed, obviously having been awakened from his sleep. 'Angel man Captain, Angel man to see you.' I did not know what to say. I had never seen it like this before. Doing my best to apologize for the intrusion, I left him details of the club. Full marks to the Captain, also Chinese, who was most gracious. Upon leaving, escorted by the watchman, I could not help thinking to myself just how impolite I would probably have been in similar circumstances and behaved like a 'Fallen Angel'.

How to give (Letter addressed to the Chaplain)

I bought a portable television in Vancouver and have used it for about five months. Tax has been paid on it and attached is the account showing all this, so there should be no difficulty with Customs for landing it. As I am proceeding home on leave from this port and will have no further use for the set, I thought perhaps that there may be some old or disabled person whom you knew of that this would benefit. Failing that I wonder if perhaps you could sell it and put the proceeds in your Mission fund for some purpose or other. I do hope this will not inconvenience you in any way or that you will not think me forward in making this suggestion. Should the set be of no use to you, it can remain on board and be disposed of in some other way, but it gave me some pleasure while in Vancouver and it may yet do to someone else.

A.M.L. Master

Today's mail

Dear Father,

Just a simple remembrance from (Filipinos) Golden Evangelistra. Please regards to all members of Seamen's club.

Yours truly

M.

When words are inadequate

Visiting on board a ship at La Point Pier, I was approached by a friendly longshoreman who felt I would like to know that half an hour earlier there had been a serious explosion on a Greek ship which was docked on the other side of the jetty. He had seen me on board this ship a couple of days earlier and knew we would be concerned. Thanking him, I said I would visit the ship right away. My arrival coincided with the return of members of the crew from the hospital where they had just left one of the engineers whose life, if it had not already ended, was fading fast. News of his death reached us a few minutes later. Everybody on board was in a complete state of shock and there was little one could do except to distribute a personal visiting card and tell them we were available if needed. I did not stay long as I sensed that the crew wished to be alone together, two of whom had their wives on board. Later that evening, non-stop from 6.30 p.m. until midnight, I booked telephone call after a call to Greece while they assured their families they were safe. It was a situation that I was familiar with, and knew from tragic personal experience just how much those phone calls would have meant to their nearest and dearest. We remained open for an extra hour to do this as they were anxious to contact their families lest the news had reached them through radio or television that there had been an explosion on board.

During the evening I discovered that on the previous night I had booked a call to his fiancée in Greece for the boy who had died as a result of the explosion. This was probably the last time he had spoken to her. Words are totally inadequate on such occasions; the most important thing, I've found, is to be available to help as needed.

TANTE

Address given by the Rev. J.D. Parker, Senior Chaplain the Missions to Seamen Vancouver, on the occasion of the funeral of Marjorie Noel Lowndes in St. James' Church, Vancouver on Wednesday 14 December 1977.

The welfare of seafarers occupies a special place in the life and history of this Parish Church of St. James, for it was under the inspired leadership of a former Rector, the Rev. Fr. Clinton, that a Seamen's Institute was opened about the year 1897 – which was later to become the Missions to Seamen with which Tante is also identified in addition to her work amongst Scandinavian seafarers.

Fr. Gardiner, the present Rector, is Vice-President of the Society, so it is appropriate that in St. James, close to the Vancouver waterfront, we commend to Almighty God's gracious keeping the soul of this great Christian lady whose work amongst seafarers became a legend in her own day.

We know very little of Tante's early life, save that she was born of British parents and raised in the Argentine where she enjoyed a happy family life as she grew to adult years. She is survived by two elderly brothers, an elderly sister and her niece. A very private person, she seldom talked about herself even to close friends.

Tante would have been in her mid-thirties when she first arrived in Vancouver. I asked a friend what she looked like in those early days. 'She was very pretty, tall and elegant, a gracious lady with a mind of her own, very active and could be great fun.'

When we consider the mammoth task to which she dedicated herself at this age and in this era, prepared to voluntarily finance her work for a number of years, which she subsequently did, we gain an insight into the character, faith and dedication of this unique woman. Tante was an individualist and like most individualists in this mould she had a powerful sense of what she ought to do. She was very determined, sincere and true to what she believed. Until the very end she retained these qualities, having learned to cope with each new situation as it arose.

She felt particularly called to dedicate herself to the welfare of

Scandinavian seafarers and dedicate herself she did. She had that biblical quality of faith which can move mountains, for that is what she did.

In time, Tante could go anywhere on board ship or on the waterfront. Slowly but surely over the years her selfless dedication became legendary amongst the crews of Scandinavian ships and she became for them the Florence Nightingale of the Vancouver waterfront. Visiting their ships upon arrival in port, distributing home town newspapers and magazines, arranging skiing trips, bus tours, and soccer games which she often refereed herself.

The sick, too, were not forgotten. She became as well known to the staff in hospitals where sick seamen were usually admitted as the hospital Chaplains. Nobody was forgotten. Like a ferret she sought them out, wrote to their families and tended their needs.

Time moved on, while Tante's value and true worth was established in the hearts of Scandinavian seafarers. Now they were concerned about her welfare. Until now she had to walk from ship to ship, and use the public transport system for her work. A collection was made amongst the Scandinavian ships and they presented her with a car.

Soon her contribution was recognized by the Swedish and Norwegian Seamen's Welfare organizations, and she was paid a small salary.

In 1957 she was honoured by the King of Norway with the title 'Knight of the Order of St. Olav'. She was similarly honoured with the Silver Medal of the Swedish Merchant Navy Welfare Council, and three years ago she shared with Norman Hacking, former Marine Editor of the Province, a unique honour: appointed an Honorary Commodore of the Port of Vancouver. In this connection, I would like to say that Mr Fred Spoke, General Manager of the National Harbours Board Port of Vancouver, telephoned personally to express his deepest regrets that he is unable to be here today. Several thousand miles away on business it is impossible; nevertheless he is officially represented.

Tante's work among Scandinavian seafarers occupied the major part of her time and it was to this work that she felt a particular call, but to say that her vision and concern for seafarers ended here would be to do her a grave injustice. Throughout the years since her arrival on the Vancouver waterfront she had an association with the Missions to Seamen. Indeed, at the time of her death she was a member of the Board of our Society. Before the opening of the new Norwegian Seamen's Centre in Burnaby a couple of years ago, she encouraged Scandinavian seafarers to make use of the entertainments and facilities at the Flying Angel Club, where for a time she served as a volunteer hostess. A friend said of her, 'She had a great understanding of the loneliness of seamen's lives,' and how true for this was the real Tante.

Serving on board Scandinavian ships are many seafarers of differing nationalities, sometimes in large number, sometimes in ones, twos and threes. True to character, Tante knew they would love to talk to someone who could speak their own language. She would seek them out, and introduce them to the Flying Angel Club, where they would be most likely to meet their fellow countrymen from other ships in port. She did likewise in the course of her hospital rounds, advising us to make sure that we attended to their needs.

Tante spoke seven languages – and often when seafarers were hospitalized or had problems we would call upon her to translate.

A few personal reminiscences of this unique lady, who with tireless energy and endless dedication brought so much light into the lives of others:

Soon after my arrival in Vancouver we first met on the job, so to speak, but this was not unusual for Tante loved what she was doing and was always on the job.

It was a shocking day with terribly heavy rain, and being unfamiliar with the waterfront I decided to walk. Almost soaked to the skin I reached my first ship, and looked about to take my bearings while the water dripped from me. A female voice called out, 'Welcome to Vancouver, you must be Padre Parker? I'm Tante.' She immediately put me at ease by introducing me to the crew. Soon the wetting was forgotten. Tante became a valued personal and family friend, upon whose wisdom and integrity I came to rely in facing the challenge of the days ahead. Many times I have thanked God for her help and guidance.

Tante's Day. I have always felt that the digits on Tante's watch comprised the arrival and departure times of Scandinavian ships. My wife and I have on occasions quietly burned the midnight oil when she visited us – for secretly we knew she would depart only to await the arrival of a ship in port, a regular occurrence in her life. Her dedication was unbelievable – she meant an awful lot to an awful lot of people.

Only recently a distressed stewardess from a Scandinavian ship, which had a quick turn-around, called my wife at the club: 'What's happened to Tante? She never came on board.' Tante and she used to have a coffee together in our club before her ship sailed from the adjacent birth. It transpired that Tante had been the mainstay during a crisis period in her life. Unaware of Tante's illness she was concerned when she did not visit her on the ship that day.

Fiercely independent and unfettered by the control of institutions or the discipline of religious orders, Tante became a mine of information. Indeed, she was an institution, a whole Mission in herself.

You know the search which always takes place for the 'Black Box' following an air crash, well, this always reminded me of Tante. Wherever she went there was the Black Bag, and inside it the Black Book to which she frequently referred. It was her memory box which contained a vast amount of vital information. The early years had taught her how to depend upon her own resources.

A recent article in the *Vancouver Sun*, beautifully written by Alan Daniles, stimulated great concern for her welfare on the waterfront. Since then, almost daily, there has been one question: How is she?'

When Alan approached me for information about her I was reluctant to co-operate for I knew she had been distressed from time to time by articles that had been published about her reasons for doing this work. Alan should know that his article gave her great comfort. She appreciated what he said, and it provided the opportunity for her countless friends to let her know how much they appreciated and valued what she was and what she did. After publication her bedroom became a flower garden.

Tante's mortal remains will be cremated. Instead of sending flowers to her funeral, friends have been asked to make a donation to the Missions to Seamen. I have been authorized to say that any money received will be used in consultation with the Norwegian Consulate General and the Swedish Consulate to perpetuate the memory of Tante. Details will be published in due course.

Tante was a great Christian, but a very human person, not easily given to pious platitudes – in her book action spoke louder than words.

A few days before she died when my wife and I called to visit her, she turned to me and said, 'I've got something for you,' and from the pocket of her dressing gown she withdrew a supplement which had appeared in the *Vancouver Sun* – Christmas Carol and Song Sheet. 'You may be asked for these. See, you can get as many as you need free.' I thanked her and promised I would.

Three days later, following our Sunday evening service an Indian Christian seafarer came to ask if it would be possible to get a few copies of well known Christmas carols. 'We want to go carol singing on board ship.'

While we pray that Tante's voice will be joined with the Angelic choir this Christmas on the highways of the sea, Indian seafarers because of her will more fully herald the coming of the King of Kings. And before she died my wife was able to tell her of how once again she had filled a need.

Our Lord Jesus Christ addressing Himself to those who would be His disciples said, 'Let your light so shine before men that they may see your good works and glorify your Father Who is in heaven' and so we pray:

> O, God of Love, we thank and praise Your Holy Name for Tante, and all seafarers who have witnessed a good profession and passed through the waters into the Heavenly Kingdom; grant that we may ever keep them in holy remembrance and bring us at last to share with them the eternal joy of Your Presence, through Jesus Christ, our Lord, Amen.

A brief sequel

It was agreed that Tante's memorial should take the form of a Trust Fund bearing her name which would be administered by the Missions to Seamen. The annual income from the trust should be used to provide entertainment for seafarers. Over the years we still received occasional donations which were added to the capital to provide further income. Until my retirement in 1993 we always used the annual income from the Trust to provide a movie show nightly on weekdays at the Flying Angel Club.

We had a large portrait of the first Florence Nightingale in our club and many of us felt that Tante had earned a similar place in the hearts of those who had frequented the Vancouver waterfront during her sojourn amongst us. A world wide search failed to produce a picture of her as apparently she always refused to co-operate with photographers. We had almost given up hope when a stewardess from a Norwegian ship heard about our search and contacted us. One day she had asked Tante to pose which she agreed to do and then promptly walked over to a window in a derelict building displaying tattered posters. With a broad smile she took her stand for the picture. It was a lovely happy picture and a true likeness. We had an artist paint out the background and with the picture blown up it is difficult to distinguish it from a portrait.

So Tante's memory is commemorated in the history of the Vancouver waterfront.

WE WERE ALL IN THIS TOGETHER

In my work with the Missions to Seamen in the port of Belfast, again and again I was called upon to visit seafarer's homes for one reason or another as a sizeable number of the population made their career at sea. Usually I was the messenger reporting on the life of a loved one who was serving on a ship overseas. In the eighteen years that I served in the port of Vancouver never once had I to fulfil this request for the simple reason I believe that few Canadians served on deep sea ships. On the other hand in my new role I was one of the sources from which these messages originated. I knew from personal experience how eagerly news was awaited by loved ones back home. One case in particular comes to mind.

A young British seafarer who had been celebrating ahead of the approaching festive season carelessly stepped off the sidewalk into the path of an approaching bus and was knocked down. It was entirely his own fault. He was taken to hospital where he remained unconscious with head injuries for several days.

Through the Master on his ship I learned that his father, an elderly widower living on his own, was his next-of-kin. What a Christmas greeting for this elderly gentleman! On my first visit to the hospital and indeed for many subsequent visits I could merely look, listen and say a prayer. On the other hand the ward staff were always optimistic and full of hope. Via our Central Office in London, England, the father was kept informed of my visits to the hospital and assured that though his son was hospitalized in a distant land he could rest assured that he was being well looked after. Dad's wait must have felt like an eternity before I was able to telephone Central Office with the best news of all. His son had regained consciousness: a wonderful Christmas present.

Appreciation
While I was the only professional clergyman in our household above the club, nevertheless as volunteers my wife and family did their share too, to which Peter's letter bears witness.

Dear Mrs Parker,

I am Peter and it is very nice to inform you that I am now in Japan. Maybe you forget my face, but anyway, I expect it wouldn't happen.

It was so good of you and your family to give my friend and me so much of your time to talk with us. We enjoyed and appreciated all your kindness to us more than we can say. We hope that we have the pleasure of seeing you and your family in our earliest convenience whenever we get a chance to Vancouver. Hereby I enclose the photo we took in the club and I expect you would like it.

It was so good being with your family and I enjoyed every moment.

With lots of love,

Peter

(Peter came from Taiwan)

The foregoing letter and the article which follows were both first published in the *Flying Angel Review* as part of our ongoing programme to keep supporters of the society informed. Rather than publish the names of those who contributed financially in support of our work we felt it would be more appreciated by them to know more about the work they were helping to support. About this time our financial situation was beginning to improve though we were understaffed. We could not yet afford to employ an experienced person yet we were very fortunate in the calibre of the young men who took time out at this early stage in life to work as student helpers with our society for very little. Without their contribution I simply do not know what we would have done. Student helpers served in the club and visited the ships. The author of the following article, Simon, lived in the basement apartment created for this purpose.

Contrary to the popular image

In the past six months since I arrived, I have found every day different in some way, so I was not surprised one morning a few months back when Mr Parker said we were off to buy a large bag of soil. All I could gather from the conversation thereafter was that it was for a seaman on a British ship who needed it for some plants. I was told to bring the camera as Mr Parker thought he might get a 'good shot' of me carrying the bag up the gangway: 'All this would be good for the *Review*,' he added. How it might be good for the *Review* I wasn't sure, but I asked no more questions. (I had a sneaking suspicion that Mr Parker felt his days of 'soil shifting' were over and that he needed somebody to do the donkey-work for him.) On finally reaching the cabin, bag of soil in hand, I realized what the camera was for. The seaman was 'Nurse-purser' on the ship and his cabin was beautifully decorated with items from around the world which he had obviously collected on his visits to numerous ports. He was pleased to see his bag of soil as it meant he could now add to his already healthy display of plants. My eyes having already settled upon a fish tank, I was considering how best to take a picture of the cabin which would in some way include the fish tank. That picture never came into being as Mr Parker told me that the seamen kept a bird for a pet as well as the fish. So a very tame canary appeared and performed before the camera for us, not seeming to mind in the slightest. The seamen said his cabin was home for most of the year so he might as well make the best of it and he certainly did.

While on a Chinese ship, I ran into the Captain who happened to be British. He invited me upstairs for a beer and I was soon to find out that his hobby was collecting seashells. He had a lot of shells on board with him, many of which he had collected on this particular voyage, but his complete collection was back home in Hong Kong. After collecting seashells (and coral) for thirty years, Captain — had over 6,000 shells and 2,400 recorded species. What is perhaps surprising is that he is now on his third collection, the other two having been given away to friends. However, this collection will probably be his last and Captain — says that he might eventually donate it to a museum, shell society or some other similar organization. Amongst his most valued shells are two which were trawled off Durban, South Africa. Both these shells are very rare since there have only been fourteen found in the whole world. I would like to have got a photograph of Captain — with his shells but unfortunately he was rather shy of having his picture taken. Needless to say though, the shells were very beautiful and although I knew nothing whatsoever about them I was extremely interested and would have liked to have stayed longer than I did. As I was leaving. Captain — mentioned that he had no shells in the area stretching from San Francisco to Alaska, so if there are budding shell collectors reading this Captain — would like to hear from you.

Both these examples I would say are contrary to the popular image of seamen. People I have met who have never come into contact with seamen usually expect them to be 'drunken vagabonds' or suchlike. I have got to admit that before I joined the Missions to Seamen my opinions of such men were very similar to that 'popular image'. Since starting work here in Vancouver, I have been greeted with many kind gestures of appreciation for the work of the Flying Angel . . . just before I started writing this article, whilst visiting an Indian ship, I got chatting with a crew member – I left the ship with a set of five hand carved elephants from India and a pair of slippers.

My image of seamen is definitely 'contrary to the popular image'.

S.R.

A volunteer writes of Christmas 1977

In Christ there is no East or West,
In Him no South or North,
But one great fellowship of love
Throughout the whole wide earth.
Join hands, then, brothers of the faith,
Whate'er your race may be;
Who serves my Father as a son
Is surely kin to me.

Christmas at the Mission was a very busy time indeed – 215 seamen signed the visitors book on Christmas Day and even more, 228 to be exact, on St. Stephen's Day; in all twenty countries were represented. Every available chair was brought out of storage and dusted off, and every corner seemed to be packed with bodies. Fortunately the remodelling work in the basement area had been completed in time, so we were able to move down there this year to sample the excellent buffets provided on both evenings by the ladies. It was very nice to see so many volunteer helpers leaving their families and come in to join us and help entertain all those seamen from far away places. Our small group of girls was augmented by a group from the YWCA, all of whom were danced off their feet by the time the end of the evening arrived. We played a few party games to get things going, and we were treated to a fine display of belly-dancing (yes, indeed – in the Mission) by Theresa from the Lebanon. No one was more surprised than a couple of young Egyptians – it was about the last thing they expected to see in Vancouver.

We ended both evenings with a brief candle-light service in the Chapel. As many of us as could get in, kneeling in front of the Altar round the Christmas Crib with Our Lady and St. Joseph to adore the Holy Child, the word made flesh, God made man, men from all around the world speaking many different languages, and from many different churches. As Fr. Parker read the Christmas gospel all the lights were turned on, for Christ is 'the true light, which lighteth every man that cometh into the world'. This was the theme of our Chaplain's address on the second evening, as he described to us Holman Hunt's famous picture, 'The Light of the World'.

B.D.K.

On this occasion a new practice was also initiated. All seafarers present received the gift of pair of socks from the Anglican Church Women of the Diocese of New Westminster. In time these were beautifully gift wrapped every year by the Ladies Guild of St. James Parish Church. Again it is interesting to note that the Anglican Church Women of the Diocese of New Westminster were major supporters of Operation Renewal since this appeal was first launched. These contributions continued to be made annually when I retired in 1993.

The Rose of Lancaster

When we first moved into the apartment above the club we put a small notice at the foot of the stairs leading to our apartment marked PRIVATE, but many seafarers did not speak English so it soon proved ineffective. We had to think again to find an acceptable method of dealing with this problem which would fit in with the decor of this lovely old heritage building. Eventually we installed a chain across the foot of the stairway to indicate that upstairs was not part of the club.

It worked well and there were no objections until Bosun George arrived on the scene. 'That damn chain does not belong in a seafarer's club like this; you ought to have a nice piece of rope work instead.' 'I believe you are right,' I said, 'but with our bank account I'm afraid we'll have to make do.' 'Leave it to me and I'll see what can be done,' says George who sailed next day. Impressive, nice idea I thought to myself. It's easy to talk.

I was wrong and completely underestimated my man. A few months later George returned to install a beautiful piece of ropework incorporating his home-country emblem the Rose of Lancaster, beautifully painted and finished. All his own handiwork and a gift from George himself.

Appreciation

We had many anonymous supporters who contributed in one way or another in support of our work. It simply was not easy to find a way to thank everybody and let them know how much their contribution was appreciated by seafarers, especially those who contributed good reading materials. We did our best to do so through the *Review* but could not be sure we were reaching everybody. The following letter illustrates how very much this service was appreciated by seafarers.

Dear Padre:

On my last visit to Vancouver, I was able to obtain from your Mission a wide selection of pocket-books. This letter is written to express my appreciation of this service. For the last five months our ship has been trading across the North Pacific to ports in the Persian Gulf and the Indian Sub-Continent, where reading material is either scarce or unobtainable. On several occasions, I have been able to exchange books with other ships, so you can understand the benefits of having a small library on board.

Will you please convey my thanks to your supporters who are kind enough to provide pocket-books for the Mission's library.

With every best wish for your continued success.

Yours sincerely,

R.A.T.

A very patient girl and a very patient horse

Occasionally on statutory holidays when a number of ships would not be loading or discharging cargo we would arrange bus tours of a scenic nature or to local places of interest. The seafarers would pay their share of the cost of chartering the bus and likewise any hostesses who accompanied us. While we were away on tour my wife together with a squad of lady volunteers usually prepared an excellent meal which awaited us upon return to the club. When the meal was fully digested we would conclude the day with a dance. These were memorable and happy occasions, not too easy to forget, and on occasion some really funny incidents took place.

I recall an occasion when we visited Fort Langley. There was a girl standing outside the Fort with her horse. I've no idea why she was there. Anyway a young seafarer talked her into allowing him to climb up into the saddle on the horse's back while his friend took his photograph. Did he start something? Practically everyone else on the bus had to do likewise. She charged no fee. One courteous girl and a very patient horse continually obliged while I apologized profusely.

What on earth goes on in there?

When we moved into the apartment above the club, Dorothy's daily routine continued as before. She is a cat lover and realized mother nature's demands have to be met. First thing every morning the cat had to be let out.

The club was located on the ground floor of the building and we lived on the second floor. No problem, Dorothy thought, I'll just sneak her out of the back door of the club and close the door. No problem, she had thought, but as soon as the cat had disappeared she wondered how she was going to get back upstairs?

The only entry to our apartment apart from going through the club was by way of the fire escape at the rear of the building and this was overlooked by a contingent of railroad workers in the spare parts storage yard adjoining our property. The escape was operated by counterweight and for security reasons was always raised at night. To lower it one had to keep walking out along the steps until one's weight counter balanced and the steps dropped to the ground. Then Pussy would be free to come and go as she pleased. No problem, Dorothy thought, and out she stepped onto the fire escape in her dressing gown. It did not drop as she had hoped and she was too scared to walk any further out. (Though I say so myself, Weight Watchers would have lost money on Dorothy at this time, for she did not have sufficient weight to drop the escape from where she stood.) One very determined lady disappeared for a moment only to return accompanied by daughter Karen, similarly clothed, and down went the escape with a bang. Pussy was now free to come and go as she pleased while our neighbours in the adjoining property wondered what on earth goes on in there?

On a more serious note. Frequently people would ask, 'Do you not feel very isolated where you live, being the only people living on the waterfront?' We loved being close to the seafarer whom we sought to serve otherwise we would not have been here. I suppose in a sense we were isolated but in another sense no, for longshoremen frequently worked through the night and directly opposite the club there was a workshop where they worked night and day maintaining equipment used on the adjoining terminal. The men who worked in this workshop were very good neighbours. My wife and our staff never hesitated to call upon them as the need arose and they never failed to respond. You cannot beat good neighbours.

To return to the goings on of our feline friends. In time our cherished Amber who was a magnificent cat was killed by a taxi cab, to be greatly mourned by seafarers and family. She was hard to replace but life goes on and our homestead so far as Dorothy was concerned was not home without a cat.

William and McIntyre took over from Amber. William was called after my friend who loved cats and McIntyre after our vet who saved his life. Can you imagine the comments on the other side of the fence when Dorothy again stood on the fire escape calling, 'WILLIAM, McINTYRE!'

SIGNS OF THINGS COMING TOGETHER
BUT STILL THERE WERE PROBLEMS

By the conclusion of the year 1978 all the signs indicated that we were making progress in the realization of our long term goal to try and re-establish the society on a more sound financial footing and expand its ministry in the region. Our directors recognized soon after taking office that in the line up for charitable funding we could expect to be placed well down the list. Organizations involved in the fight against cancer, with deprived children at home and overseas, the blind and other human casualties would naturally take precedence over our need. In this light it was essential to conserve capital which invested could generate income and likewise make the best possible use of the resources at our disposal to generate income. We must spend wisely and avoid increasing our debt load which is always difficult to repay.

One of the very first signs of progress to notice was an increase in the use being made of the club. Almost 20,000 seafarers signed our visitors book this year emanating from 63 countries. We anticipated this number would continue to increase as we extended the services we had to offer and made the availability of these more widely known on board ships.

We were convinced at board level that there was the potential for a further increase in the use made of the club. To achieve this goal it was decided to use the proceeds from the next Operation Renewal Appeal to produce a new brochure about the club which for the first time included a map of the surrounding area in relation to the club, details of local bus services, and the new sea bus service linking the north shore with the south shore of the port. The brochure was by no means perfect but at least it did constitute a recognition on our part of a very definite need. In time we hoped to do better but in the meantime attendance continued to increase.

The Operation Renewal Appeal became a life saver over the years. Our club, being located in an industrial area, was not serviced by cablevision. It was a constant irritation to seafarers who visited the club to view a particular programme to discover that this would not be possible as we could only provide two channels. Recently the cablevision service had been extended to cover a residential block of apartments at the top of our street which was run by the city. To avail ourselves of the service we were informed that our society would have to pay the cost of extending the cable to our location. Our directors decided we should make this our project for the next Operation Renewal Appeal. We did too, circulating the *Review* which contained the appeal far and wide to solicit support. An influential gentleman well disposed towards our work was disgusted at the charge quoted by the cable company and took over negotiations on our behalf, with the result that the work was undertaken for a fraction of the original estimate. Now we had money in hand which we used to purchase of a large 28" TV and a VCR. Things were definitely looking up.

The introduction of the sale of Canadian souvenirs in our Canteen Souvenir Shop was a success from the start and profitable. It was one way in which seafarers could contribute towards their own welfare programme. Our prices were competitive with downtown stores and we were open when most stores were closed. Seafarers welcomed this new service and were happy to patronize the Mission for this reason alone, knowing they would get a good buy.

The backbone of our work I have always claimed is ship visiting. Neglect to visit seafarers on board ship and in time they will neglect to visit you. There is no substitute for personal contact. On the other hand it's been a very poor visit when there is little evidence left behind to show that a visitor has been on board from the Mission as it's impossible to speak to everybody on board. Our brochure should be posted in the mess rooms and on all bulletin boards by the visitor before going ashore. Just as our board members carry fiscal responsibility for administering the affairs of the society so too all those involved in ministry have a particular responsibility in this connection.

Up to now I have neglected to mention another change which we implemented. Our accounts were being kept by a local firm when our present directors were appointed. It was realized that if our reorganization programme were to be successful in the long term it would cost much less to operate our own accounting system. This change, it was felt, while it would be a little more expensive in the initial stage would save money in the long term. We looked to people to support our work and our directors felt that a person in the office rather than a computer would make sense. A person could fulfil many functions in addition to bookkeeping. The ladies who occupied this position over the years were worth their weight in gold and their contribution to our work was appreciated by Chaplains, volunteers and supporters alike.

The business through our Canteen-shop continued to increase and we were fortunate to be able to recruit enough volunteers to serve our patrons from 6.00 p.m. to 11.00 p.m. nightly, which increased profitability enormously. The purchasing, checking of goods inwards, pricing for resale and display was handled by my wife and myself but owing to the increasing turnover this task was becoming more than we could cope with, in addition to other responsibilities which were also increasing.

We depended upon a number of volunteers to operate the shop and to make it simple for them our marked resale price included the various taxes applicable. When recruiting volunteers for the Canteen-shop the fact that we did this simplified the task we were asking them to do, much to the relief of everyone. It also saved the seafarer from confusion as the price marked was all he had to pay.

Again about this time we began to experience difficulty keeping up with the demand for international telephone calls. While we could depend upon volunteers to a large extent to operate the Canteen-shop it was impossible for the telephone service. If someone could not turn up for duty at the last moment we were in trouble as all operators had to be trained before we could delegate this responsibility to them. In a sense, overall we had become victims of our own success. It was time to review our progress. We needed more staff.

While we pondered where to go from here something wonderful happened beyond our wildest dreams. The directors of the British Sailors Society (now called the International Sailors Society) after a long and honourable history of service on the Vancouver waterfront decided to close down their club and use the income from invested capital to render financial assistance on a non-denominational basis to Associations and Societies serving seafarers throughout Canada. Vancouver being Canada's major port and our society having to face the greatest challenge in service to seafarers, we were awarded a substantial grant annually for a duration of three years thereafter subject to review.

This generous contribution by the British Sailors Society was unsolicited and came as quite a surprise to us. Our former partners in the ecumenical ministry from whom we had separated were now coming to our aid. Troubled waters of some years earlier were openly calmed by this magnificent gesture. Our directors immediately decided that the British Sailors Society be asked to nominate a person to serve on our board and that their logo appear on our ship visiting brochure and be displayed outside our club.

We needed more staff but did not have sufficient funds to hire without going into further debt which we were reluctant to do while in the long term we realized that increased income depended primarily on an increase in revenue from club services which in turn now depended upon an increase in staff. The British Sailors Society intervention was timely.

Once again it was time for a careful analysis of the overall situation from a practical operational point of view and financial cost before a decision could be made. It was decided that instead of doing our own cleaning, to contract out to a janitorial service. We would employ two part-time people to operate the reception desk and international telephone service. They were assigned additional duties as well in relation to the Canteen-shop formally undertaken by my wife and me with the exception of buying stock and display which we would continue to do. We also decided that it was now time to keep a variety of on-going statistics relating to our work, which would be of help with decision making in the future. These could also be kept by these people.

Thanks to the BSS grant we could go ahead and hire these two people on a part-time basis, one from 12.00 noon to 6.00 p.m. and the other from 6.00 p.m. until 11.00 p.m. Prior to now the club opened daily at 9.00 a.m but after a careful study of attendance we found it was rarely used before 12.00 noon. As a charitable society we could no longer justify paying wages to open earlier.

We were making progress just as the hymn says,

> God moves in a mysterious way
> His wonders to perform;
> He plants his footsteps in the sea,
> And rides upon the storm.

Whate'er misfortune may befall us on our way through life the clouds we so much dread will eventually break with mercy on our head if we can keep faith.

Another ecumenical development also took place about this time. The Rev. I Shim Ro, a minister of the Korean Presbyterian Church, approached me to enquire if it were possible for him to become involved in our work. In this respect I was a man under authority and was honour bound to address his question to my Bishop. He turned to me and asked, 'Can you speak Korean?' I replied, 'No.' Then turning to me he said, 'If no in your case then why not Mr Shim Ro?' Just the answer I wanted to hear and soon Mr Shim Ro joined our staff on a part-time basis. While his ministry was in the main addressed to Korean seafarers he could also speak fluent Japanese.

Mr Shim Ro's enthusiasm and obvious sincerity was boundless making him a valuable member of our team.

These were pioneering days at 50 North Dunlevy Avenue compared with what was to follow.

In some respects it could be said that we operated in very primitive surroundings. By now my wife had lined up a good support team to assist with the preparation and serving of banquets.

Attendance had increased to the extent that it was no longer feasible to serve these on the ground floor of the building, as all of this space was required for entertainment, so we had to resort to the basement. Dorothy and her ladies met the challenge by decorating an area of the basement for this purpose normally used as a temporary measure by the Company of Master Mariners. They removed furniture to accommodate the maximum number of people and the food was tastefully set out on tables in the corridor.

Our kitchen was primitive, a small two burner electric stove, a single sink in a corner with double draining boards, total area approximately 8 ft. x 8 ft. The food, all of which was donated free and pre-cooked, consisted of turkey, ham, cold meat plates, fish, salads, desserts, assorted cakes, pop, wine, tea and coffee.

Now for the punch line: directly off the corridor where the food was so painstakingly and tastefully set out on large tables for the seafarers to help themselves were the ladies and gents washrooms. The meal was hardly over when calamity struck. Someone rushed me into the men's washroom where I could hardly believe the sight of my own eyes. All the toilets were backing up and overflowing onto the floor! To appreciate fully the catastrophe, about 65 per cent of our guests could speak little English. My memory is a little hazy and confused about the order and procedures which followed. What I do remember is the arrival of the General Manager of the port, the Manager of the Maintenance Department and several of his staff. It was a very unfortunate occurrence: our sewerage was below street level and the lifting mechanism had jammed. Measures were taken immediately to prevent it happening again. This story speaks well for the port authorities on Christmas night when most people have a tendency to be wrapped up in their own well being. I have no recollection who was first contacted or by whom. It may have been me, but one way or another their arrival brought relief.

SOME MEMORIES ARE HUMOROUS, OTHERS SAD, OTHERS INSPIRING

Listen to the Father

The Rev. Canon Bill Down, General Secretary of the Missions to Seamen, Central Office, London contacted me to say that an Anglican Priest from Newfoundland had just joined the society's world wide staff and that he would like him to do his training in Vancouver. While Central Office would be prepared to pay his stipend we would have to provide accommodation. Dollars were a very scarce commodity at this time and however attractive it might be to have an addition to our staff, which we could certainly use, our spending had to be kept within budget. The only accommodation we could offer was the temporary make do apartment in our basement which was noisy and lacked privacy. (It has since been demolished and this whole area redeveloped.) Canon Down appreciating our situation said before we call the proposal off the man himself ought to be made aware of the accommodation problem. The possibility of him doing his training in Vancouver was mentioned and it could well be that he might yet still choose to do so. A man of rare worth and character, this is exactly what he decided to do.

My colleague from Newfoundland turned out to be a wonderful Pastor; seafarers of every race and creed dearly loved him, especially Polish fishermen, who at this time were frequenting the port in large numbers. A kind and compassionate person, he never spared himself to serve their needs. These fishermen were very poorly paid and had to spend long periods in port while their vessels underwent dry docking and repairs.

The plight of these men, far from home and earning poor wages by Canadian standards and with little to spend, won the sympathy of my colleague.

One episode in his many attempts to help them is worth repeating if for no other reason than to record one response to his kindness which was very humorous.

Vancouver is one of the most beautiful harbours in the world from a scenic point of view. One sight these Poles had to watch daily was the cable cars ascending and descending Grouse Mountain. This trip is a must for most tourists and not only to ski but from the summit one is afforded a panoramic view of the city and greater Vancouver in general, a photographer's dream. On the summit there are a number of trails to follow, a ski resort, a souvenir shop and a magnificent restaurant. However, on the wages of a Polish fisherman this trip was a long way off until Charles Babb got to thinking about it.

Charles organized a day's outing for the fishermen and arranged for them to bring plenty of food. When they had all assembled, Charles arrived with the Mission's VW micro-bus which carried six persons and then began to ferry them in stages to the base of the mountain. The party set out on foot on a pre arranged route. Charles returned again and again to pick up another load until he got them all there. Next they climbed the mountain following the route underneath the cable car.

I could hardly believe my ears when I first heard of this feat, for my colleague was by no means a small man. When I tried to commend him for such a valiant effort, he made light of it by saying, 'The grub was good; actually they brought half a pig and we were ready for it by the time we reached the top!' Now for the punchlines – about this time I had to enter hospital for emergency surgery and Charles took over my duties while I recuperated. Living upstairs my wife had grown close to our volunteers and she would invariably say hello to whoever was on duty. It's no exaggeration to say that these volunteers saved the Mission thousands of dollars annually and Dorothy always liked to show appreciation. When she entered the kitchen on this occasion she noticed the sinks were blocked. The ladies assured her that Charles had the situation in hand and would be back soon with an engineer from a Polish ship to take care of the problem. Knowing that I acted as general handyman about the club Dorothy suggested I take a look before the others arrived.

Still nursing my wound from surgery I managed to get down very slowly to look underneath the sinks. I was wearing an open neck shirt and still peering at the trap beneath one sink when Charles returned accompanied by two Polish engineers carrying the largest wrench I have ever seen! One look at that wrench spelled catastrophe to me unless I could convey to the handler that our pipes were made of plastic and could crack. I did my best but we had a language problem. Suddenly one of the two pushed me flat on my back and instructed me, 'Listen to the Father.' He had no idea who I was but one thing for certain, he had come to help the Father and nobody was going to get in the way! Slowly and painfully I got up from the floor and made myself scarce. Charles had won their hearts. They cleared the blockage okay but next day we paid a whopping plumber's bill for replacing sections of plastic pipe and joints which had been broken.

Halloween
The following article was first published in the *Flying Angel Review.*

We had quite a party on Halloween night. Some weeks before, the members of our Lightkeepers Guild decided that we would have square dancing and games and the club would be appropriately decorated – witches, black cats, skeletons, pumpkins and all the spooky paraphernalia one associates with parties at this time of year.

An Italian ship had been at anchor in port for several weeks preceding the party waiting to load grain. Our club had become home away from home for the crew who got to know the staff, Lightkeepers and other volunteer workers by name. When a group of Lightkeepers decided that it would be a good idea to have an afternoon practice run for the square dancing the Italians were an obvious choice for partners. After the practice, the ladies provided them with a delicious supper.

The party got under way about 8.15 p.m. with the Italians leading the floor when Cindy began calling the square dancing. Uninhibited, other nationalities soon followed and while the steps and movements weren't always according to the book the atmosphere and fellowship left nothing to be desired for the remainder of the evening. Two courageous Lightkeepers, Valerie and Karen, were almost drowned bobbing for apples in competition with the men. The excitement reached its peak with the swift arrival of a slightly rotund Count Dracula, alias Padre Charles Babb, who enveloped those nearest to him in his swirling black cloak. Our chief concern for the remainder of the evening was that Charles would melt in our midst as seaman after seaman clutched tightly to be photographed with the celebrity! A wonderful time was had by all.

A few days later we said good-bye to our Italian friends. Their parting gesture was to take up a collection on board ship for the club which amounted to $176.00. A letter dropped into our post box the night before sailing by a member of the crew enclosed a further $20.00 and '*A thank you for everything you have done for us . . .* '

The least we could do
The tragedy of the MV *Lee Wang Zin* will be familiar to most people in British Columbia, having received extensive coverage in the press and on

television. The *Lee Wang Zin* loaded a full cargo of iron ore pellets at Tasu on Christmas Day and was lost with all hands only hours after leaving port. Two bodies were later recovered.

I was asked to officiate at the funeral of Lee Ai Hwei, mess boy on the ill fated vessel. Though I have officiated at many funerals of seafarers who have died away from home during my years as a Chaplain with the Missions to Seamen, this one was different from all others save one in that there were no shipmates present. The congregation included Captain Chen (Manager Marine Department representing the owners of the ship, Key Yej Maritime Co. Ltd., Taipei), Mr R.H. Kao, President of the Taiwanese Association of Vancouver, his wife and myself. It was a very sad occasion when our thoughts were focused upon the families of all those who had died in this terrible tragedy. At Captain Chen's request the funeral director took some pictures of our small group beside the casket to send to the deceased family.

After the funeral service we discussed the bereaved families generally. Being conscious of the fact that all but two would not even have a picture to mark the passing of their nearest and dearest I offered to hold a memorial service in our Chapel and invite the Rev. Peter Pang, and Father Leahy of St. Paul's Roman Catholic Church (who had conducted the funeral service for the other member of the crew) to participate. Captain Chen immediately accepted the offer and re-scheduled his return flight to Taipei so that he could be present. Mr Kao assured me of the full support of the Taiwanese Association.

The service took place two days later and was attended by over eighty people, the majority being members of the Taiwanese Association of Vancouver, the Clergy of St. Paul's Church and our own staff. The bible reading and address was given in Chinese by the Rev. Peter Pang, while Fr. Leahy and I also officiated in English. The Roll of Honour listing all those who died was read in Chinese by Mr Kao with the congregation standing; following a brief period of silence a member of the Taiwanese Association read a tribute in Chinese which he himself had composed. Refreshments were provided after the service, when the congregation had an opportunity to meet Captain Chen.

The congregation was asked to sign an attendance list and we also took a number of photographs. The members of the Taiwanese Association had adorned the Church with a number of magnificent floral tributes. These together with all records of the service, photographs, etc. were used to print for the families a Memorial Book. 'We present this book of memories with the hope that it will be of comfort to you in the years to come.' Thirty copies were later dispatched to Captain Chen by registered mail for distribution to the families of the deceased. Beautifully inscribed throughout in English and Chinese by Miss Helen Moore of St. James Parish, Vancouver and Mr K.H. Kao, President of the Taiwanese Association, the text concluded with the following prayer.

> O God of love, we thank and praise Thy holy name for all seafarers who have witnessed a good profession and passed through the waters into the heavenly Kingdom. Grant that we may ever keep them in holy remembrance and bring us at last to share with them the eternal joy of Thy presence; through Jesus Christ our Lord. AMEN.

Vaya con Dios (Go with God)

The following tragic and inspiring story occurred just before the tragedy recorded in the previous story.

From time to time a seafarer visiting the Flying Angel Club leaves a very special mark. Such a person was Ronald Boorman, assistant steward on the MV *Wild Cormorant*. He made several visits to the club and came to Church one Sunday. It was uplifting and inspiring to see the way he participated in worship. He made no secret of the fact that his faith was the most cherished of all his possessions, without which life would be unbearable.

Ronald was no stranger to the society's clubs. He expressed overwhelming gratitude to the Missions to Seamen for what the Society had meant to him during his career at sea.

As a member of the Society's Seafarers' Fellowship he kept in touch with the secretary of the Fellowship Prebendary, Tom Kerfoot, and he was a particular friend of Melbourne Assistant Chaplain Robert Long with whom he corresponded regularly. 'Ronald was an active member of the Seafarers Fellowship and made every effort to follow the Rule of Life. He had a very "wide and comprehensive" view of the Church and welcomed his port contact with Chaplains with whom he maintained regular correspondence. They were his pastoral friends as he was theirs,' said Prebendary Kerfoot.

Ronald frequently contributed poems he had written to the Seafarers Fellowship newsletter. When with us, he presented us with one he had written about Christmas, and gave us permission to publish it.

The late Ronald, author of 'Thank Goodness it's Christmas',
with the Rev. Charles Babb (left) and the author.

A few days after he left Vancouver he wrote thanking us for our hospitality on behalf of everyone on his ship and wished us a happy Christmas. This letter concluded, *'as it's said in Spanish – Vaya con Dios (Go with God). Best wishes to all. Ronald.'* On the outside of the envelope he had written 'A Merry Christmas and a Happy New Year to all postal workers everywhere.'

It was the last time we were to hear from Ronald. He was lost overboard from his ship a few months later.

There must be many like Dorothy, Charles Babb and myself who were uplifted by the living faith of this sensitive man who in his poetry proclaims such thankfulness to the King of Kings.

'Thank goodness it's Christmas'
by Ronald Boorman

Thank goodness it's Christmas, I heard someone say
Did they think of Jesus, with nowhere to lay?
Thought they of Bethlehem, a long time ago
Where Mary and Joseph trudge through the snow?

One sings songs of Christmas, of hope and of joy
To celebrate the birth of one little boy.
While angels in heaven, all sang and proclaimed
That he is God's son, and is fully ordained.

Those shepherds who heard it, all felt ill at ease
And that blinding light did nothing to please.
Peace to you on Earth, the angels now sung
And welcome this gift, of God's only son.

He has not come to rule you, but only to save
For we were unenlightened, and sorely afraid.
The stars in the bright sky were dim on that night
As one brilliant star shone forth with great light.

Three kings in the east, they saw it too
We must go and pay homage, it's the right thing to do.
With gifts to the newborn, on that Christmas Day
Have been doing it since, in a round about way.

So Caspar and Melchior, and Balthazar too
Went onwards to Bethlehem, to honour Him true.
The snow still fell silent, as to deaden each sound
And the cattle lowed softly, stood idly around.

May your Christmas be merry, and days just as bright
But remember the story of that Christmas night.
Resolve to be righteous, Christian duty to do
For the babe in that manger would die just for you.

As the years lay before us, many things we can do
Help less fortunate ones, show the way that is true.
Think not of your riches, your pies, and your cakes
Look outwards with pity, for our Jesus' sake.

Thank goodness it's Christmas, I heard someone say
Was he thinking of Jesus, asleep on the hay?

An oasis on the waterfront

The Flying Angel Club on 50 North Dunlevy Avenue has been compared
with an oasis in the desert.

This beautiful old heritage building was once the office of Hasting's Mill,
one of the very first industries in the port around which the City of
Vancouver was built. It is surrounded by a small park – a tiny green belt on
the waterfront. In the park stands a cairn placed there some years earlier by

the Historic Society. The wording on the cairn commemorates the first export of lumber on 25 July 1867 to Australia.

When I arrived in Vancouver in 1975 with the support of my wife it was to create in this building a home of welcome for seafarers. We were to discover that we had also inherited another task as we had become custodians of this beautiful old heritage building. This second charge we took equally seriously. If we could not enhance we would not destroy in terms of heritage.

Our society was hard pressed financially at this time but we resolved to do our best. The tiny park which surrounded the building would have offered enormous possibilities for a professional gardener to develop, but for us amateurs it was going to require a lot of effort before we finally got it knocked into shape. My wife made the suggestions (as usually happens in these circumstances) while I did the work and was assisted with the grass cutting by various members of staff from time to time.

The pain of my life were two large flowering cherry trees which had been pruned so many times that the stumps looked bulky and ugly and the roots spread out all over the place. I decided they would have to come down. We were left with two large stumps. How in heaven's name was I to get rid of these? A seafarer came to my rescue with a gadget called a 'come along' and together we extracted them from the ground.

Now my hidden agenda could be revealed. We could now use the park for barbecues and games. Another item was thus added to our entertainment programme.

Some years later when my grass cutting years were behind me save in an emergency I was invited to say grace at dinner during a conference organized by the port authority at Canada Place.

One after dinner speaker was an executive with the Longshoremen's Union. Looking across the room in my direction he went on to say something to this effect, 'The Reverend may not remember me now but I'm unlikely to forget him. One day a few years ago as he was mowing the grass outside the Mission the engine on the mower cut out and however hard he tried it refused to start. Soon he was down on his knees but it was not to pray but rather to express himself as most men do in this type of situation, only he was doing it on his knees. I won't repeat what he was saying for I wasn't suppose to be listening but it will suffice for me to say that I fixed the mower for him and in the employer's time too.' One can never be too careful!

'THE THREE MUSKETEERS'

The following article was first published in the *Port of Vancouver News*. It immediately attracted my attention as all three men were at this time also members of the board of the Missions to Seamen and they contributed unsparingly of themselves in support of our work I nicknamed them 'The Three Musketeers'. The Missions to Seamen in the Diocese of New Westminster owes a debt of gratitude to the members of the Vancouver Division of the Company of Master Mariners of Canada for their fervent loyalty and support in good times and bad times.

One of the founding members of the Company of Master Mariners of Canada comes by his interest in maritime matters by inheritance. Capt. Allan N. Cabot, national secretary, is a direct descendant of the daring adventurer who discovered Newfoundland, Giovanni Cabotto (John Cabot in our history books), born in Genoa, Italy, and a fellow citizen of Christopher Columbus.

Cabot made his remarkable voyage to the New World in 1497, like Columbus, in search of Cathay. Cabot disappears from the nautical records of England after a second voyage, but his name was carried on by three sons, one of them Ludovici (Lewis) from whom Allan Cabot is descended. The line is traced in an unbroken pattern in a family tree which took more than 20 years to complete.

Allan Cabot is a Liverpudlian, having been born in a suburb of Liverpool from which he went to sea in 1924. He served in British merchant ships, then as a captain with Western Canada Steamships. During the Second World War in 1943 he was an instructor on the famous old wooden ship-of-the-line HMS *Conway*.

In keeping with a tradition that has extended across the centuries, Capt. Cabot wears a gold ring with the original Cabot family crest on its face, the right of the first-born male in all Cabot families.

His executive associates in the Company's national headquarters here are two other well-known West Coast seamen, Assistant Master Capt. Neil Gow and Treasurer Capt. W.E. Ellis. Capt. Gow is Scottish-born, a descendant of the famous Scottish fiddler of the same name who wrote the music to Comin' Thru the Rye, among other things, and was a close friend of the poet Robert Burns.

After British merchant navy experience, Capt. Gow came to Canada and served for five years on the MacKenzie River and in the Delta of the Arctic.

He later joined Greer Shipping, where he became a vice-president prior to his retirement six years ago, and where he is still retained as a part-time consultant.

Capt. Ellis is a native of Aberystwyth, Wales. He went to sea in 1928 and was in the British merchant fleet until coming to Canada. In Vancouver he was associated with Seaboard Shipping, in the deep sea trade.

Recollections of life in a British tramp

Capt. W.E. Ellis, a member of the Board of Directors of the Missions to Seamen, wrote the following for inclusion in the quarterly newsletter of the Company of Master Mariners of Canada, Vancouver Division.

In the middle 1930s, there was a considerable movement of cargo from Soviet Black Sea ports to Vladivostok. Manufactured goods mainly, intended, no doubt, to ease the burden on the Trans Siberian Railway. At that time, Britain was still the world's carrier, and most of the ships chartered by the Soviets for this trade flew the red duster. They were the tramp vessels of the day, about 9,000 tons deadweight, 9 to 10 knots, mainly flush decked with raised forecastle head, or entirely flush decked, having finally graduated from the earlier three-island design, and crews now lived aft instead of forward.

Many UK tramp companies took part in this trade, and ships owned by Reardon Smith, Court Line, Radcliffes of Cardiff, Denholms, Dalglies and Runciman were familiar sights in Soviet ports. Having loaded their cargoes, they would plod their way through the Bosphorus, the Red Sea, and Indian Ocean, bunkering at Colombo, Sabang in Sumatra, or Singapore. Having discharged their cargo, they would either load soya beans in Vladivostok or Dairen, or steam down to an Australian port for grain, or come across in ballast to B.C. for lumber, all for discharge in the UK or Continent.

One such ship was the *Temple Bar* owned by Lambert Bros. Ltd., London, and one of the ABs was a chap named W.E. Ellis.

It was very hot in Vladivostok in July 1934, and eight or nine British ships were alongside discharging or loading. One day, an official of the International Seamen's Club boarded each ship and invited all hands to the funeral, the following day, of a motorman from the Norwegian tanker *Belita*. How the Masters of the ships ever agreed to so many crew members getting the afternoon off I will never know, but the next day a crowd of seamen, about 150 strong, converged upon the International Club. In those days, the Soviet Government had created these clubs to take care of visiting seamen, not with any humanitarian motive in mind but as a means of disseminating their ideology. The clubs were usually housed in palatial buildings formerly occupied by gentry, prosperous merchants, etc. Food and drink were available, and the best looking girls in town were roped into dancing with the seamen to lively Russian music. Girls who, I was told, were sternly enjoined to avoid 'hanky panky' with the guests. Each day, lectures were given on the Revolution of 1917, or 'the struggle' as they termed it. It was all very intriguing, and all very new to us, brought up as we were in a straightforward society. But the walls, plastered as they were with distasteful caricatures of the leaders of the democracies, seemed to blaze with hate, that indispensable ingredient of Marxist philosophy. Masters, mates and engineers were never invited, as they were 'bourgeois'. But I never heard of any converts amongst seamen. Far preferable to us were the Missions to Seamen which flourished in all the major ports, where one could be sure of a warm welcome, a home away from home, with no strings attached.

On entering the palatial building, we were ushered into a large ballroom type room. In the centre of the room, surrounded by a mass of flowers stood the motorman's casket entirely draped in red cloth. Standing obediently round the casket were a number of young ladies of substantial proportions.

In charge of operations was an Englishman named Smalley, or Comrade Smalley to be precise. To find a Britisher in such surroundings was somewhat of a shock, indeed embarrassing. Distinctly 'working class' as we were, enduring long hours, living in poor conditions, and eating ghastly food, we regarded Comrade Smalley with some distaste. Of course, he had every right to think that Lenin was the greatest and, although we did not know it at the time, intelligentsia at British Universities were even then tinkering with the new philosophy.

After all hands had arrived, the casket was carried down the ornate front steps of the building, and placed on a truck. The flowers were also put on the truck and the funeral procession started for the cemetery, four miles away; the dutiful young ladies walked alongside the truck, and the seamen tagged along behind. The seamen were all dressed in their Sunday best which, in those days, was almost always a blue serge suit, cloth cap, and often, brown shoes. It was a dusty gruelling walk in the heat.

My watch mate in the *Temple Bar* was a fellow Welshman named William Thomas Evans. Evans hailed from Portmadoc in North Wales and for some reason was known there as 'Will Science'. He was short and stocky, a very likable chap, and had a tendency to the bottle. To a Welshman a funeral was a big event usually ending up with a great burst of hymn singing, and certainly an event for which one should be suitably primed. Evans had already had a few before we started, so that, with the heat, and the effects of the beer, the procession became too much for him, and in the end we had to lift poor Evans on to the truck, to repose amongst the flowers.

But Evans was by no means completely 'out'. From time to time he would call out to me, in Welsh, asking where the preacher was. I had not thought about it really, but looking around, there was no one who looked remotely like a preacher. Could it be that there was no preacher? Could it be that the Norwegian motorman was to be laid to rest without a preacher of some sort? In all Welsh villages and towns, the local minister, be he Anglican, Presbyterian, Methodist or Baptist, was greatly revered, and was certainly the central figure in any funeral. It was unthinkable that anyone should be buried without a minister being present. Still, I thought, he may turn up at the cemetery.

The cemetery was on a hill. The graves were marked by steel framework headstones, each one surmounted with a red star. The Revolution was only seventeen years old in that year, and I wondered who reposed under the red stars. Were they loyal adherents to the new ideology, or were they non-adherents who had no choice?

Strong arms lifted the casket off the truck. Evans took his place with me as we all stood round the open grave. The young ladies all displayed an exemplary air of solemnity. It soon became obvious that comrade Smalley was in charge of operations, and there was no sign of anyone in clerical garb. Evans got more agitated as the moments went by, especially as comrade Smalley began to drone the same old things we heard at the International Seamen's Club: 'Workers of the world unite against fascism and war' etc. 'Where's the preacher, where's the preacher?' cried Evans as he hung on to my arms. This was indeed a crisis of major importance. How could we stand here and see this happen? How could we allow the Norwegian motorman to be consigned to the earth without even a word of prayer? I made up my mind. I was going to say something, and I desperately hoped for an opportunity.

As luck would have it comrade Smalley, having delivered his speech said, 'Would any of his fellow seamen like to say a few words?' I held up my hand and stepped forward. Thanking comrade Smalley for the opportunity to speak, and thanking him for the splendid arrangements he had made for the funeral, I spoke briefly in general terms, pointing out that as far as the seamen were concerned we were all brought up in the Christian faith, and believed the Norwegian seaman had been too, and felt it was right that the seaman should be afforded a Christian burial. I said we believed that whatever our ideology, we were nonetheless children of God. I then asked the men to bow their heads in prayer, and tried to remember what our local minister would have said under such circumstances. I rounded off my efforts by leading the men in the Lord's Prayer, which very few of them could recite anyway, but which Evans loudly, though falteringly intoned in Welsh.

Satisfied that all was done that could be done, Will Science collapsed, and was put on the truck for the march back to the International Club. As for me, I wondered whether the Norwegian motorman would also spend his last long sleep under a red star.

REASONS TO BE TRULY THANKFUL

During 1981 we welcomed the appointment of Fr. Roland Joncas as the first full-time Roman Catholic Chaplain in the port. Our directors invited him to be our guest at the Flying Angel Club and make full use of our facilities in support of his ministry, ecumenical cooperation of this nature having become the norm in many of the world's ports by this date. Being new to this work he was assured of our full support and cooperation. Having worked together unofficially for several months it was a great joy for all of us when the decision was made for him to base his ministry at the Flying Angel Club on a permanent basis.

Fr. Joncas exercised his ministry under the auspices of the Apostleship of the Sea (which is the Roman Catholic Church's equivalent of the Missions to Seamen). Our arrangement was such that while working together we would each continue to preserve the identity of our own society. A generous grant was pledged annually in support of the upkeep of the Flying Angel Club by the Roman Catholic Archdiocese of Vancouver. Needless to say this development was cause for thanksgiving on all of our parts, representing as it did the voluntary restoration of our earlier ecumenical partnership. Once more our three societies represented world wide were working together in Vancouver in the service of seafarers.

The practical application of our agreement was as follows: Fr. Joncas' first priority would be to minister to the needs of his own flock. He would then assist with the general ship visiting programme. Cooperating together we would keep each other informed where one or other of the staff could be of particular help to a visiting seafarer. He would be provided with office accommodation and have access to all of the facilities in the club. The Missions to Seamen as the sponsoring body of the Flying Angel Club would continue to be responsible for its daily operation, management and financing.

By now our whole operation was calling for a more sophisticated approach to Ministry if we were to make full use of the skills of our Chaplaincy staff while ship visiting. Now Fr. Joncas needed to be able to locate Roman Catholic seafarers quickly upon arrival in port. We devised a system whereby we kept a record of the nationality and majority religion of personnel on all ships and upon their return Chaplains visited accordingly.

We looked to the ships' agents to provide us with these details for all new arrivals in port. Eventually our list became quite comprehensive. Though by no means perfect it was nonetheless very useful.

One million dollar birthday present

The *Flying Angel Review* had by now become an established fact in the life of the society. In the fall 1981 issue there was a report which must have rejoiced the hearts of all our supporters even though it had been covered previously by the press and was also shown on television. The report published in the *Review* was substantially based upon *Port News*, a publication of the National Harbours Board port of Vancouver.

> A million dollars worth of waterfront property changed hands for a dollar in a recent ceremony that left the Flying Angel Club of the world-wide Anglican Missions to Seamen very pleased and excited.
>
> The occasion was the official transfer of the deed to the Club property at 50 North Dunlevy Avenue, Vancouver. Involved is the heritage building erected in 1906 as a show place for B.C. Mills Timber and Trading Company and for eight years the home of the Flying Angel Club operated by the local Missions to Seamen.
>
> Before an appreciative audience of Mission officials and workers, and a large group of leaders from the maritime community of Vancouver, the Mission received the formal deed to the property from Mr F.J.N. Spoke, General Manger of the port of Vancouver.
>
> Accepting the gift on behalf of the Mission was its President The Most Reverend Douglas Hambidge, Archbishop of New Westminster.
>
> The Archbishop, Mr Spoke and Captain Alan Cabot, Chairman of the Mission's Executive Committee and Secretary of the Canadian Company of Master Mariners, jointly signed the transfer documents. The transaction was made legal by the payment of one dollar by the Archbishop to the National Harbours Board which led His Grace to remark that this was one of the genuine bargains of a difficult economic time.
>
> The club was established in 1897 as an adjunct to St. James Church, and became part of the world-wide Missions to Seamen in 1904. It had leased the property from the National Harbours Board since 1973.
>
> Mr Spoke, in presenting the gift, stressed the longstanding good relationship between the port authorities and the Mission, and praised the society for its contribution to the welfare of thousands of seafarers – 24,278 from 70 countries were registered by the club in 1980 – who visited the port.
>
> Archbishop Hambidge, noting the happy coincidence of the 125th anniversary celebrating of the founding of the Missions to Seamen, thanked

the National Harbours Board for its magnificent gift. He made reference to the ecumenical nature of the ministry being carried on in Vancouver where the Rev. Joe Parker, Senior Chaplain, works in happy partnership with Father Roland Joncas, the city's first full-time Roman Catholic port Chaplain, the Rev. I Shim Ro, a Presbyterian Minister fluent in Korean and Japanese, and the Rev. Robert Young, Anglican, who is fluent in Cantonese and Mandarin.

The Rev. William J.D. Down, General Secretary of the Missions to Seamen, London, England also spoke briefly and expressed the delight of the global organization at this handsome gift. He told of the wide communion of fellowship available to sailors throughout the world in the society's outposts.

Tail-piece. Lest our readers have got the impression that should the Mission run into hard times at some future date and decide to sell this property, this will not be possible. Ownership reverts back to the National Harbours Board 'upon the property or any part thereof not being used for the purpose of religious, social and recreational activities for seafarers visiting the port of Vancouver'.

It should be acknowledged here that the exterior of the building was extensively refurbished by the National Harbours Board prior to being gifted to the Missions to Seamen. A new shake roof had been applied to the building, complete with new flashings throughout, and the entrance stairs, both front and rear, were rebuilt and renewed as required. The entire exterior was cleaned, primed and repainted.

So thanks to the generosity of the National Harbours Board of Canada once more we had a place to call our own with ample space for expansion to cater for future needs when the basement area was developed.

A few days later we met in St. James Church by the waterfront where our ministry had its beginnings in the port of Vancouver to give thanks to Almighty God for '125 years of service willingly and lovingly offered to seafarers of every race, rank and religion in ports all over the world by members of the Flying Angel family of the Missions to Seamen' of which we became a member in 1904.

The special preacher for the occasion was the Rev. W.J.D. Down, General Secretary of the world-wide body from the Central Office in London. Having outlined the many reasons for thanksgiving world wide in relation to the society, Mr Down went on to underline that we too had good cause for thanksgiving on our own doorsteps so to speak and went on to list some of these.

'We give thanks for seventy-seven years of service to seafarers of the world given by the Missions to Seamen in Vancouver. The Vancouver station is a model of what a seafarers' centre can and should be. It is an attractive building, well maintained. It is beautifully furnished without losing a homey atmosphere. It is superbly equipped without giving an impression of luxury. At its heart is a simple and beautiful Chapel, the powerhouse from which its outreach springs. The people who work there – voluntary helpers, lay staff and Chaplains – extend a welcome that is renowned the world over. The members of the board are people with the Church's and the Mission's good at heart. The Church is at the heart of the operation. The Archbishop of New Westminster is President of the Missions to Seamen in the Diocese of New Westminster, and the Roman Catholic Archdiocese of Vancouver became associated with the work with the appointment of Father Roland Joncas in 1980. The non-denominational British Sailors' Society supports the centre financially. The Anglican Church Women of the Diocese of New Westminster and many parishes and congregations give substantial assistance. The shipping community is also vitally involved. This is instanced by the marvellously generous gift of the Flying Angel Club, valued at one million dollars, to the Missions to Seamen by the National Harbours Board last Tuesday. The Chaplaincy team is ecumenical and international. The Senior Chaplain, Joe Parker, an Anglican, comes originally from Ireland, the Assistant Chaplain Robert Young from Hong Kong, the Roman Catholic Chaplain, Father Roland Joncas, is a Canadian by birth, and the Presbyterian Chaplain, the Rev. I Shim Ro, comes from Korea. Assisting them is an Anglican layman from Melbourne, Australia, Brian Winnett. In 1980 they visited 2,734 deep sea ships, made 142 visits to seafarers in hospital, and welcomed 24,278 at the Flying Angel Club. When you get to the Flying Angel Club, study the full statistics for 1980, they make rewarding reading. In 1980 Father Joncas has said Mass on board ship an average of every other day.'

While the weather was foul for our 125th celebration service in St. James nevertheless the church was almost full to capacity and likewise the club for the open house which followed. We were making progress in the re-establishment of our work on a much broader base than ever before. Our directors had every reason to be thankful but we realized there was yet much distance to go before we were in sight of our goal.

In 1975 a total of 12,711 seafarers signed our visitors book while in 1980 this total had reached 24,278 and our board anticipated this number had not yet reached its peak. We booked 1,790 international telephone calls in 1975 while by 1980 this total had reached 6,749; again this number would continue to increase in the years ahead as more and more households installed a telephone. On the financial side the income from club services increased from $7,090 in 1975 to $42,052 in 1980.

When in 1975 Ted Jones, one of our directors, through the Burrard Dry Dock Company made the gift of a display counter and two show cases to introduce the sale of souvenirs through our Canteen-shop, few at that time would have realized that this project would prove an unbounded success. Earlier this year we extended to make way for additional display and storage area and installed the equipment to cook and serve savoury snacks and ice cream. Our architect friend, Bob Troughton, did the designing, free of charge. Now to conclude our celebrations, Mr Tom McGrath, President, Local 400, Canadian Brotherhood of Railway and Transport Workers Union was here, to present Archbishop Hambidge with a cheque for the sum of $6,460 to cover the cost of these improvements on behalf of The International Transport Federation. Yes, we had many reasons for which to be thankful.

SEA SUNDAY IS BORN

It's been said that a week is a long time in politics, in other words be prepared for a change in fortune from day to day. Well, the same could be said of our work in the Missions to Seamen. We made unbelievable progress these past few years as was recounted in our 125th celebrations, but we were by no means out of the woods yet. Soon we realized that our income was insufficient to continue to support the full-time employment of an Anglican Chinese Chaplain and we had to let him go. This came as a disappointment but perhaps we were a little ahead of ourselves in making the appointment in the first place. He might have left anyway for within weeks he was appointed to a very good living in Hong Kong. Having come to terms with this setback, hopefully our expenditure was now more in line with our income and we could soon look forward to balancing the two in the not too distant future.

Life is a great teacher, experience is something which cannot be bought. The coming together of everyone associated with our work for the 125th Anniversary Celebration in St. James Church and afterwards for open house at the Flying Angel Club was followed by one question asked repeatedly by supporters of our work. Why don't we do this more often?

The Anglican, Free Churches and Roman Catholic Church in the United Kingdom had agreed to set aside one Sunday annually when prayers were offered for all seafarers and the work of those societies who cared for their welfare. I thought to myself, why couldn't we do likewise? Here was the obvious answer to this request and it would also provide a wonderful opportunity to raise the profile of our work at Church and community level.

I spoke to our President, Archbishop Hambidge, about the idea and he was enthusiastic in his support. Sea Sunday was born in our diocese. He agreed to introduce the concept of Sea Sunday, as it was called in the United Kingdom. Annually I was instructed to prepare a package with a selection of suitable prayers and illustrations about our work and the Archbishop himself would enclose a letter of commendation which was circulated to all parochial clergy. In addition it was agreed that an ecumenical service would be held in St. James in the afternoon to bring together all who supported this ministry. All clergy in the Diocese of New Westminster and known supporters of our work would receive a personal invitation to this service which would be followed by open house at the Flying Angel Club. Year by year the attendance continued to increase as our work became more widely known.

The Archbishop went out of his way to commend the work of the Mission at all times and it is largely thanks to him that Sea Sunday was to become a major event in our calendar, reminding all Christians that we had a sacred duty to care for the stranger in our midst. Through the *Flying Angel Review* our supporters always received advance notice so that they could make long term plans to be present. In this respect the Archbishop was a joy to work with as he was very organized in the long term and together we could plan accordingly.

The Archbishop usually chose the preacher for the service in St. James. I'm sure he will forgive me for drawing attention to a bit of a boob which occurred on one occasion in this connection and caused a lot of amusement. A local Church dignitary had been asked to preach and throughout his sermon he kept on referring to the Blue Angel instead of the Flying Angel. It was embarrassing at the reception which followed when one person after another kept saying to me, 'Tell him it's the Flying Angel and not the Blue Angel.'

The Flying Angel Club faces west and from our windows on this side of the building we enjoyed a view of sunsets which were indescribable in their majestic beauty. The club was bathed in a sea of pure gold as each day would draw to a close and become history. It was in this setting following the Sea Sunday service in St. James in the fall of 1982 that Mr Fred Spoke at the request of Archbishop Hambidge unveiled in the grounds of the club historic notes on this beautiful old heritage building to complete the final act of the handing over ceremony.

Sea Sunday provided a wonderful opportunity for our supporters on these memorable occasions to share in the growth and development of our work which would have been impossible without them.

Once again we relied upon the genius of our architect friend, Bob Troughton, to come up with an original design which would be easy to read and not detract from this beautiful building in the background. He did too. Walking, the notes were easy to read without the slightest effort; the cyclist could do likewise and rest a foot on the kerb; all the motorist had to do was stop by the kerb, remain seated and read.

The notes provide accurate and detailed historic information about the building and site, special features, some unique in today's world, e.g. the wood support beams in the basement are 47 ft. long, as sound today as when they were first installed. Once the office of Hastings Mill, the site is one of historic value for around it the City of Vancouver was built. These notes contain a lot of information in great detail. This building is of considerable architectural merit and for this reason always attracted attention but now with the addition of these historic notes it attracted even more amongst visitors to the area.

When the Vancouver Port Corporation introduced Port's Day as an annual event to give members of the general public an opportunity to visit the various areas of the port in conjunction with this event, we kept open house at the Flying Angel. We always had a very good attendance and frequently people would come who had previously read the notes which aroused their interest to see inside the building.

This first celebration of Sea Sunday which was to become an annual event was not only marked by the unveiling of these notes but also by the fact that our visiting preacher was the Most Rev. Lawrence Sabatini, Episcopal Promoter, Apostleship of the Sea in Canada. It was fitting that he should be here on this historic occasion and see the notes unveiled.

A LONG OVERDUE DEBT, STILL UNPAID

by Terry Walsh
(First published in the *Flying Angel Review*)

From the time I joined the Royal Mail Lines at the age of sixteen until I jumped ship in New Zealand at eighteen, my shipmates and I spent a great number of our shore hours at the Flying Angel. It was, to use the words of the cynics, a give-and-take relationship. The Mission gave and we took.

Our short-sighted selfishness was not due entirely to greed or the shallow-thinking of youth. It just never occurred to us that we were meant to make any contribution. The Mission was there and in ports where they were no missions we felt cheated by what we considered was downright meanness.

The trick of getting the most out of the Mission was to arrive after the service had been started. God always seemed so dreadfully inconvenient. I remember baby-faced padres smiling hopefully, until their jaws must have ached, wandering around the lounge, first asking and then almost pleading, 'Would you boys like to come to service?' We stuck our heads deeper into the free magazines, looking across the tops of the pages at each other and smirking. Some padres would even try to make a special offer, 'It will only take a few minutes.' And then a slight threat, 'After that we'll be able to re-open the canteen.'

They did not fool us. We knew that no matter what happened, they always re-opened the canteen. They would not dare to do otherwise. We knew our rights.

Occasionally some of the old civvies (they always seemed old) would come around and ask us where we were from. We never quite knew what to say and when they became silent and wandered away we sniggered at each other.

Of course, we did not always go to the Mission. Sometimes we had money, and other places would welcome us.

I recall a conversation a group of us had with an elderly philosophical pantry-man whom we regarded as the source of all wisdom. We asked him about the padres with their posh voices. Were they queer? He did not think so. He said their real job was to keep you out of bars and save you from getting poxed up. We concluded that was probably worthwhile work.

Turn the clock forward 30 years

An editor had sent me to write a piece on a walk along the Vancouver waterfront. It has to be among the most beautiful harbours in the world. At certain times of the year snow skiers criss-cross the mountains while water skiers slice through the deep blue of the Burrard Inlet.

Hidden between the old salmon canneries and giant new container cranes I came upon a large, old wooden house painted deep blue and neatly trimmed with white, its shrubs and clipped lawn completely out of context with the dock gates and railway tracks. It was a calm and windless day and the Angel on the flag seemed to be nuzzling up to the mast, rather than flying.

For no better reason than I needed a few paragraphs to fill out my article, I ambled along the veranda and went through the double doors. It was early in the morning, and the first time I had ever seen a Mission without seamen; it was like being backstage at a theatre when there is no audience, an opportunity to study the mechanisms and the unglamorous practical aspects of the operation. Reverend Joe Parker took me on a tour, lilting away in his Irish brogue, and adding dabs of humour that made me think he would have made a wonderful innkeeper but for his inverted interest in the welfare of his customers. For my research he recited the tasks of fund-raising that he, his wife Dorothy, and their tiny band of volunteers must undertake just to keep the Mission ticking over. Back in my office, when I went over the list, it occurred to me the Anti-Slave Laws must have been very loosely worded.

After the magazine came out my wife said, 'If they are looking for supporters, why don't you lend a hand, you got enough out of them when you were a boy.' Agreeing to lend a hand, and actually getting down to doing it took four years.

Early last December, Ingrid, my wife, telephoned Mrs Parker and asked if they needed any helpers over Christmas. I don't know what skilful brand of brain-washing detergent Dorothy Parker uses but by the time my wife came off the telephone she had promised our services, homemade cakes, large salads, a flagon of wine and the services of our daughter and her friends to act as hostesses. It seems that in the Vancouver Flying Angel you do not just offer time, you also barter goods to ensure acceptance.

When we arrived in the main lounge, small lounges, nooks and crannies were filled with seamen. I slipped off my coat and wandered around as if I had founded the Mission, beaming at groups, welcoming them and asking them where they came from. My attempts to ignite conversation failed miserably. The skill of small talk among young seamen had not improved since my days. I suddenly felt how embarrassing it must have been for those kind people who had, years before, tried to befriend me, only to find I ran dry after mumbling that I was from London.

I did much better with a couple of Indians. I took them to be around twenty. Both were Chief Officers, married, with larger families than my own.

An invitation to play Santa patched my self-esteem. The uniform was plastic so it was like wearing a crimson garbage bag. None of the seamen minded. They opened their brightly-coloured gift packs, and examined their two pairs of socks with genuine surprise and pleasure. The long buffet table heaped with large salmon, chicken portions, sliced turkey, curry, cakes, pies and trifle was actually better stocked than the spread offered at one of the main Vancouver hotels I had been to for Christmas lunch.

At the end of the evening, when even the dancers looked a little tired, Joe and Dorothy mentioned they could do with a bit of help with the New Year's party. Could we come?

On the following Friday, there were more hostesses than before, partly as a response to the invitation that had been pinned up in the YWCA. Interestingly, the girls were not swept off their feet. Although young seamen may fantasize and boast about women, their most dominant characteristic is shyness.

Perhaps there was less homesickness than at Christmas. Everything about the evening seemed to move at a faster pace, except my efforts at conversation. 'Here, have a little Beaujolais,' I said to a Greek stoker, handing him a glass of red wine. He took a slow thoughtful sip. 'I think it's a Bordeaux,' he said before turning back to his gesticulating circle of friends. I looked at the label. He was right.

Joe seemed particularly thrilled at one point during the evening and was dashing about trying to find a camera. A Chinese deck hand he had baptized in Belfast ten years before had walked through the door. His convert wanted a record of their reunion.

Ten minutes before midnight the chapel filled without any urging by the staff and the windows were opened so that the vibrations of the ships' hooters flowed into the chapel to sound in the New Year. A wonderful feeling of hope ran around the building. Men who had been silent all night smiled, chatted and shook hands. If only that feeling of goodwill could be maintained for the whole year maybe the divisive insanity of international politics could be abandoned.

As we were leaving we gave a lift to a girl who was staying at the YWCA. She was from New York, touring the West Coast on a perilously tight budget. She was Jewish and this was the first time she had spent the season in a Christian environment. She had been invited to spend the Christmas weekend with a Christian family in Seattle and had been appalled by the gloating over gifts, and what she considered was the sheer selfishness of the celebration.

When she found out about the volunteer work at the Mission, and how all the unused food was donated to a soup kitchen, and what the Flying Angel did, it rebalanced her brief experience of the spirit of Christmas. Before leaving she made a donation from her dwindling resources.

I knew exactly how she felt. My own attempt to repay a debt from my youth had not really worked. I came away feeling I had received far more out of the evening than I could ever have contributed.

LIGHTER MOMENTS

Living on the job, so to speak, I was advised that it was absolutely essential for me to take a regular day off otherwise all work and no play would make Joe a very dull boy. This was good advice which I followed save on those rare occasions when it was impossible for me to do so. By those rare occasions I mean when there was a ship to bless or a reception to attend related to my work. Occasionally when we were exceptionally busy time would have to be pinched from my day off for one reason or another but this was not frequent.

My wife Dorothy worked part-time with Vancouver Public Library. We eventually settled upon Saturday as being the most convenient and beneficial day for me to take off and we planned accordingly. Throughout the whole of my time as Senior Chaplain in the port of Vancouver, my wife acted as coordinator of our volunteers, and she knew each one intimately. Saturday afternoons could be very busy in the club, especially during the summer months, the cruise ship season when many seafarers would call to telephone home or merely to get a break away from the ship. We needed one of our most reliable volunteers on duty in the Canteen-shop on Saturday afternoons. Dorothy chose Sally Hames, always dependable. In the evenings we arranged for my lay colleague to take over from Sally at 6.00 p.m. So having ensured that all stations were manned, we were footloose and fancy free to make the day our own.

Saturday morning one could lie on in bed and relax except when the seagulls went on the rampage cracking shells upon the roof of the building. I don't mind saying that on these occasions, much to the amusement of our son and daughter, my wife and I very nearly went nuts. However, there was always Stanley Park and the beach which was our habitat when the weather was fine. We could reach the park via the waterfront road in about fifteen minutes as we frequently did when it was gull time over the club: one of the advantages of being a port waterfront resident in the seventies, eighties and part of the nineties. Stanley Park is one of the most beautiful parks in the world.

We would bring our lunch with us to eat on the beach. Sometimes we would eat out in the evenings, returning to the club fully refreshed after a very pleasant day. On other occasions we would barbecue on the beach.

Dorothy would prepare the food in advance and leave it ready in the refrigerator to collect when she would also arrange to give Sally Hames a ride home on her way back to the park where Sally lived close by. These were wonderful days.

One of my chores in the evening was to raise the fire escape at the rear of the club for security purposes. This was a duty which I sometimes forgot to perform, to the annoyance of my wife.

On this occasion I had forgotten to do my chore and looking through the door of an adjoining room there before my eyes at the top of the fire escape stood a large female and she appeared to be mouthing through the glass door what looked like the word Father. I was spellbound for it was a great height from the ground and if she toppled over it was unlikely she would survive.

My sin of omission having caught up with me and thoroughly scared I called my wife. What am I to do? A much more virtuous person than me, she resisted the temptation to remonstrate with me and said, 'Just call the Harbour Police and they will know what to do for if you go out there and she overbalances you will feel terrible.'

I did as she suggested and returned to observe developments from a position where I could not be seen. Suddenly Madam threw one leg after the other over the protective rail which separated the escape from the roof and proceeded to climb the roof in an upward direction. I looked down to see what caused the panic. On the ground, a Harbour Police officer had apprehended her boyfriend and, now in handcuffs, he was being escorted to a waiting car. (We were later to learn that he was high from sniffing glue.)

The fun had just begun. The officer called for back up as this was dangerous territory. Soon the fire service arrived with an extension ladder, a massive contraption to say the least. Madam took one look and threatened to jump if anyone went near her.

The first Harbour Police officer to arrive on the scene asked me if we had a step ladder which he could borrow which would enable him to reach the top of a porch at the rear of the building. 'I'll try and talk her down from there,' he said and he did.

While this excitement took place on the roof my daughter Karen was soaking in the bath. When she dressed and came out of her bedroom she said to her mother, 'Mum, I now know what you and Dad mean by the gulls cracking shells on the roof over your head. I must apologize for being so insensitive for I had no idea they could be so loud but having just now heard the pounding on the roof I understand what you mean.' Dorothy could only reply, 'That was no gull . . .' and proceeded to fill in the rest of the story.

Why a ship is called a she

Karen was spending a few days on vacation in Victoria, B.C. when she came across an Irish linen tea towel. It had a poem on it which was so humorous that she purchased one for me. I immediately felt this would be a best seller if we could obtain supplies for our Canteen shop, and it was too. I trust readers will appreciate the poem as well:

Why a ship is called she

A ship is called a 'SHE' because there is
always a great deal of bustle about her;
There is usually a gang of men about.
She has waste and stays;
It takes a lot of paint to keep her good looking;
It is not the initial expense that breaks you, it is the upkeep;
She can be all decked out;
It takes an experienced man to handle her correctly:
And without an experienced man at the helm, she is
    absolutely uncontrollable.
She shows her top side, hides her bottom and,
When coming into port, always heads for the boys.

Where is your faith?

It was one of those days when I got delayed every time I tried to leave the club to go ship visiting. I had a lot of visits to make and could not afford to lose time. Driving through Vanterm I heard a noise underneath my vehicle as if something had attached itself to the vehicle. Thinking to myself, it's one of those days, and somewhat irritated I stopped and got out to inspect underneath the vehicle where I found that a large nail with a metal band attached had penetrated a tyre.

My immediate reaction was to exclaim to myself, 'Blast, it would happen now just when I'm pushed for time. A voice came back, 'I'm surprised to hear a man of the cloth talk like that.' I tried to explain my predicament to this longshoreman, who listened attentively. Poker faced, he replied, 'I'm still surprised, Padre, where is your faith? Your boss could walk on water but your faith won't take you two or three blocks, to get a puncture mended!'

The pink elephant

The telephone rang and Vicki answered. The caller said, 'We have a pink elephant and he is about 6 ft. tall . . . ' To Vicki it sounded as if he was joking so she responded, 'Oh really?' Suspecting that he was not being taken seriously the caller decided to sound more impressive, 'I'm telephoning on behalf of the Master and Officers of the Motor Vessel — [naming a regular trader to the port]. We won this elephant in a competition overseas and he takes up so much space in our lounge that we've decided to ask the Padre to donate him to some worthy cause on our behalf, preferably a children's hospital.'

He wasn't joking, it was for real. Brian Winnett, our lay worker, was detailed to collect Jumbo and bring him to the club. The first problem Brian encountered was a very natural one. Jumbo had beautifully clean pink fur and white feet. Brian realized that he could not put him on the floor of the van where he would get dirty. Now here is where Brian made his mistake. Instead of placing Jumbo on a rear seat in the van secured by a safety belt Brian gave him pride of place in the front passenger seat beside himself.

One could not claim that Brian was a big man with the result that he was completely overshadowed by his passenger who was larger and taller than himself. Brian's passenger, sitting tall in the seat beside him, distracted so many passing drivers that Brian literally began to fear that his life was in danger, particularly as he drove through the shipping terminal and then over the long expanse of the Second Narrows bridge. Had Brian thought about the situation he might have done otherwise. Him driving a van bearing the name Flying Angel and with a pink elephant for a passenger: what else could he expect from approaching drivers be they drunk or sober?

We found a very good home for Jumbo at Sunny Hill Children's Hospital, Vancouver. Within minutes of his arrival once again he occupied centre stage.

Toe-tapping with the Lightkeepers

Note: The following article was first published in the *Flying Angel Review*.

Imagine a geisha girl offering a tray of sushi or a punjabi-suited redhead offering samosas. Imagine smoking barbeques and three-legged races, toasted marshmallows and hula hooping Filipinos. Imagine partners swinging to the virginia reel or the syrto with Zorba the Greek. Imagine these and you conjure up a summer of fun with the Flying Angel Club Lightkeepers Guild.

To arrange an entertaining social evening at the Mission every Sunday of the year is not an easy task. Disco music can be boring for even the most avid rocker. We put our heads together and came up with a special theme party for each month, complete with costumes, food, games and music for each evening. The Mission Chaplains advertise our events by putting up a poster on each ship so the seafarers are warned of our masquerades! It's exciting to gather the props, hang the streamers, plan crazy games and with our costumes surprise one another as well as the seafarers!

International night was a wonderful success and the Lightkeepers went to a great deal of trouble to dress up in national dress of different countries and to prepare a tray of cuisine.

Serving food always seems to make people more relaxed. A group mixes well around the buffet table – everyone's favourite spot! To enjoy both the summer weather and the lovely Mission grounds, we planned two summer barbeques – a new idea and a great success. Barbeques are an essential part of a Vancouver summer. It is fun to share them with seafarers who might not otherwise have an opportunity to enjoy a Canadian family treat – hamburgers, salads, cakes, ice cream. To work off the calories, we had the traditional three-legged race, egg and spoon race, pass the parcel, and a hilarious balloon popping race.

We had our usual Sunday service at 7.30 p.m. in the Chapel followed by dancing. On the warm summer nights next year, it would be fun to dance in the setting sun and under the stars in the garden.

The Lightkeepers are always eager to have new members join our group – any women aged 16 and up who enjoy dancing, socializing and welcoming seafarers who are far from home. Do drop in any Sunday for the service at 7.30 p.m. and for the dance/party at 8.15 p.m. or phone the Missions to Seamen Chaplain for more information. We need your support especially as the busy Christmas season approaches.

Thank you.

Alison J. Brookfield

Lightkeepers Guild Secretary

AN ECUMENICAL APPROACH

There was absolutely no doubt whatsoever that in this twentieth century in the port of Vancouver a duplication of club facilities for visiting seafarers could not be justified. Any branch of the Christian Church that wanted to go it alone and establish a club in our region would have difficulty financing such a venture in the long term. This was a lesson which those of us involved in this work some years earlier had to learn the hard way.

Thankfully we had all come to terms with this fact and were now working together in a genuine spirit of Christian partnership. I was very fortunate in that both Archbishop Somerville and his successor Archbishop Hambidge welcomed and encouraged this development from the start. It was a meaningful development.

A perfect example surfaced soon after we had to let our Chinese Anglican chaplain go because we could not afford to continue to employ him full-time. The Presbyterian Church had a Minister who had arrived in Canada from Brazil and as yet had not been placed. His English was somewhat limited but he was learning fast and also spoke Mandarin, Cantonese and Japanese. If we could support his ministry half time in the port there was every possibility his own Church would eventually support his Ministry full time. We agreed to do so for a time and eventually the Presbyterian Church funded his Ministry full time in the port.

In selecting people to preach on Sea Sunday Archbishop Hambidge made certain that this choice was always extended to include representatives from our ecumenical partners in Mission. Again we always reproduced the content of their sermon in the *Flying Angel Review*. On one occasion three Chaplains were each asked to give a brief address. These addresses are interesting in that they reflect how each one saw his Mission in the port at that time.

A brief address by the Rev. Paul Tong, Presbyterian Chaplain
May the Lord's blessing be with you all, brothers and sisters in Christ. AMEN.

Since I started to preach the gospel to seamen in 1983, I can tell you that I have only wonderful words of thanks to our God.

First of all, I thank God for calling and selecting me, so that I have the opportunity to do this very important missionary work.

Secondly, thanks to the Seamen's Club Senior Chaplain, Rev. Parker, for his guidance and all of my fellow workers who work with me in the Mission.

Thirdly, I thank the Rev. Metzger, Rev. Garvin and all of the congregation members of our Presbyterian Church and Anglican Church members for the support and prayer, which give me a lot of strength and courage to carry on this very important work. All these only encourage me to do my job with love and enthusiasm so that we can see more and more seamen come to believe in God.

My commitment and belief to the preaching of the gospel is based on the words of Jesus Christ to his disciples before he ascended to Heaven, 'Go and preach the gospel to every part of the earth.' According to our scripture, Acts 1, verses 6-10, says, 'When the Holy Spirit comes upon you, you will be filled with power, and you will be witnesses for me in Jerusalem, in all Judea and Samaria, and to the ends of the earth.'

How can we preach the gospel to every part of the earth?

1) From the closest to the far away. From Jerusalem, in all of Judea and Samaria, and to the ends of the earth. I was born in Taiwan and in 1955 I became a Minister after I graduated from Theological College. I ministered for ten years and in 1965, I was sent by the Presbyterian Church in Taiwan to go to Singapore where I ministered for a local Presbyterian Church for four years. In 1969, I moved to Rio de Janeiro, Brazil, where I established the first Presbyterian Church. I worked very hard without receiving a salary since I didn't have any financial support from anywhere. After ten years, when the Church was financially independent, I then left to come to Vancouver, Canada. In my prayers, God gave me his guidance for me to commit myself with the preaching of the gospel to seamen.

2) Jesus told his disciples to start preaching the gospel from Jerusalem to their fellow countrymen. That is exactly what I did when I was a minister in Taiwan, Singapore and Brazil when I had the opportunity to preach the gospel to my fellow countrymen.

3) Preaching the gospel to the ends of the earth. In the Seamen's Club, our important mission is the preaching of the gospel to all seamen from all over the world who come to Vancouver. I feel this is a very exciting and precious opportunity to spread the gospel to every part of the world. May the Lord continue to guide me and give me strength

and courage so that I am able to bring more and more seamen to know Jesus Christ.

I thank God for the blessing of speaking four dialects in Chinese, and also Japanese, Portuguese, Spanish and English, so I can easily communicate with lots of seamen and this way I am able to preach God's word to them. The majority of seamen, in order to make their living, have to leave their wives, children and families. Their jobs are very dangerous and highly risky work. There is a very high incidence of accidents happening in their daily work. Some problems they face are: their own safety when the weather conditions worsen, financial difficulties when the ship's company faces financial crisis. They worry about their wives, children and families. All these besides other problems cause them to work under constant pressure and disturbance. The only way we can care about them is to treat them like our own family members, so that they can feel the love we spread and share with them, like Jesus loves us.

Thank you once again for your concern and prayers, brothers and sisters. I continue to ask for your support and prayers with this very important mission that God has committed to us in the Missions to Seamen. May His name be praised.

A brief address by the Rev. Fr. R. Joncas, Roman Catholic Chaplain

The Chaplains of the Missions to Seamen Club form a wonderful team to serve the seafarers of the many ships that come to the Port of Vancouver from all over the world. These ships with their crews from over eighty countries form an important life-line to bring Canadian goods, grains and bulk raw-materials to feed hundreds of millions of people where food is in short supply, and to serve the industrial needs of nearly every nation across the world. The visitors, the seafarers who come to our shores, are for the most part poor people from the 'Third World' who consider themselves very fortunate to have jobs on the sea, as they are paid much more than they could earn at home. Their wages on the sea for even the lowest paid may be as much as government officials, important business people, and even doctors make in their own countries. This makes it possible for them to take care of their families in much better homes, and to educate most of their children through university in their own countries. But the price they pay to go to sea is a costly one. It takes them away from home under conditions of special hardship, of long separations from their families, up to a year at a time. Some of the men will even stay on a ship two or three years at a time to make sure that there is no interruption in the funds that are putting their sons and daughters through college and university. They often work under very harsh conditions of winter and storms at sea. The Polish fishermen, of whom thousands visit our port every year, usually spend five months at a stretch fishing in the Bering Sea. Their ships are continually tossed about twenty-four hours a day by stormy waters most of the time while they are fishing. They handle heavy nets as high as fifteen story buildings and 60 metres or 200 feet across with all the heavy weights to sink them as far as 1,000 metres down as they travel the ocean bed. They haul their nets up with all their heavy equipment, and a catch of 40 tons of fish at a time while their ship tosses at sea. It is a dangerous game. All the ships have a doctor and an average of 10 per cent of the men get a serious injury and sometimes death during their five months at sea. All they may see during that time are stormy ocean waters, no land, in a sea that is rarely calm. This is the North Pacific. In the bitter cold of the northern winter, there is no worse place to be. When these fishermen come back to the Port of Vancouver, they come back rejoicing, having had good fishing and made good money, and glad to have their feet back on land.

They are ready to relax and to fly home for five or six months to be with their families. When they come back from the storms of the Bering Sea, what better place to go than to the relaxing, pleasant and homelike surroundings of the Missions to Seamen Club where one of their first pleasant duties will be to phone home to find out how everything is going there. Sometimes, their ships will stay in port for two and even three months for repairs. While they are here, they will make the Missions to Seamen Club their home away from home. Their ships will be visited by one of our chaplains every three or four days. If they are here for Christmas, there will be gifts for all, and parties at the club where they will be entertained and dined by our staff of generous volunteers and workers in a 'royal' manner.

The hard life at sea of the Polish fisherman can be applied in varying degrees and different circumstances to *all* the seafarers who come to the Port of Vancouver. For all of them, their life is hard and sometimes dangerous. For all of them, their life is lonely. For all of them, the Seamen's Club is that haven of rest, relaxation and friendly welcome that makes them feel at 'home away from home'.

All this spirit of home coming for the seafarers which the club affords them, begins with the work of the dedicated team of Chaplains who visit them on the ships and welcome them to the club. Our team of Chaplains is second to none on the Pacific Coast. The Chaplains' spirit of co-operation and mutual help in serving the seafarers is *tops*, and can only be admired, in the ministry we share.

All those who contribute to the success of the Seamen's Club, can be *proud* of the work we do. May God continue to bless our work and all those who make the Missions to Seamen Club a success.

A brief address by the Rev. J.D. Parker –
The Missions to Seamen

Displayed on the right hand side of this pulpit are three flags: the Flag of Apostleship of the Sea, our Roman Catholic colleagues in this Ministry; the flag of the British Sailors' Society, a non-denominational Society caring for the welfare of seafarers; and the flag of the Missions to Seamen, the official Society of the Anglican Communion which caters for the welfare of Seafarers world-wide.

Today increasingly throughout the world this ministry is exercised on an ecumenical basis and the seafarer in his travels may find himself in a club run by one or the other of these three organizations with an ecumenical chaplaincy team operating out of this club.

Here in the Port of Vancouver, the Missions to Seamen is the host society, so to speak, and it is from our Flying Angel Club that this ecumenical ministry is exercised in this port. One could add that one of our strengths is the variety of training and experiences which we have available within our chaplaincy team.

In an article published a few months ago in the *Flying Angel Review* on the place of the Chapel in the life of the Flying Angel Club, I stated that 'we would be concerned to learn from any seafarer using the Club that he felt under subtle pressure to attend chapel services or convert to our way of thinking.'

Though nobody has actually said so, nevertheless, at the time of writing I can remember thinking how some Christians might find difficulty with a statement of this nature, believing that in every situation and on every available opportunity we should, so to speak, put in a verbal plug for the claims of the Lord, Jesus Christ. It's called Witnessing. To witness for the Lord in this sense, it would appear that other people's feelings are of no consequence so long as we use the opportunity to make our point.

I must honestly confess that I find myself as intolerant of this attitude of mind as those who hold it would appear to be insensitive to other people's feelings, especially Seafarers, strangers in our midst. Though in my heart I know that neither attitude will reflect the love of Christ to the stranger in our midst.

Our Lord, Jesus Christ, left us in no doubt about the manner in which we are to treat the stranger. Read Verse 40 of the 25th Chapter of the gospel according to St. Matthew, also the preceding and following verses. It's not a long and complicated theological statement but a command briefly summed up in Verse 40, 'I tell you this! Anything you did for one of my brothers here, however humble, you did for me.'

I once had the privilege of baptizing a seafarer who came to believe in the Christian faith because his heart was touched again and again by the kindness experienced at the hands of Chaplains and volunteer workers in Missions all over the world. Why me? he would ask himself. Eventually, he was to discover that this love had a converting power. It was freely given and could be received. As the hymn writer puts it: Love Divine, all loves excelling.' In certain circumstances the Christian is called upon to be a person of deeds rather than words.

Action speaks louder than words. *Christian love can be very costly.* Good Friday tells us this: endless caring. St. Paul would say, 'There is nothing love cannot face; there is no limit to its faith, its hope and its endurance.' 1 Cor. 13, v. 7.

Why am I saying these things? What made me think about these things? A seafarer stepped into my office one evening a few months ago and told me that he was a Moslem from Turkey. 'Where can I pray?' he asked. My first thought was the chapel, which is always open, and as I took him there we passed what we call 'The Green Lounge', a most beautifully furnished, comfortable, inviting and quiet room. 'This will do,' he said; but next door was the chapel which I thought might be better. He took one look at the chapel and said, 'No, not for me, this is better,' and he walked back into the Green Lounge. Now quite naturally he took a compass out of his pocket to find his location and then faced Mecca. 'Would you like the door closed?' I asked. 'It doesn't matter to me; this place is very nice,' he replied. I left him to say his prayers. He left the club soon after.

When I was a younger man, I might have been tempted to get a word in about the claims of Christ before he left the Club, but not now. In coming to our Club, this man was responding to an invitation extended to all seafarers irrespective of race, creed or colour; that at the Flying Angel Club they will find a home of welcome for the stranger. God already knew that this man took us at our word. The seed had been sown. Love has its own converting power, freely we have received and freely we must give. To love is an act of faith.

So in the words of our Lord, Jesus Christ, I would conclude by saying to all our volunteer workers and supporters, 'Let your light so shine before men that they may see your good works and glorify your Father who is in heaven.

A visitor from Poland

Having just read through Father Joncas' sermon for Sea Sunday I was reminded of the following story. Canon Nakayama, though officially retired at this point in his life, in another sense never retired. Time and again he came to our aid in the Missions to Seamen before we had a chaplain who could speak Japanese. Here we see him continuing to care and meeting a need irrespective of race or creed. He was a wonderful example.

Some eight years ago outside a Greyhound bus depot in Sudbury, Ontario, Canon Nakayama, a Priest serving with the Anglican Church of Canada, noticed another clergyman in the crowd who looked worried and forlorn. He immediately decided to befriend this stranger and made himself known to him. The stranger turned out to be a Roman Catholic Priest from Poland by name Romuald Szumiers who was visiting Canada. Until this summer when they met for a second time the two had corresponded regularly.

'It's been a long journey right across Canada by bus but it's been worth it for me to be able to spend two days with Dad,' said Father Romuald (meaning the Canon) upon being introduced to me at the Flying Angel Club. He was visiting New York but could not go back to Poland without seeing his friend so he chose the cheapest means to travel to Vancouver.

Aware of the many Polish fishermen visiting the club at this time, characteristically the Canon brought his friend down to enquire if he could help in any way. We were able to introduce him to Father Roland Joncas, our Roman Catholic colleague who ministered to the spiritual needs of Polish fishermen.

Father Romuald has since written, 'I am very happy that I could visit the Missions to Seamen last summer. Thank you so much for your kindness . . . my mind and my heart is with you because your work is beautiful . . . I will send you two Polish prayer books for Polish seamen, a gift from me . . . '

I should have mentioned earlier that Canon Nakayama, though retired, served on our board for a time: a legendary figure whose faith and dedication was an inspiration to many. Like many fellow Japanese he spent the years of the second world war in an internment camp in Canada, even though he was a Canadian citizen. There was no bitterness for the Canon not only talked about Christianity, he embodied it.

FIRE PROTECTION ESSENTIAL

Whenever I look back to the beginning of the eighties, one activity always comes to mind: Captain Ellis on one telephone and Captain Cabot on another and both unceasingly canvassing for funds in support of the Mission. While the demand for our services at the Mission and the use being made of our club continued to increase we were having great difficulty balancing our books. We ended the year 1981 with a small surplus of $278. Apart from the daily cost of operating our welfare programme we also had to think in terms of necessary development costs. We needed the perseverance of men like Captains Ellis and Cabot and other committee members whose vision of the future goal kept them going. Their perseverance did pay off eventually.

Thursday 23 June 1983 was something of a 'Red Letter' day at the Flying Angel Club when Captain Alan Cabot, Chairman of our executive committee, and other directors hosted a luncheon to express our grateful thanks to the British Columbia Masonic Foundation and the British Columbia Heritage Trust, each of whom each donated $20,000 to install a sprinkler system throughout our building.

One of Captain Cabot's requests for funding stimulated this response from the British Columbia Masonic Foundation which was subsequently matched by the British Columbia Heritage Trust.

Fire was the major hazard we faced. Our building was classified as a heritage structure by the city, and we had many artifacts which required protection, not to mention our patrons and residents. We were reluctant to increase our debt load but now thanks to our two generous benefactors we could preserve the past and make good the future. A plaque was unveiled on the veranda acknowledging these generous gifts towards the cost of installing fire protection.

The Flying Angel Club, like many other church establishments, inherited some valuable and beautiful artifacts from those who served before us, a goodly heritage. Forming the reredos in our chapel are three wood panels skillfully carved by a former fisherman, Mr Samuel Burich, which tell the story of the first Mission to Seamen.

When facing the altar, the left side panel shows the disciples in their boat with the empty net after their fruitless night's fishing. The panel at the right

These beautiful carvings form the reredos in the Chapel of the
Flying Angel Club, Vancouver, B.C.

shows the same scene after the nets have been cast on the 'right' side of the
ship. Here are portrayed the catch of 153 fishes and Simon Peter kneeling
at the feet of our Lord. The centre panel tells the story of this first Mission
as contained in the ninth verse of the 21st Chapter of St. John's Gospel: 'As
soon as they were come to land they saw a fire of coals there, and fish laid
thereon, and bread.'

Our Lord thought of the material needs of those fishermen who were
wet and cold and hungry, just as the Missions to Seamen today tries to
think of the material needs of those who must always endure the loneliness
and separation that goes with their calling.

The symbolism of this meal and its link with the Holy Communion is
seen in the inset carving of the chalice and paten under our Lord's hands.
These are actual copies of the vessels used in the Vancouver chapel.

The whole concept of this story has been modernized. The fishing boat
of Galilee gives place to the British Columbia scene; while, mingling with
the apostles, are the navy men, merchant seamen and fishermen.

Originally dedicated by Archbishop Gower on 4 May 1958, these panels
were fixed to one of the walls in the chapel of the Mission building that
once stood on the site of 1195 West Hastings Street, Vancouver. The Rev.
Canon Stanley Smith, Senior Chaplain at that time, was I believe

responsible for the preparation of the brochure from which the foregoing explanatory text has been taken. When the society moved here in the fall of 1973 these panels were then fixed to the south wall of our present chapel but when some refurbishing work was later undertaken they were moved to their present location behind the altar.

The vestibule to this beautiful little chapel was a later creation when we were refurbishing. Many years ago our society operated a club in association with Holy Trinity Cathedral Church, New Westminster. When the club closed, a beautiful set of five stained glass windows were given over to Holy Trinity for safe keeping. These windows, a memorial, were later transferred to us.

Having consulted a number of authorities about adapting these windows for us in our heritage building, we were advised to convert the small vestry room at the rear of the chapel into a vestibule entrance and close off the other entrance halfway up the side of the church. It was then suggested that four of the stained glass windows be put together to form one window, as one wall in the vestibule, and lighted from behind. Apart from preserving these very valuable windows and perpetuating the memorial, our chapel was greatly enhanced. The entrance to the vestibule was open from the club side where everyone had an unobstructed view of these beautiful windows. The other window depicted the Flying Angel and was appropriately found a place over the entrance door to the club.

A brief history of the Mariners' Rest

Though the Mariners' Rest officially came into being in 1979 and we took over custody of the Memorial Record in 1988, I am including the story here which seems appropriate as we cover some of the reasons for fire protection.

Through the efforts of Captain William York Higgs of Gibsons, B.C. and by his personal negotiations with the Provincial Secretary and various government departments, and assisted by the Company of Master Mariners of Canada, and the Canadian Merchant Service Guild, the unsurveyed islet in front of Lot 6169, Group 1, New Westminster District formerly referred to as 'Steamboat Rock' situated in Thornborough Channel off the west coast of Gambier Island in Howe Sound, British Columbia was set aside by the Government of British Columbia as a heritage reserve, and renamed 'The Mariners Rest'.

On Sunday 26 August 1979, at the request of the Company of Master Mariners of Canada, the Rev. J.D. Parker (their Hon. Chaplain), Senior

Chaplain of the Missions to Seamen in the Diocese of New Westminster officiated at the ceremony which dedicated the Mariners' Rest as an official marker for the committal of ashes at sea.

A stainless steel cross, donated by the Higgs family, now marks the islet as consecrated ground. All services must be conducted offshore and only ashes will be accepted, no one may go ashore there, add or secure anything to the islet.

To the best of the writer's knowledge this facility (if one may call it such) is the only one of its kind worldwide. If not it is certainly unusual.

In the immediate years following dedication, a problem arose with regard to the keeping of a record of those whose ashes had been committed at Mariners' Rest, finally a permanent solution was agreed between Captain William York Higgs, the Company of Master Mariners of Canada and the Missions to Seamen in the Diocese of New Westminster for the latter to keep a permanent record on the following conditions.

The Memorial Record

1) To accept custodianship and administration of records relating to the islet as a committal site by entering (the names) in a Memorial Record of persons whose ashes are scattered at Mariners' Rest.
2) To keep the Memorial Record up-to-date and on display at the Mission during the hours when the Mission is open, where it can be viewed by friends and relatives of persons whose ashes are scattered at Mariners' Rest.
3) To send a copy of names as recorded in the Memorial Record to the town hall at Gibsons, British Columbia.
4) To collect a fee of $50.00 for entering a name in the Memorial Record.
5) Providing these functions are being carried out the proceeds from the fees shall be used by the Mission for its work on behalf of seafarers, after payment of all expenses involved in carrying out these functions.
6) The Missions to Seamen shall bear no responsibility or liability arising from or relating to any monies paid by relatives and friends of persons whose ashes are scattered at the islet which are not paid or transferred to the Mission.

We were provided with the original records for the creation of the Memorial Book by Captain Alan Cabot after carefully checking these in consultation with Captain Higgs. Miss Alison Brookfield, a member of the Board of the Missions to Seamen, painstakingly in calligraphy entered every name. Our architect friend, Bob Troughton designed a wall mounting unit to hold the Memorial book and Vancouver Shipyard manufactured this unit and presented it as a gift to the Mission. The unit containing the Memorial Record was appropriately mounted in the MacMillan Room of the Flying Angel Club. I say appropriately mounted because in this room on the ground floor of the club, the Canadian Company of Master Mariners met twice weekly. A page is turned every day. Here at the request of Captain Alan Cabot, Archbishop Douglas Hambidge, our President dedicated the Memorial Record.

Some time after the Memorial Record had been installed and dedicated, Captain Richard Wilson of the Canadian Company of Master Mariners came up with the following which without doubt added a finishing touch to the Memorial Record and was reproduced on a plaque and displayed in the area.

In memory of a fallen shipmate.

God saw you were getting tired
And cure was not to be
So he put his arms around you
And whispered 'Come to me'
With tearful eyes we watched you
And saw you pass away
Although we loved you dearly
We could not make you stay
A golden heart stopped beating
Hard working hands at rest
God broke our hearts to prove to us
He only takes the best.

On all the oceans, white caps flow
They have no crosses, row on row,
but they who sleep beneath the sea
Sleep in peace, for our country's free.

WE WILL REMEMBER THEM
(Canadian Merchant Navy Association)
(R.C.N.A.)

Mariners' Rest brings back memories

Writing about the Mariners' Rest brought to mind many seafarers whom I've known and as the prayer says 'witnessed a good profession' and passed on through the waters into the Heavenly Kingdom. A number had their ashes committed at Mariners' Rest and I had the privilege of officiating at these simple services.

In this connection it is not the story of a seafarer which I wish to recall for you but the conclusion to a life from which seafarers benefited throughout. She was a lifelong supporter of the Missions to Seamen, the Anglican Church Women of the Diocese of New Westminster and many other charitable causes. She requested before her death that her ashes be committed at Mariners' Rest.

Throughout her life Irene was joined in her support of the Missions to Seamen by her husband Fred. When they could no longer participate in the life of the club they did their thing from home. They say 'the best way to a man's heart is through his tummy.' Irene must have believed this, for over the years until she could bake no more, she baked thousands of mince pies for our Christmas parties and they came as her free gift. Dorothy, my wife, used to say, 'Without Irene's pies, it didn't feel like Christmas.'

Fittingly, 'In sure and certain hope of the resurrection to eternal life' we committed Irene's ashes to the deep at Mariners' Rest one beautiful summer evening, just as she had asked.

LAUNCH OUT, DO WE? OR DO WE NOT?

There were very few associated with the Missions to Seamen who did not regret the retirement of Mr Fred Spoke as General Manager of the port of Vancouver. Of all the people associated with the shipping industry, he had a great feel for the work of the Missions to Seamen and was able to access its value to the port. He was a leader and a man who had the courage of his convictions. Indeed I have always believed that he was the prime mover behind the decision of the National Harbours Board to gift 50 North Dunlevy Avenue to the Mission. He was truly our friend to whom we could turn at any time for help and advice.

Our President, Archbishop Hambidge, shared our opinion of Fred Spoke and organized a luncheon at the University Club at which Mr and Mrs Spoke were the guests of honour. Attending were Chaplains, members of the Board of the Missions to Seamen, Diocesan executives and my wife Dorothy.

When all had eaten, Captain Alan Cabot, Chairman of our executive committee, presented Mr Spoke with a certificate declaring his election as an Honorary member of the Missions to Seamen in the Diocese of New Westminster. Before handing the certificate over to Mr Spoke, Captain Cabot read from the citation thereon, 'In recognition of and an expression of our deep appreciation for your outstanding contribution to the work of the Missions to Seamen.'

Replying, Mr Spoke said, 'The work of the Missions to Seamen has always been very close to my heart and during my retirement I look forward to being able to continue my interest and of increasing my support.' He concluded by saying that he deeply appreciated the honour the Society had bestowed upon him.

Archbishop Hambidge referred all present to that wise saying, 'Behind every great man is a woman.' He then called upon Dorothy Parker to make a presentation to Mrs Spoke. (A pair of Native Indian ceramic figures.)

Searching deep

We had by now reached what was perhaps the most crucial period in our programme to re-establish the society on a more sound financial basis. 26,280 seafarers had signed our visitors book during 1981 and we were all convinced that the potential for further growth existed. Yet we ended the year 1982 with a deficit of $13,659 in our income and expenditure account, and a reduction of 142 in the number who signed our visitors book.

On the other hand the income from club services which depended upon the use being made of the club had increased from $49,124 in 1981 to $55,333 in 1982. 9,289 international telephone calls were booked through the club in 1982, an increase of 1,259 over the previous year. 146 seafarers signed our visitors book on Christmas Day. 123 seafarers signed our visitors book on St. Stephen's Day. 202 seafarers signed our visitors book on New Year's Eve. A total of 2,703 seafarers used the club during the month of December. These statistics represented but a few of the services we were providing, most of which showed the same potential for future growth. Very reluctantly, in the light of these statistics it was agreed that we had no alternative but to budget once again for a deficit in 1983.

However at board level we realized this situation could not continue after 1983 without some provision being made to bridge this gap between income and expenditure in the long term. There was no doubt that there was a need for the Mission, a fact statistics proved beyond doubt. There was also ample evidence to show that seafarers were now contributing substantially towards operating costs and this contribution would likely increase in the years ahead. Yet there would still be a gap in income to close.

Our directors were in a sense trustees of the Society's future and all of us realized that there would be no future if we permitted that future to be whittled away by continuing to borrow without a definite plan for repayment. We must balance our expenditure against income. Everybody put on their thinking cap to try and come up with a practical way out of our difficulty. We had never squandered funds and had no reason to fear reproach on this account. Our income must increase if there was not to be a cutback in services which most would be reluctant to bring about.

Feelers went out far and wide to find a solution and the answer when it came exceeded our wildest dreams. We were invited by the Vancouver Foundation to become involved in a self help project by setting up an Endowment Fund in the name of the Missions to Seamen in the Diocese of New Westminster within the Foundation. They offered to match dollar for dollar in a fund-raising drive, up to a maximum of $300,000 over a three year period. The capital sum contributed to the Endowment Fund plus matching dollars would be held and managed by the Foundation in perpetuity and the earned income paid over to the Mission as agreed.

The purpose of this generous offer was to enable us to launch a major fund-raising drive on the most favourable of terms. Every dollar donated to the Mission for the Endowment Fund was to be matched by the Foundation with another dollar.

A life saver: needless to say our board did not hesitate in accepting this generous offer. One of the very first members to accept with real enthusiasm was Mr Fred Spoke, the former port General Manager who, true to his word, when he retired continued his interest in the work of the society and was now serving on the board. He was joined with equal enthusiasm by Captain Hank Vondette, former Harbour Master, and Capt. Alan Cabot. Together they spear-headed plans for the fund-raising drive. A professional fund-raising consultant was engaged to direct the campaign which we would carry out ourselves. It was agreed that we should attempt to raise a sum of $400,000, of which sum $100,000 would be used to cover the short-fall in income until such time as we were in receipt of regular interest payments from the Foundation.

The next formidable task to face our board was to choose a fund-raising programme chairman. There was little doubt in anybody's mind as to where this choice should rest: Mr Fred Spoke who had championed our cause over many years. While it would be a demanding and responsible task he generously agreed to act. In the special brochure produced for the occasion he wrote, 'The work of the Missions to Seamen is so vital for the well being of our great Port and community that I have gladly agreed to be the Programme Chairman for our major fund-raising effort. The Missions to Seamen contribute significantly to making our port a happy one, and a port with that kind of reputation is better able to attract increased international trade – a crucial objective for Canada. The motto of the City of Vancouver's coat of arms expresses this very well: "By sea, land and air we prosper." Every happy seafarer is in fact a good-will ambassador for our port, province and country. I shall actively and to the best of my ability contribute towards our fund-raising programme. I trust that my many friends in the community and corporations will also contribute generously.'

Many times throughout this narrative I have mentioned the enormous contribution made annually by the supporters of Operation Renewal, principally the Anglican Church Women of the Diocese of New Westminster, other Church groups and some individuals. Ever faithful, the supporters of this appeal accepted a contribution to the Endowment Fund as their project over the next three years. Many corporate bodies in shipping and otherwise, Parish groups, Parishes and individuals also contributed to the fund-raising drive. By the time the intensive phase of the campaign was over, the total pledged had reached $350,000 and it was hoped to eventually reach the target figure of $400,000 plus expenses. Captain Hank Vondette took over as continuation Chairman while another member of our board, Miss Ella Sim, took on the position of comptroller of the Endowment Fund account for the three year period.

Our President Archbishop Hambidge, at the conclusion of the intensive phase of the programme, invited those who occupied a leadership role in the campaign to have lunch with him at the University Club when he presented each one with a certificate marking his election as an Honorary Member of the Missions to Seamen in the Diocese of New Westminster, the highest honour the Society can bestow its benefactors. Those so honoured are listed as follows: Captain Hank Vondette, former Harbour Master, Port of Vancouver; Mr Ray Williams, Corporate Vice-President C.N. Rail, Western Canada; Mr Clyde Jacobs, Vice-President of Shipping, Seaboard Shipping Co. Ltd.; Mr Greg McKay, President Western Stevedoring Co. Ltd.; Mr Gordon Diamond, President, West Coast Reduction; Mr Alan Grimston, President, Anglo Canadian Shipping Co. Ltd; Mr George Adams, President, Canadian Transport Co. Ltd. Unavoidably absent were Mr Fred Spoke and Mr Tim Chapman.

I need hardly add that the success of this campaign took a great weight off the shoulders of our directors at this time. We could now run a deficit with an easy mind knowing that within three years the gap would be bridged.

'If you love life, give life'

Some time ago my telephone rang and the caller enquired, 'Is that you, Joe, I wonder if you can help me?'

Almost fourteen years earlier on a beautiful Sunday evening in July, in the Chapel of the Missions to Seamen in Belfast Northern Ireland, I had had the privilege of baptizing this seafarer. I later gave him his first confirmation class before commending him to the Chaplain in his next port of call to continue his instruction.

When seeking baptism he made no secret of the esteem in which he held the Mission and of his appreciation of the hospitality and fellowship which he had enjoyed world-wide enabling him to grow in knowledge and understanding of the Christian faith.

His experiences reminded me again of those few words St. Paul had written to the young Church at Corinth many years ago. 'One plants, another waters, but God gives the increase.' God uses ordinary people to bring others to faith, in this instance the anonymous staff and volunteer workers of the Missions to Seamen world-wide by doing what they considered natural: being kind to the stranger.

The real joy of the Christian faith is experienced when like the Master we too learn how to give without counting the cost. To echo many old hands, volunteer workers of the Missions to Seamen, 'It's in giving that we receive.' My seafaring friend had made this discovery too, as we shall see later in the story.

Dark clouds were already overshadowing my native land when this man was baptized; indeed this service was to be the last service in this life in which our family unit as a whole would participate. A few days later our beloved second son, Stephen, was killed by a bomb, an innocent victim of a terrorist outrage. We were not to meet again until a few years later when he appeared at one of our Christmas parties in Vancouver.

A lot of water had flowed down the River Lagan in Belfast since we first met. Now he sought my help again. In port for a brief time he asked, 'I wonder can you help me?' Now a blood donor, he wanted me to transport him to the nearest transfusion clinic where he could donate his tenth unit of blood. Time was precious and he could not make it without my help. How could I refuse?

A man with a problem

Randy (not his real name) had a problem. Almost one year earlier he had paid over in cash a large sum of money to a bank in the United States of America with instructions for this money to be forwarded to his family in Sri Lanka.

His instructions were either insufficient or indistinct with the result that the draft was returned from Sri Lanka. On several occasions the bank wrote to Randy for further clarification but the misunderstanding continued. It took months for these letters to reach Randy on board ship and for his replies to reach the United States. Eventually the bank got fed up with the problem and returned Randy's money by bank draft to him.

Now this is where we enter the story. Randy now turned to us for help. Unknown in Vancouver, he could not find a bank to cash his US bank draft. He still had a problem understanding why his original bank draft did not make it home and was scared of a repetition as he now wished to add a further $800 in US funds. Could we help him?

I went along with him to see our bank manager who listened carefully to the whole story. He suggested that Randy leave his US bank draft with him to be placed on collection. When this money arrived he would call me and we could then forward the total amount to his family in Sri Lanka. Everything worked as planned and some time later we received the following letter from Randy, thanking us for our help in the circumstances.

I am in quite good health and wish you the same and may the Almighty bless you.

First of all I take this opportunity to thank you for your kind help in recovering my money from the American bank which has been going around the world for the last year. I received a letter from my parents acknowledging the cheque together with your statement of account which was very self explanatory and interesting.

Of course, my parents were pleased of the same and they were really wondering about the statement since it was unexpected and unwanted.

Further we are now loading iron from here to Greece and as soon as we reach there I hope to go on my vacation as I am now completing two years by mid February.

I am looking forward to be in my mother country and with my parents. Hope that we shall have a chance of meeting each other if I happen to continue my seaman life.

The Lord is my Pilot

There was a message awaiting me when I returned from ship visiting one Sunday. A senior officer had died suddenly on board a ship en route to Vancouver. The ship had now arrived and was at anchor in the port. The deceased's widow was on board having accompanied her husband on the voyage. The Captain requested that a memorial service be held on board before the vessel berthed.

A launch had been chartered for 6.30 p.m. to take a shore side party out to the ship. Would I confirm with the shipping agents whether or not I wished to avail myself of this offer. Though it meant a last minute reorganization of our Sunday evening programme at the Mission, in the circumstances I gladly accepted the offer of transport.

Despite the tragedy certain formalities had to be observed. Officials from the Coroner's office, police, immigration and the shipping agents all shared this launch, each with a particular task to fulfil. We were all taken to the Captain's office upon arrival on board. Introductions completed, the Captain had me escorted to the widow's cabin while he took care of the other formalities.

Almost two hours later the Captain entered the cabin and was able to inform us that the remains had been taken ashore where a post mortem would take place followed by an inquest which would be held next day. Arrangements were being made to have the body flown back to the United Kingdom on the same flight as the widow.

The long period I was able to spend alone with this bereaved lady was of mutual benefit. A committed Christian, it gave her time to talk about her new situation and come to terms with this sudden change in her circumstances. While there is not a lot one can say in these circumstances without sounding as if one were reeling off pious platitudes, on the other hand for the bereaved's benefit to be a good listener can be therapeutic. I felt that she was more relaxed when I left to go ashore. Afforded this opportunity to talk about her married life so suddenly drawn to a conclusion helped me too and I felt more equipped in knowledge to conduct the memorial service next day.

Before leaving I made a note of her daughter's telephone number in the United Kingdom and I promised to telephone her and assure her that her Mum was coping: a small gesture which was overwhelmingly appreciated by all concerned.

The memorial service was held in the crew's mess. Apart from those on essential duty the entire ship's company was present. At the conclusion in a very touching scene the widow thanked the Indians for standing vigil over her husband's body from the moment of death until his body had been taken ashore.

On occasions like this I always make provisions during the service to read the seafarers' version of psalm 23 by Captain J. Rogers. It's meaningful and full of hope. It reads as follows.

Seamen's version of the Twenty-third Psalm

The Lord is my pilot, I shall not drift. He lighteth me across the dark waters: He steereth me in the deep channels. He keepeth my log; He guideth me by the Star of Holiness for His Name's sake. Yea, though I sail 'mid the thunders and tempests of life, I shall dread no danger; for Thou art with me; Thy love and Thy care they shelter me. Thou preparest a harbour before me in the homeland of eternity: Thou anointest the waves with oil; my ship rideth calmly. Surely sunlight and starlight shall favour me on the voyage I take; and I will rest in the port of my God forever.

Captain J. Rodgers

Compliments of the Missions to Seamen, The Flying Angel Club, 50 North Dunlevy Avenue, Vancouver, Canada V6A 3R1. Remember: Our beautiful chapel is always open for private prayer and meditation. Worship services are held daily to which all seafarers are invited.

A MEMORABLE YEAR

It began with an announcement in February at our annual general meeting that the society had been awarded a grant of $100,000 by the trustees of the H.R. MacMillan Estate Charitable Trust to develop the basement area of our club and carry out a refurbishing programme to the exterior of the building. Captain Hank Vondette, now Chairman of our executive committee, architect Bill Milne, a former seafarer, and retired builder Win Maynard must be given most of the credit for what was achieved. To get the maximum benefit from the grant it was decided wherever possible to use direct labour. Hank became Man Friday on the job and whatever needed doing he did it; he was first to arrive in the morning and last to leave at night.

The basement area of the club had been left until last as we carefully adapted this beautiful old heritage building for our purpose. The reader will already have come to realize that in their whole approach to this ministry our directors never lost sight of the fact that our society was not the only deserving cause and that we were honour bound to recoup operating expenses wherever possible from our patrons. It would not be honourable to do otherwise and we acted accordingly to the benefit of the society financially. It did not end here; we also had a clearly defined duty to ensure that all expenditure was kept in check and was justified. We could never have tackled this project until we knew that we could pay for it without going into debt.

Our long term plans for development were not formulated by amateurs but by experienced people, some of whom had sailed the high seas themselves, who continued to serve the industry ashore and who were in an ideal position to access our future needs with experience and knowledge. I myself had spent a great portion of my life in this Ministry. During the previous year almost 27,000 seafarers had signed into our club representing almost 100 per cent increase since 1975, ample evidence that we were moving in the right direction. While it might not be the choice of every Chaplain to live in an apartment above the club, the gains to the society were substantial in monetary terms and for me as Chaplain. My world was expanded for the exercise of my ministry. My wife and I felt at home in this setting. The space required to create this apartment would not be required for future growth and development. All of our studies confirmed this fact.

The practical administration of a club such as ours with a view to reducing operating costs had to be of concern to a charitable society. A pragmatic approach to administration and job sharing was essential in both planning and implementation. Let me illustrate.

Seafarers, upon entering our club, would be greeted by a receptionist through a hatch on the left side of the entrance door where he and the telephone booths were located. The receptionist was responsible for booking international telephone calls. When the club was not very busy in the daytime the receptionist-telephone operator also took care of the Canteen souvenir-shop. This meant that the reception desk would be vacated while he was away. Our secretary/bookkeeper was located in an office adjoining the reception desk from where it was possible to observe and attend to anyone entering the club while the receptionist was absent. This person could also assist with a telephone call should the need arise. Again when supporters of the society called to make contributions, the secretary could immediately identify them from her office and admit them to the club. Many people who called to make donations were advancing in years and did not wish to climb stairs so having the office located near the door was a blessing in disguise with no stairs to climb. My own office was close by the secretary's office and I had a full view of all the activity taking place in the main area of the club. Here I could be seen and easily reached by anybody needing me. No escort was necessary. Design and location of staff helped reduce operating costs.

Our Canteen-shop faced into the main area of the club and was highly visible, its displays attractive to look upon. Leading off this main area were a billiard room, table-tennis and other games. The Chapel was easy recognizable by the beautiful stained glass windows in the vestibule and also a comfortably furnished lounge which was frequently used by ladies travelling with their husbands on board ship and by lady seafarers serving on the cruise ships. Again lay out and design were given very careful consideration when we planned.

The main area was furnished with a number of comfortable lounge chairs, and upright chairs and tables for those who preferred to sit at a table. There was a large 28" colour TV and video recorder, where a movie was shown every night except on Sunday. (The cost of providing these movies was paid by Tante's Memorial Trust Fund.) We made a dancing area by rolling back a section of carpet on Sunday night. Those who wanted to watch TV could still do so in the lounge. Apart from a section of the table tennis room the club was now carpeted throughout.

Having lived in the building for a number of years, I had one concern which I wished to see addressed when the basement was developed. A couple of years earlier I had been awakened in the early hours of one morning by the buzzing of our house telephone. It was my namesake Joe, a student helper who was at this time living in the temporary apartment we had constructed in the basement. When he first woke up I think he thought that he was dreaming and a passenger in Noah's ark. He woke up to find himself surrounded by water and everything around him beginning to float. Could I come down and take a look? I did too and for the next few hours the two Joe's continued to bail water out until the floor was clear. We had a couple of repeat performances and eventually discovered that we had a back up problem. A drain had never been fitted with an automatic valve to prevent this happening when the foundations were laid about the year 1906. At this time we were experiencing record high tides and heavy rainfall well in excess of what was anticipated in 1906. These factors together with later development in the area had all contributed to the problem. The appropriate device to prevent back up for all time was now installed and proved absolutely satisfactory. Nevertheless living on the premises I wanted to be absolutely sure before we developed the basement that we would be protected against a surprise of this nature in the future.

In Captain Hank Vondette, who had served on the North Atlantic convoys in World War II, I had a sympathetic ear. Like many of the survivors of these tragic years he had learned that you should never ignore a warning, 'to be forewarned is to be forearmed.' Together with our architect and Mr Win Maynard they carried out a thorough investigation of the basement area and no defects were found. They did however identify one possible weakness against which a precautionary measure was advisable. The basement area was partly below ground level and entrance from outside was gained by walking down a slope leading to the exterior door. A large catchment drain was designed to take away the water which ran down this slope. It was fitted in a corner outside the door. As a precautionary measure we installed a sump pump into the catchment area to take away excessive water in the event of heavy rainfall or flooding. Provided this catchment drain was cleaned out regularly we would have no reason to fear flooding at some future date.

We did not need experts to advise about the use of space when the area had been gutted out. Our architect was a former seafarer and a member of our board so he was well qualified to access our needs for years to come. Whatever the requirements of the Mission, we were all agreed that within this framework we should continue to make provision if at all possible to accommodate the needs of the Canadian Company of Master Mariners who had proved themselves to be good and loyal supporters of our work. We could not boast of better friends for in countless ways they had come to our assistance over the years.

Sea Sunday, 26 September, was scheduled for the official opening of our newly developed basement area by Mrs G.T. Southam, daughter of our benefactor, the late H.R. MacMillan. News of the event which was to follow the Sea Sunday service in St. James' Church was made known to all of our supporters who were invited and it was later covered extensively in the *Flying Angel Review.*

In a room packed to capacity, our president Archbishop Hambidge introduced Mrs Southam and asked her to unveil a large bronze plaque mounted on one of the walls which told the story of our good fortune. 'This room is named in honour of a generous benefactor of The Missions to Seamen over many years. H.R. MACMILLAN – on the occasion of the completion of an extensive programme of redevelopment and refurbishing at the Flying Angel Club which was funded by a substantial grant from the H.R. MacMillan Estate Charitable Trust. His daughter, Mrs G.T. Southam, graciously unveiled this plaque on Sunday, September 21st 1986.'

The MacMillan Room resembled a ship's wardroom in that it was panelled throughout though of course much larger in size. Our architect had been very innovative: in one alcove he located a small lock up business office for the Master Mariners, and their filing cabinets, copying machine, etc., were accommodated in a space running alongside the room where there was low headroom and so could be used for little else. This resembled a walk-in closet accessed by folding doors finished in panelling to match the other walls. Another larger alcove was developed in such a manner that it could be used for office accommodation in the future should the need ever arise, being fitted out with a folding door which covered one wall but which for our immediate use remained open. Indeed the original office furniture, desk, bookcase, waste paper basket, etc. from the Port Managers office when the port occupied 50 North Dunlevy Avenue were later gifted to the Mission and found a home here. A beautiful office furnished with antiques here awaited a tenant. In the main body of the room we now had ample space to serve our Christmas and other banquets, indeed more space than we had required to date. Sea Sunday receptions could be catered for in this room too, our annual meeting could be held here and gatherings of one kind or another.

So far as the lady volunteers were concerned our new kitchen was a dream by comparison with the conditions under which they had laboured over the years, yet never failing to provide those Christmas banquets for which the Vancouver Flying Angel Club was renowned. It's been said that 'everything comes to him who waits'. Well, these ladies had waited a long time; all the while the quality and quantity of the food donated free continued to increase and improve. We had a number of old refrigerators which needed defrosting from time to time. An argument could have been made to get rid of the lot in favour of one large unit with automatic defrost, but not so with our ladies, unless we had money to burn. Instead we all became experts at segregating one kind of food from another into different refrigerators. Adjoining the MacMillan room, this spacious kitchen was long overdue.

Up to now I have elaborated mainly on the basement area of the club which meant so much to us at the time. The idea of using direct labour meant that overall much more was achieved which would not have been possible otherwise. In addition to developing the basement, the building throughout received a complete facelift. Some knotty problems were taken care of such as the installation of an emergency lighting system to comply fully with fire regulations. Overall the following work was undertaken:

Exterior of the building: defective wood siding was replaced, window sills and sashes repaired or replaced, together with an extensive glazing programme carried out specifically at the request of the Heritage Advisory Committee; defective wood on the veranda deck and side entrance steps was replaced; the roof was cleaned and sprayed with a moss preventative solution; the exterior had also been completely repainted.

Interior of the building: the H.R. MacMillan Room and adjoining kitchen facility were developed; a laundry room, cleaner's store room and ladies' powder room were also developed; the men's washroom was refurbished replacing amongst other fixtures wood cisterns which probably dated back to the turn of the century and of course plumbing; the stairway to this area was redesigned to provide easier access to the library and basement area as a whole; a major problem with ventilation in the vault games recreation area was corrected and an effective ventilation system was installed in the main reception area of the club; the entire roof space in the building was insulated; an additional emergency exit door from the basement was installed together with an emergency lighting system throughout the building.

It should be appreciated that this work also involved extensive updating of plumbing and electrical wiring as necessary throughout the building.

This was a wonderful occasion, the realization of a dream.

Expo 86

The year 1986 was beyond doubt memorable for the Missions to Seamen. It was an eventful year for Vancouver too, being the year of Expo 86 in which we also played a small part.

There was a great feeling of expectation throughout the whole community in the year prior to this; some were very positive in their attitude towards this forthcoming event while others were more negative viewing preparations for Expo 86 with more than a little apprehension.

Now with the benefit of hindsight we know that Expo 86 was very successful, the overall attendance exceeding twenty-two million, one hundred and eleven thousand. The people of Canada, British Columbia and Vancouver in particular can feel justifiable proud of this magnificent achievement.

While our contribution could not be described as mammoth by any stretch of the imagination, nevertheless we did play our part by cooperating and helping in those areas where we were qualified. The Rev. Paul Tong and I were privileged to have been invited to conduct in Japanese and English the religious part of the ceremony, 'Salute to Sailors', held in the Plaza of Nations, Sunday, 20 July on the Expo site. There was a very large attendance from the Japanese sail training vessel *Nippon Maru* and the Korean training ship *Hanbada* amongst others. Throughout the Exposition the crews from visiting naval ships and the additional cruise ships laid on for Expo all used the Flying Angel Club, contributing significantly in helping us to reach the all time record of 31,783 persons to sign into the club, an increase of 6,072 over the previous year.

Ambassador Patrick Reid, Commissioner General of the Exposition, graciously joined us for the Annual Seafarers' Service held in St. James.

When the Exposition drew to a close Captain Mike Williamson, Supervisor Marine Events, wrote:

> As Expo 86 draws to a close, I would like to take this opportunity to thank both you personally and all the staff at the Mission for the support and tremendous assistance we received.

The overall success of the specialized periods of Expo 86 was in no small part due to your participation and specifically, to the support you provided to the crews of the many visiting ships to our port during Expo. My very best wishes for the continued success of the Mission. Fair winds and smooth seas.

Our directors felt that Expo 86 was an historic occasion and to mark for future generations our society's participation Captain Williamson's letter, photographs and other memorabilia should be mounted, framed and displayed in the club. In due course this was done and displayed in the MacMillan room which almost immediately after completion had become home to various historical artifacts and memorabilia.

A SIGN OF THE TIMES – TRAGEDY AND A PROBLEM

The year 1986 was, as stated earlier, a memorable year for the people of Vancouver. It was said in advance of Expo 86 that this Exposition would put Vancouver on the map. Certainly the port of Vancouver was never to be the same again. I speak of the latest addition to the port and its development from this year on, the forty million dollar cruise ship facility. Incorporated into the Canada Place complex against a backdrop of Stanley Park and the coast mountains this development enhanced an already beautiful sea-port and a gateway to the city and set in motion the development of what was to become a major industry.

Somehow almost from the moment of completion one had a very positive feeling about this development. It represented progress. Until my retirement in 1993 the cruise ship business continued to expand, eventually overflowing onto Ballantyne Pier where I understand an additional facility has since been constructed. It was a development which was to add greatly to our work load at the Flying Angel Club during the cruising season, May to September. The number of cruise ships in port varied from day to day, Saturday being the busiest when we might have three to four vessels. Some had a crew complement of three hundred, others less depending upon the size of the vessel, the smallest number being about eighty five of which there were few.

When I use the term crew in relation to cruise ships it should be borne in mind that in context this term includes everybody employed on board, both male and female. Crews were invariably multinational and came from a variety of religious backgrounds. Some because of their duty on board were unable to go ashore. The duration in port was a matter of hours. Arriving in the early morning when passengers had disembarked, the ship had to be made ready for the new passengers embarking in the afternoon to join the next cruise. Some crew members were free to go ashore earlier than others but had to return before embarkation time, while others would go ashore later and return before sailing time. Others were free to remain ashore while the ship was in port. It would be difficult to estimate how many crew members were ashore at any one time as this depended upon the nature of their duties and the duration of the ship's stay in port.

One question always presented itself with regard to ships having a quick turn-around (or to put it in other words a brief stay in port): how can we be of help? In my experience gained over many years there was one universal need. In and out of port like a yo-yo, the people serving on ships with a quick turn around had difficulty keeping in touch with their families and for many the arrival and departure of mail was erratic to say the least. If there was a problem within the family, a telephone call could relieve a lot of anxiety. This need we could satisfy. While prior to 1986 we did have a number of cruise ships calling into the port, after 1986 the number continued to increase. In the year 1987 the number of international telephone calls processed in the club increased by 963 which I attribute to the expansion of the number of container and cruise ships using the port.

Another aspect of our work which of necessity must remain confidential is our Pastoral Ministry. Those who sail the seas and spend long periods separated from their loved ones like the rest of us who live ashore have problems from time to time. Sometimes they have need of a shoulder to lean upon and as we all know it's not everyone that we can feel free to open up our heart to. It could be a job related problem, a family problem, a very personal problem or whatever. In my capacity as a Chaplain with the Missions to Seamen and responsible for the coordination of an ecumenical ministry I was obligated to ensure that we Chaplains as far as possible rotated our visits to cruise and other ships which returned frequently so that those on board would have a choice in whom they would confide. We Chaplains were supportive of one another and in some circumstances would refer crew members from one to the other. Again lest those on board felt that our outreach was wholly dominated by 'Religion' our ship visiting team included lay-workers too. In this connection I do not mean that our lay workers were people without religion but as one would hope with Clergy too, they were people who did not wear their religion on their sleeve and only look for instant converts. 'One person's meat can be another person's poison.' Sometimes a change of diet can be a help and provide another perspective.

The response in the number from each ship to use the club varied but whatever the response one of us always went on board. It was obvious even though there were coin operated telephone booths on the terminals that the service we provided was meeting a need. Many welcomed an opportunity to get a break away from the ship, even for a brief time, in an atmosphere where they could relax, play a game of billiards, table tennis, or merely watch TV over a quiet beer.

The growth of the cruise ship business out of the Port of Vancouver literally transformed the life of our club from May to September. Provision had to be made to cope with this influx of people every afternoon. We did not have the financial resources to hire more staff so it had to be volunteers. Our Day-Steward was fully occupied processing international telephone calls and simply could not manage to operate the Canteen-shop at the same time. My wife Dorothy got busy and recruited annually a team of people to take care of this need. The Missions to Seamen in service can do little without volunteers.

It's not always realized that many seafarers have a language problem and indeed sometimes a currency problem when it comes to using the public telephone system ashore. Of all the services we provided this must have been the most taxing for our operators. It called for compassion, endless patience and above all the grace of perseverance. On average calls were dialled at least five times before connection was made. In cases of illness, bereavement or of a particular concern some calls have been dialled fifteen times. Everybody's in a hurry and patience is not a virtue. Many had difficulty realizing a number can be busy. Our operators were frequently the first ashore to learn of a birth and offer congratulations or of a family bereavement when they would introduce the Chaplain on duty to minister to the bereaved seafarer. If there was no Chaplain on duty in the club, living upstairs I was within easy reach.

Repetitive but rewarding

How does the old saying go? Patience is a virtue, possess it if you can, seldom in a man but never in a woman!' or is it 'Patience is a virtue, possess it if you can, seldom in a women but never in a man!,' I like to think that it works both ways depending on of whom you speak. Certainly within the context in which I write this has been my experience.

This afternoon, Margaret McLellan was on duty when a Polish seafarer arrived in the club. It was his first day back on board ship from vacation. A telephone call home to advise his family of his safe arrival meant everything and he was prepared to wait all afternoon and evening to be connected. Margaret tried thirty-five times before she finally managed to process his call. Her patience and perseverance finally was rewarded.

This commendable effort was interrupted for a space when another Polish seafarer arrived in the club. He appeared visibly troubled, his gaunt face as white as a sheet. He came to the point immediately, informing Margaret that he had just returned from the fishing grounds in the Bering Sea having been advised that his nineteen year old daughter had been killed in a motor accident near his home in Poland. His family were waiting to hear whether or not they could expect him for the funeral. Arrangements were on hold until he telephoned.

By coincidence the other Polish seafarer mentioned earlier, whose telephone call Margaret was having so much difficulty processing, turned out to be a neighbour of the bereaved father, a kindly man who knew the deceased and her father personally. He succeeded in keeping the bereaved father in conversation while Margaret tried to connect him with his family.

A mother with two young daughters of her own, you can imagine how Margaret must have felt at this moment, especially knowing that for hours she had been trying without success to process this other seafarer's telephone call to the same town.

Margaret said a quick prayer, kept her cool, tried six times before she got through to the family. Quietly and with equal tact she involved me in the situation. Having travelled down a similar road myself a few years ago with the sudden tragic loss of my own son I knew there was nothing I could contribute in the circumstances save to ensure that what Margaret had initiated was completed. Action speaks louder than words at a time like this so it was my privilege to tell Margaret, 'There's to be no charge for this call.' Polish fishermen did not earn a big wage.

The problems can be repetitive but thankfully our staff and volunteers do not give up easily, earning a special place in the hearts of seafarers and their families across the globe. This must have something to do with the wonderful reception we Chaplains always receive on board ship. Today I viewed a collection of Iranian stamps, coins and a beautifully coloured card given Brian Kaneen by a grateful seafarer from Iran: one man's way of saying thank you, Brian, for your patience and kindness in helping me speak to my family back home.

A victim of circumstances but a happy ending

Manuel (not his real name) was an ordinary seafarer serving on a Greek freighter and came from El Salvador. He was a visitor to the Flying Angel Club whenever his ship returned to port. On this occasion his ship had just docked, having been at anchor in English Bay for some little time. I was paying my first visit on board since they docked.

One afternoon earlier when his ship was at anchor in English Bay, Manuel managed to get ashore by launch for a few hours. Visiting a local bank he purchased three money orders; one was for $50, one for $200 and one for $300.

Upon leaving the bank he mailed the $50 and $300 orders to his family and put the two stubs in a small hand bag he carried together with the remaining money order for $200. Later in the afternoon he either mislaid the hand bag or it was stolen from his person. Unfortunately the bank had closed for the day when he returned to report his loss.

The unfortunate man's difficulty was compounded by the fact that his ship was anchored in English Bay and it would be several days before he would be able to get ashore again and report his loss to the bank. He also had something of a language problem.

The loss of the bag meant the loss of his personal record of any transactions with the bank, making it impossible for the bank to place a stop payment order on the missing money order. There was nothing anyone could do in the circumstances as he was to discover when he finally went ashore. A family man and not earning a large wage, this was a devastating loss for him to suffer.

Having slowly and carefully explained the difficulties to him I happened to remark that if only someone else on the ship had accompanied him and purchased a money order at the same time it would have helped the bank to trace his purchase of the three money orders. It so happened that he was accompanied by another seafarer who did in fact purchase a money order at the same time.

The Chief Officer gave Manuel permission to accompany me to the bank and now armed with the stub from his friend's purchase we set off with the renewed hope of success. When we arrived at the bank and explained the situation to the supervisor she was both sympathetic and helpful. Eventually his purchase was located and it was established that the $200 money order had not been cashed and it was not too late for a stop payment order to be placed.

The bank agreed to issue a replacement money order for $200 and having signed the necessary papers a very relieved and happy seafarer left the bank full of gratitude for all the trouble taken on his behalf, while the Flying Angel had gained a friend for life.

ECONOMICS

I have always felt that however rosy the economic climate may appear it is unwise to borrow in order to spend unless one has an absolute guarantee that there will be the income to pay back what has been borrowed and not have to remain in a perpetual state of debt paying high interest rates. The funds we were entrusted to manage on behalf of the society are a sacred trust and our successors should be able to expect to inherit a society which is financially solvent and not a pile of debt. Good management demands this. In my opinion this trusteeship is even more important than the management of one's personal finances.

Our Canteen-shop was manned largely by voluntary help. We did not seek a large mark up, so prices were competitive and it was well patronized by visiting seafarers. We found it impossible to operate an international telephone service using voluntary help alone, as a degree of training was required. If a volunteer did not show up for duty it was difficult to find a trained replacement at short notice so we had to operate largely with paid staff in this area. In the circumstances, in an attempt to recover some of our costs we added a small service charge. We also made a charge of 25 cents per half hour for the use of the billiard table. It was hoped this charge would deter complete amateurs from using the table and tearing the fabric. While they did not always do so at least we derived sufficient income to maintain the table in good condition for use by those who appreciate the game. Apart from these charges everything else was provided free in the club.

The food for all banquets was donated free by supporters of the Mission. Transport to special social functions was always provided free and all seafarers would be notified in advance. A video film was shown free every night (Monday to Saturday).

On Sunday night immediately after Church the Lightkeepers took over the evening by organizing 'Disco Dancing' and this was the most popular entertainment of the week.

Our expenditure was always related to income; we spent what we could afford to spend.

Over the years as we visited ships we began to notice an increase in the number of non English speaking seafarers using the port, for instance over

4,000 from one nation who were very poorly paid. One year there was a temporary drop of $7,000 in income from club services though the number of people who signed into the club had increased. We immediately concluded that we were beginning to experience a reduction in the number of seafarers from traditional maritime countries who earning higher wages could spend more in our souvenir shop and use the telephone service more frequently. This accounted for some of the drop in revenue.

There was more bad news to come at this time. Though our fund-raising drive had been an unqualified success we still had a little time to go before the income from our Endowment Fund with the Vancouver Foundation kicked in to wipe the slate clean. Now we were advised to expect a substantial cut in two of our operating grants. It seemed as if it were impossible to win.

To add to our problems, concern was being expressed about the cost to seafarers of bus fares in reaching us and that non English speaking seafarers because of the limitation of language were having difficulty coming. Upon making enquiries overseas we found that a free bus service was being provided by many similar establishments to our own from ship to shore (e.g. clubs). However upon making further enquiries we were to discover that in many overseas countries any person in possession of a non-professional driver's licence was permitted to drive a 12-passenger minibus and in some instances a 15-passenger vehicle. Here in Canada a professional driver's licence was required by any person driving a minibus for transporting passengers.

We found it impossible to recruit volunteers prepared to qualify for a professional licence. Our circumstances differed radically from overseas and if we were to introduce a free service of this nature we would have to hire two professional drivers on a part time basis in addition to the other costs. Economically speaking we simply could not afford to finance a free service of this nature.

We continued our investigations to see if we could come up with a reasonably practical solution. An appeal to the Diocese of New Westminster resulted in a grant to cover two thirds of the cost of purchasing a new bus. We then decided to set up a bus service charging a small fare which would be available upon request to serve all areas including Port Moody, Robert's Bank and Fraser Port. It was appreciated that the money raised in fares would not be sufficient to meet all overheads but it would at least generate a fair proportion of the cost. So the Flying Angel Pick Up Service was born. While we could not afford to provide a free service we did the next best thing with the financial resources at our disposal. We set a very low tariff, much less than the public transport or taxi services. A grant from the International Transport Workers Federation enabled us to purchase a second 12-seater bus as a back up. This was driven largely by me and our lay assistant, particularly last thing at night when the club was closing. We had both qualified for a professional licence so our contribution did not cost the Mission anything.

The introduction of this service underlined the need to update our ship visiting brochure to include this new service. The brochure was produced in a basic English text with cartoon figures used to illustrate the services and recreation facilities we provided. We also used the opportunity to update all of our maps.

We were very fortunate in the latter respect in that Alison Brookfield, a member of our Lightkeeper's Guild, was an experienced cartographer and she produced the new maps. Another reality now had to be faced. A high proportion of seafarers did not speak English. We now had all of the foregoing information translated into fourteen languages, each printed separately to accompany the English text as necessary. Once again the Operation Renewal Appeal enabled us to pay the cost of printing and updating.

When language is no barrier

We've spent quite a time in this chapter dealing with the economics of our situation which our directors, as responsible people, could not ignore. So now we will go for a change of subject.

One evening recently my Korean colleague, the Rev. I Shim Ro, informed me that he would shortly administer the sacrament of Holy Baptism in the Mission Chapel. Though the service would be conducted in the Korean language I would be most welcome.

Being an Anglican Priest I'm familiar with the words of this office in my own branch of the Church and have a mental picture of the various stages leading up to the climax: 'the actual baptism'. However, I was not familiar with the Presbyterian Rite and with it being conducted in the Korean language I did not expect to participate. I could pray quietly in my own language. I wished to support my colleague and the candidate so I decided to attend.

Throughout there was an atmosphere of reverence which I could sense even though I didn't speak the language but when we came to the climax 'the actual baptism' language was no barrier, there were the outward and visible signs – water and the signing with the sign of the Cross – in the name of The Father and of The Son and of The Holy Spirit.

This baptismal hymn puts it very beautifully.

> And in token that thou shalt not fear
> Christ crucified to own
> We print the cross upon thee here
> and stamp thee His alone
>
> Thus outwardly and visibly
> We seal thee for His own
> And may the brow that wears His cross
> Hereafter share His crown.
>
> Amen

1864 PORT VANCOUVER 1989

Happy 125 Years

Just pause and look around you
At Vancouver's lovely sights
View rugged North Shore Mountains
And the harbour lights at night

Imagine old Vancouver
Imagine if you can
See many folks from far off lands
And the Genius of Man

The line of foreign merchant ships
Tied along her many piers
And the memories of sailing ships
Of a hundred passing years

Shades of wooden cabins
Along the southern shore
And stacks of new hewn lumber
By old Hastings Mill and store

A fleet of little fishboats
Their colours never match
The lilt of many accents
As varied as their catch

The corrugated elevators
The silos reach the sky
Their bellies filled with Prairie fare
With barley, wheat and rye

The harbours philharmonic
The sound of winch and steam
The rhapsody of rail cars
The seagulls' hearty scream

The quaint cafés of Chinatown
The song of Cantonese
Mediterranean sounds from Grandview Heights
And musical chords like these

A blend of many countries
Passed through our azure door
A home for tens of thousands
From every far off shore

Thank God for all their foresight
And the benefits we share
They gave us lots to start with
Let's show we really care

We're going to build a city
The likes you've never seen
We'll call her Port Vancouver
And crown the Pacific Queen

We'll celebrate her Birthday
Greet guests from nations all
Welcome to Vancouver
The greatest Port of all

E. Glennie

*(Published with the kind permission of the author,
a longshoreman and a poet)*

History Past and Present

The casual visitor driving along the stretch of the Vancouver waterfront
road from Canada Place to the Main Street overpass in 1989 would soon
become aware of the fact that Port Vancouver was in the midst of
celebrating its 125th Anniversary. A blaze of colour announced the fact
from banners mounted on the roadside lamp standards.

An anniversary of this nature would never have come to fruition were it
not for the principal players, the seafarers. It's no exaggeration to say that
were it not for ships and seamanship down the years the overwhelming
majority of Canada's emigrant population would not have made it here. Yet
I'm not aware of any monument commemorating the immeasurable
contribution to our welfare made by countless seafarers of the world's
mercantile marine. When the War Memorial was being constructed in
North Vancouver to commemorate those who had participated, some
recognition was given to the men of the Mercantile Marine who had served
in these hostilities. Someone contacted me at this time and asked if I could
suggest suitable wording for the Merchant Navy Plaque at this memorial. I
could think of no more suitable words than these which came from a

prayer of thanksgiving we use in the Missions to Seamen. 'Give us grateful hearts for ships and seamanship whereby the estranging oceans of the world have become highways of commerce and bonds of fellowship between the nations.' These words were approved and used.

One has only to look to the wording on the official emblem of the City of Vancouver to realize the truth of what I have been saying, 'By sea, land and air we prosper.' Where would Canada be without the men who go down to the sea in ships and occupy their business in the great waters? We would have no imports and we would have no exports. People the world over are inclined to take for granted the enormous contribution seafarers make towards the well being of their fellow man by transporting imports and exports across the oceans of the world in fair weather and foul weather, enduring long periods of separation from family and friends.

I don't mind admitting that when I first saw the banners on the waterfront road I wondered in what way the seafarer would be involved in these celebrations? On Saturday 1 July, Canada Day, by prior arrangement the port Corporation hosted a massive party at the Flying Angel Club for visiting seafarers, all expenses paid. It took the form of a Square Dance and Bar-B-Q.

A large marquee 40 ft. x 60 ft. was erected in the car park adjoining the club. It and the club were both illuminated with party lights and the whole area fenced off for the occasion. Free transport was provided for all seafarers in port. Our task at the Flying Angel Club was to organize the party, and to provide volunteers and hostesses for dancing.

This was a great occasion. We were honoured to be chosen to play our part and all stops were pulled out to ensure an enjoyable time would be had by all.

When the marquee was being erected on the eve of the party, there was such a strong gale blowing that additional precautions had to be taken to make sure the structure did not collapse. Then the rain began to fall and it continued for two whole days, sometimes very heavy. On the morning of the party I had one question. How can we bar-b-q in this downpour? We had expected to be able to bar-b-q outside but we would not be able to do this because of the heavy rain. If we tried to operate inside the marquee it would fill the area with smoke. Being a national holiday everywhere was closed. At least a couple of hundred people would show up for the party. What to do? By 12.00 noon we were getting close to panic.

There was a standard practice we always resorted to on these occasions: consult the boys in the Canadian Stevedoring Company's garage-workshop, opposite the club, and see if they could come up with a solution. My prayers were answered; they came to the rescue by providing a large canopy which they transported to the car park and placed alongside the marquee. One problem remained: the sides of the canopy were open to the elements and would have to be closed off to protect the food and our chefs from the wind and rain. My daughter Karen and I spent the remainder of the afternoon lashing tarps onto the sides and back to form a semi enclosed area for the bar-b-q. Prior to this we had managed to furnish the marquee with chairs, tables, refrigerators and a stage platform. My wife got the food and refreshments ready to await volunteers.

Our chefs were a mixed bunch whose experience was limited to the domestic situation; nevertheless they had the one quality necessary to function in this type of situation. They did not seek a job description but were flexible in their approach. All were volunteers – Captain R.C. Stevens, Director The B.C. Chamber of Shipping; Captain D.W. Bachelor, Superintendent Pacific Pilot Authority; Bob Trouton, Architect, many times friend to the Mission; and Captain B.R. Wilson, Company of Master Mariners of Canada. The burgers were delicious and nobody got food poisoning.

Captain Norman Stark, Deputy Port Manager and Chief Operations Officer, welcomed the guests and thanked the volunteers on behalf of the Port Corporation.

We estimated some 350 people participated: seafarers, our staff and some board members, representatives from the Port Corporation, Lightkeepers and volunteers. Seafarers present came from the following countries: Poland, India, Brazil, Korea, Philippines, Japan, People's Republic of China, USSR, Yugoslavia and Canada. We had a wonderful response from young ladies invited to join our Lightkeepers and act as hostesses for the occasion.

While we could not claim that the square dancing was exactly professional nevertheless we were all agreed that it was a truly fun evening and had a wonderful atmosphere. We had twenty-seven draws for prizes and one presented by the Port Corporation found its way to the USSR.

It was appropriate that this celebration should be held at the Flying Angel Club for around this site the City of Vancouver was built. It was fitting of the Port Corporation to include the seafarer in their celebrations.

The old dog for the hard road. When you have been down the track before you usually learn what to worry about and what not to worry about, and what precautions ought to be taken and what precautions can be ignored. Well, we already had our dry run organizing the bar-b-q and square dance for the 125th Anniversary celebration of the Port of Vancouver and we had managed to survive.

Just three years later, Canada Day 1992 – commemorating 125 years of Confederation and the 200th Anniversary of the arrival of Captain George Vancouver – we were invited by the Port Corporation to do the same again. Thankfully all went well.

BY WAY OF CONTRAST

During my early years with the Missions to Seamen one of the first things I noticed was that there was an awful lot to be desired by way of improvement in the accommodation and working conditions on board many ships. Compared with shore based employment one sometimes wondered why men continued to go to sea. There appeared to be no logical answer to this question save to guess. In some mystical way it seems some are born to go to sea and here they find fulfilment; others like the challenge battling against the elements; others suffer from itchy feet and like to travel, but for all it's a means of livelihood to keep body and soul together and for some to also support a wife and family. The sea acts as a magnet to these brave souls and rather tragically society is apt to take them for granted, yet over the centuries men still come forward to face the elements.

Though there have always been concerned employers, nevertheless it took the activity of the trade union movement to demand decent standards in accommodation and wages as a norm for those who go down to the sea in ships. I lived through these years and witnessed the struggle as these men sought proper recognition from ship owners and state alike. Though some ship owners were an example of how employers ought to treat their employees, others lived in everlasting disgrace. By the time I settled in Canada a career at sea was desirable and sought after by many despite some obvious disadvantages, the chief one being a life of separation from family and friends. Many chose to live with this now that regular leave was guaranteed to spend with their families.

The past decade has seen a great change in the nationality of the people who serve at sea and a vast decrease in the number of ships registered in traditional maritime countries in favour of registration under flags of convenience such as Liberia, Panama, Bermuda and Cyprus.

The seafarer serving upon a ship registered in a traditional maritime country almost always has the benefit of union membership and protection, whereas those employed on ships registered under flags of convenience are open to exploitation. Generally speaking ships registered under flags of convenience pay smaller wages, give reduced benefits, if any, and working conditions are generally speaking inferior. The owners pay much less in the way of taxes to the flag of convenience country in which they register.

Invariably ships registered under flags of convenience employ people from under developed nations for small wages. Economics, it's been said, rule the world, hence ship owners from traditional maritime nations could not compete in this market, so they changed to register under flags of convenience. This created a lot of unemployment amongst highly skilled seafarers in traditional maritime countries.

It's interesting to note how this worldwide phenomenon was reflected at local level in Vancouver by the year 1989. The United Kingdom was a traditional maritime nation in the early part of the century and had one of the largest fleets in the world employing primarily their own nationals and some nationals from Commonwealth countries. As a result of flagging out this fleet became tiny by comparison. Only 218 seafarers from the United Kingdom signed into the Flying Angel Club in 1989. When we compare this number with 1,135 in 1978 when these changes were already in progress we have some measure of the effect. Years ago Greek seafarers were always in the majority of those who visited our club annually. In 1989 they occupied third place with 1,540 down from 1,961 in 1988 and from 3,637 in 1978.

While this development at first provided something of an employment bonanza for people in underdeveloped countries, likewise it also provided a massive opportunity for unscrupulous ship owners to take advantage of cheap labour as these men new to seafaring were unaware of the pitfalls and an easy prey until the International Transport Federation took up their cause and began to bat for them. I always felt this was not a job for the Missions to Seamen for we had neither the financial resources nor the expertise of the trade union movement. On the other hand we could support them in their endeavours. When the International Transport Federation became involved I was delighted. Eventually the International Transport Federation settled upon a form of contract for seafarers serving on these vessels.

When I retired in 1993 the international community was still wrestling with the enforcement of various safety regulations for the protection and safety of life at sea and training standards.

Seafarers who arrived in a port in British Columbia on a ship registered under a flag of convenience and had a work related problem were very fortunate. Our first International Transport Federation inspector was to the best of my knowledge a volunteer, Tom McGrath, whom I secretly referred to as the friend of the friendless. Whatever the hour, day or night, if a seafarer needed Tom's help or advice he was available. President of Local

400, Seafarers Section, Canadian Brotherhood of Railway and Transport Workers Union, Tom, a dedicated trade unionist, pioneered this work in this region for a number of years. In job related problems totally outside the scope of my expertise I remember Tom as a fearless champion of the underdog and beyond doubt his zeal and dedication led to the appointment of Gerry McCullough as full time International Transport Federation inspector in British Columbia when Tom was transferred to Ottawa.

There were many cases dealt with by these gentlemen over the years, some of which resulted in big cash settlements and received a lot of publicity in the press and on television. Again there were many settlements where the truly needy were quietly helped along the way. I recall one such case. Two seafarers were hospitalized in Vancouver suffering from tuberculosis. I visited them on a regular basis and eventually one was allowed to return home. Some weeks later the hospital telephoned me to say that the one who remained in hospital had become very depressed and nobody could shake him out of it, which was not good for someone in his condition. I promised to call and see him.

When his colleague returned home and visited this man's family it was to find them in dire poverty and none of the verbal promises which had been given to him by the owners had been fulfilled. I explained the situation to Gerry McCullough and having first visited the man in question he was later to return with a substantial cheque, though by no means as much as he would have earned had he sailed under an International Transport Federation contract. It did, I believe, cover the time he had spent in hospital at this rate. A couple of years later I met his colleague, now fully recovered and back at sea. Subsequently his friend returned home but never fully recovered and later died.

I mentioned earlier about some of the enormous cash settlements made to seafarers as a result of International Transport Federation backing. These cases were taken to court with the International Transport Federation underwriting the entire legal costs at no charge to individual seafarers, the only condition being that if successful, each seafarer would make a voluntary contribution to a Trust fund set up by the Union to assist welfare organizations similar to the Missions to Seamen. You will have read in this narrative how on several occasions we received substantial grants from this fund.

I have written at some length about the activities of the International Transport Federation in response to abuses perpetrated under the flag of convenience. I do not wish my comments to be interpreted as meaning that every ship registered under a flag of convenience falls within this category, which would be very far from the truth. However, it's been my experience that these conditions existed from time to time. I have no doubt in my mind that many reputable ship owners, in order to survive, had to register under a flag of convenience but nevertheless they did not go in for near slave labour or use substandard ships.

Portrait

Included in a previous chapter is a poem by Eddie Glennie entitled '1864 Port Vancouver 1989'. Happy 125 years. Eddie was born in Scotland and served in the British Merchant Navy before he emigrated to Canada. Though he swallowed the anchor and came ashore he never lost his love of the sea, and things and people associated with the sea.

I first made his acquaintance when he accompanied Bosun George to install the rope barrier on our stairs in the Mission. We have been friends ever since and in countless small ways he has helped me in my work in the Missions to Seamen.

A man of accomplishment, he is not only a poet, a seafarer, and a longshoreman, but an artist too and his work in this respect is unusual, preserving an ancient craft associated with seafaring. When Eddie first went to sea, rope was the in thing and like his peers he had to know how to work with it by learning how to splice and knot as required of a seafarer in those days. There were those who like Eddie made this into an art form using rope for many artistic creations: an art form pretty well lost by today's seafarer.

In the Missions to Seamen we were very privileged to have been presented by Eddie with two outstanding pieces of his work which we took great care to preserve for future generations. The first was a knot board illustrating a variety of knots made from rope mounted and framed. This board, though beautifully mounted and framed, did not have a glass. In time, tobacco smoke stained the white rope yellow, disfiguring this once beautiful creation. I had noticed on many ships where this had happened that the cure seemed to be to paint the ropework in white and have the display re-framed in a sealed unit for protection with clear glass for viewing. Preserved thus this became part of our heritage at the Missions to Seamen. The second creation was equally beautiful and original. A memorial to the members of the Canadian Mercantile Marine who served in the Second World War, it consisted of a magnificent creation in white rope of various nautical objects, anchor, lighthouse, etc. mounted on a royal blue background. Realizing that in this memorial we had something rare and unique which ought to be displayed for everyone to see, Vic Watts, one of our volunteers, incorporated it into the well of a glass top table where it was preserved for everyone to see.

A man of the people, Eddie covered a lot of subjects in his poetry: people, their lives and times. His subjects present a fair commentary on the environment which he inhabited in his adopted land. I understand an attempt is being made to gather together in one book his works with a view to publication.

LIGHTER MOMENTS AND A BEAUTIFUL CHRISTMAS EXPERIENCE

Living in a cosmopolitan society as one did in Vancouver there was ample opportunity to learn gainfully from people who like ourselves had settled here from another country. One's family got introduced to all sorts of ideas which even for parents could prove tempting.

While attending University my son had a part-time job in one of the principal hotels downtown. A number of his colleagues in the hotel were of Italian origin and like many of their fellow countrymen they liked to drink wine but did not care too much to pay the fancy prices being asked for a bottle of wine in the liquor store. So they made their own. 'Dad, it's dead simple, all you have to do is to buy a pail (5 gallons) of grape juice and give it time to ferment.' He was so enthusiastic that we went into production for domestic consumption. One problem though was carrying these pails up to our apartment on the top floor of the building; however with practice we managed and were encouraged every time someone said how much they liked the wine. We chose our own brand names, 'Harbour Dew' and 'Parson's Poison'.

When fermentation was complete I had learned from my instructors that it was a waste of time going through a whole session bottling in individual bottles when you were going to use the stuff for your own consumption. Instead I learned when fermentation was complete to transfer into 1 gallon jugs for storage and consumption.

On one occasion my production was not quite up to standard. It was immediately prior to the port authority making a gift of the building to the Missions to Seamen and they decided to install a new roof. Every day the roofers would strip off a section of the old shingles to replace them. It could get quite hot up top so my production had to be moved almost daily for protection. What I was not aware of at the time was that I had transferred five gallons prematurely (not fully fermented) into 1 gallon jugs.

Our Canteen-shop was usually operated by a volunteer at night and before they turned up for duty frequently a member of staff would hold the fort until the volunteer arrived. On this occasion our Lay Worker, Brian Winnett, was holding the fort when his attention was drawn towards a Korean seafarer simply spellbound, the white of his eyes showing as he gazed up into a display case. He saw Brian looking at him and remarked, 'BLOOD.' 'Never mind,' said Brian, 'It's only the Padre beating the wife, he does that from time to time.' Brian's remark was so funny that when we heard the story we forgot to enquire about the Korean's reaction. Brian shared our secret. Up top a gallon jug bottled prematurely had exploded. Next day for my sins I had a paint job on my hands, to remove the evidence.

Me Catholic
The overwhelming majority of seafarers' clubs worldwide owe their origin to one branch or other of the Christian Church. While we might all claim to worship the same God, I believe it's true to say that we don't always behave alike, which can sometimes be a wee bit confusing for the unbeliever.

Some seafarer's establishments are none too keen on dancing and as for a club being licensed to sell beer, it too is a no no. I believe it's also true to say that most of these establishments are on the Protestant side of the fence. Yet seafarers rarely found these people lacking compassion for those in need though their mode of thinking, however well intended, sometimes gave rise to confusion.

One day while visiting on board a Korean ship a young seafarer came up to me and asked, 'You Christian?' but before I got a chance to reply he went on to say, 'Me no Christian, Christian no dance, no smoke, no drink, no go film, no do nothing. Me Catholic, me believe, me do plenty.'

Some 30,966 seafarers from 80 countries signed into our club this year.

One dream we never want again
'I'm dreaming of a white Christmas.' That song sounded lovely until Christmas 1990 when we got a taste of the real thing but from then on we did not want to hear any more.

It all began a few days before Christmas when we arose one morning to find our water pipes were frozen throughout the building. We had experienced this problem a few years earlier but when we received the MacMillan grant with the upgrading programme the roof space and other exposed areas of the building were lagged and we had no recurrence until now. I have always been reluctant to run up a big bill trying to investigate something like this if it could be avoided. A bit of a Jack of all trades I was prepared to have a go myself first and if I failed no harm would be done when we could then call in the professionals. I began by consulting our friends across the road when they wisely asked, 'Have you been doing any work recently under the veranda and forgotten to replace the lagging on a pipe?' Personally I was not guilty but I found the culprit. A technician had been installing a new water meter a few days earlier and had left exposed the water pipe which he should have lagged and buried. I applied heat at this point and soon the water began to flow. Next I lagged the offending pipe and buried it. I will not elaborate on what I said to the offending technician. Suffice to say he was lucky it was me who found the cause as I was not too expensive to hire. The job was just completed when the weather forecast said snow.

It's no exaggeration to say that a snowfall usually wrought chaos in its wake throughout Vancouver, especially when followed by a big freeze up. Though it was now some years since we had left the Emerald Isle and its gentle climate this forecast was enough to put the fear of God into people of our background. However there could be no escape.

Dorothy's telephone got busier and busier but it was not with people calling to volunteer their help but with people calling to say they were sorry and unable to make it. The membership in our Lightkeepers Guild had never been so low and of this small number several had already indicated that they would be away over Christmas. Though we had made an arrangement to hire a large bus to transport seafarers on Christmas Day, St. Stephen's Day and New Year's Eve, the weather forecasts were so threatening that we finally decided to cancel the bus for St. Stephen's Day and New Year's Eve.

Despite the problems Dorothy together with a small core of volunteers still managed to produce those Christmas banquets for which our club had become famous. The remainder of us, a faithful staff and a small band of Lightkeepers, did our utmost to organize and keep an entertainment programme going. Alan Thompson, our magician, proved to be no fair weather friend. His show was greatly appreciated and he could have gone on for hours and nobody would have minded.

Perhaps the greatest tribute I could pay to our tiny band of helpers over these difficult and trying days when we tried to function as normal is to publish here the number of seafarers who availed themselves of our hospitality. 174 seafarers signed into the club on Christmas Day; 97 seafarers signed into the club on St. Stephen's Day; 112 seafarers signed into the club on New Year's Eve.

As if to test our faith to the utmost we had a couple of other problems to contend with at this time. Our international telephone service went on the blink on the day of New Year's Eve. This was not supposed to happen! Men would walk miles to reach the club simply to connect with home on this night of the year. I made an appeal to the British Columbia telephone company explaining our circumstances and to their great credit all systems were soon operational again despite the snowfall. The night before we had a problem with our fire protection unit and at 2.30 a.m. on the morning of New Year's Eve I said good morning or good night, whichever you prefer, to the technician who responded to our emergency call.

Panic stations

The previous story brings to mind a couple of other occasions when Dorothy must have felt like pushing the panic button but resisted and kept her cool. Nothing to do with snow on these occasions.

From the day we landed in Canada until the day of my retirement Dorothy acted as coordinator of the Mission's army of volunteers. Quite literally she was my other half, many would say my better half but I will spare her blushes. She also had a part-time job to hold down and being wife and mother she had more than her share of responsibility. Christmas could be very challenging.

Dorothy was a very good beggar and usually managed to scrounge a variety of food free of charge for our banquets over the Christmas festive season. She was not the least bit slow in asking a favour. Having received a gift of cold meats to feed a hundred people or so she waylaid a butcher in our neighbourhood whom she persuaded to slice these as his Christmas gift to the Mission. It was agreed that she would collect at the last moment before closing time.

When Dorothy returned to the shop it was locked up and everybody had gone home. She had mistaken the closing time. Enquiries in the neighbourhood and a search through the telephone directory failed to produce the butcher's home address. All we knew was that the proprietor had his son working for him and that he lived at home with his parents.

Over two hundred seafarers would be turning up at the Mission expecting to be fed over the next two days so we had no time to lose. Burning rubber we made it to Woodward's meat counter as they were about to close. A hurried explanation of her predicament to the staff on duty and being Christmas Eve one staff member after another stayed behind to fulfil her requirements.

Panic situations elsewhere too. When the butcher got home and sat down to his evening meal with his son he asked the boy, 'Did you fix that

The Flying Angel Club, Vancouver.
One of the many banquets; seafarers help themselves.

lady up with her meat during the rush this afternoon?' 'No,' replied the boy, 'I thought you were looking after that yourself.' 'O, my God,' the father replied, 'and she's probably got a couple of hundred to feed over the next two days and I've no idea where she lives except that it's somewhere along the waterfront. I'll have to find it somehow and deliver the meat.' After a search he did too. All is well that ends well and we could eat.

One cannot expect to feed a multitude over the festive season for eighteen years and never have a ripple on the pond, so to speak.

Before the development of our basement one almost required a shoehorn to fit into our tiny kitchen where all of the food was laid out in preparation before being moved out into the corridor and put on display for the men to help themselves. A volunteer squeezed into the kitchen to put something on the stove to boil, came out and locked the keys inside. There was no spare key.

Once again Dorothy kept her cool. She quietly explained the problem to a seafarer whom she knew and who was an engineer. A resourceful man, within seconds he had the door off, with no damage either.

On another occasion we had a power failure on Christmas Day. All of our refrigerators were packed with food. Some food had yet to be cooked, turkeys were farmed out to friends of the Mission to be cooked and carved. We could expect to have to feed a couple of hundred people.

A public announcement was given over the radio. Everything possible was being done to restore power but no idea could be given as to how long the power outage would last. People were warned not to open their refrigerators and to keep the cold inside to protect the food.

After about three hours power was restored. Dorothy was so grateful and thankful that a major catastrophe had been averted that she immediately telephoned BC Hydro to say thanks. They'd had a mountain of complaints but her one call to say thanks made their day.

A beautiful Christmas experience

Some years earlier I first noticed him, in my hasty judgement an eccentric old tramp, who come hail, rain or snow slept rough in a warehouse doorway in our neighbourhood nightly throughout the year. He was an odd character who wore a wool toque on his head which he promptly pulled down over his face the moment another human appeared, myself included.

Every time I drove by, his face would be promptly covered. In time I began to feel like the priest who passed by on the other side having more important duties connected with the temple to attend to (which we read about in the Gospel story of the Good Samaritan). Though there was one significant difference: this man made it perfectly clear that he did not want my help. He looked the picture of health and appeared to be well nourished. With niggling doubt I decided for a time to respect his privacy and leave him alone.

Along came Christmas and somehow I felt it would be wrong to pass by on the other side on this day of days. I mentioned to my wife Dorothy that I was going to call and greet the toque man on my way to visit the ships on the North Shore of the port. She made up a parcel of Christmas goodies to which we added a few dollars for me to take along with me. When I arrived at the scene and explained the purpose of my visit, immediately the toque was removed and I was greeted like a long lost brother. The ice was broken and from that day forward his face was never covered to greet me again.

The following Christmas morning something arose which prevented me from calling to see my new found friend. Instead Dorothy said that she would take my place as she had already prepared a parcel for him. He knew Dorothy and as soon as she arrived, greeted her with these words, 'So the old bug . . . couldn't make it himself and sent you instead.'

Message received. I made a point of going the next year myself. When I arrived it was obvious that he was waiting for me as he immediately handed me, with a toothless grin, a yellow dirty piece of newspaper, and passed some remark which I could not understand. The paper smelled high but afraid of causing offence I decided to look inside. To my utter astonishment it contained a one hundred dollar bank note in Canadian currency.

I tried to protest by saying I could not accept such a large sum of money. He replied, 'Don't spoil my giving – I've been saving up to do this.' I still felt badly about taking so much money and tried to say to him that there was no need for him to do this. Now it was his turn to teach. 'Sir, you have a problem, you know how to give but you do not know how to receive. Take my gift, use it for the wife or the fellows around the corner that you're suppose to be helping.'

One year later our friend had died, leaving with us this message.

ON A PERSONAL LEVEL

Throughout this book readers will have become familiar with certain names coming out of the woodwork from time to time: those of my family. We have been described as a Mission family which is I suppose true: Dorothy my wife, my sons Roger and Stephen and my daughter Karen.

Probably no man has been more blessed in marriage than myself for throughout my life Dorothy has been my constant companion, support and guide. With the children I can truthfully say that she has been all things to all of us. We had to say good-bye to our beloved Stephen very early in life and his passing brought the rest of us very close together. I will never forget the support I received from the rest of my family following emigration, for without them I doubt that I could have survived.

Like their mother, Roger and Karen soon became very involved in the work of the Missions to Seamen in the Diocese of New Westminster, especially during those struggling years. Roger filled many roles as the need arose but two in particular during those early years while attending University. He was janitor and also receptionist-telephone operator. Another skill he acquired during his part-time employment in the hotel industry was to learn how to carve and cater for large numbers. Soon his Mum recruited him and he became her chief authority on banquets. While attending University in England, Roger was always booked up in advance at the hotel in Vancouver over the Christmas season. However, his Mum still used him; he was elevated to the position of Chief Carver for all Mission banquets.

Karen literally grew up living over the Mission. She was a member of our Lightkeepers Guild in Vancouver (a hostess) under the watchful eye of her parents before she should really have been doing so. During her nursing training, when not on duty she frequently was to be found helping in the club and enjoying every moment of it. After graduation she nursed for a time in the United Kingdom before returning to University in Victoria, Canada, where she eventually sat her degree in Nursing before returning home to live above the club once more and actively participate as a Lightkeeper. However, it was different this time for without my knowledge it transpired Cupid had been to Victoria and soon life would never be the same again. She was to be married.

Karen had been baptized in the Chapel of the Missions to Seamen located on Eden Quay in the City of Dublin in the Republic of Ireland. She had come a long way in life under the umbrella of the Missions to Seamen and felt a very strong affinity with these roots. Now a new phase in her life was about to begin and where else but in a Chapel of the Missions to Seamen, where it all began. The following article was first published in the *Flying Angel Review*.

One of the family

The wedding took place on Saturday, May 18th, 1991, in the Chapel of The Missions to Seamen, Vancouver, of Karen Louise Parker and Anthony Guy Yip. The Rev. Fr. Gordon Gardener officiated and the bride was given away by her father, The Rev. Parker, Senior Chaplain.

The bride was attended by Mrs Nancy Hilderbrand, Matron of Honour and Miss Christine Corwell, both nursing friends of Karen's. Tony's friends Colin Dalglish and Mark Burran acted as Groomsmen. The Ushers were Masters Shawn and Neill McKay whom Karen babysat as children. Karen's brother Roger acted as Master of Ceremonies at the reception which followed in the Flying Angel Club.

It was appropriate, indeed Karen's choice, that this great occasion in her life should be celebrated at the Mission. Only daughter of Dorothy and Joe Parker, Karen's very much a part of the worldwide Missions to Seamen family. She was baptized in the Chapel of the former Missions to Seamen station in Dublin and grew up within the fellowship of the Society in Belfast, Northern Ireland and Vancouver, British Columbia. Save for her time attending University in Victoria, British Columbia, Karen has lived with her parents in their apartment above the club. Karen has been an active member of the Lightkeepers Guild and regularly attended Sunday worship in the Mission Chapel.

The Ministry to Seafarers in the port of Vancouver had its beginning in St. James Church in which parish the present club is located. Fr. Gardener, now retired from the active Ministry, was formerly rector of St. James and Vice President of The Missions to Seamen in the Diocese of New Westminster and being Karen's Parish Priest prepared and presented her for confirmation. Once more Karen declared her preference and Fr. Gardener graciously consented to officiate at her wedding.

People attending St. James Parish church frequently speak of the magnificent floral arrangements by Mrs Marguerite Hornby. The Mission Chapel was similarly adorned by Marguerite for Karen's wedding with two of the most beautiful and artistic floral arrangements we have ever seen.

So, at the Flying Angel Club in Vancouver with the good wishes of family and friends, Karen and Tony began their new life together.

IT'S TIME TO SAY 'THANK YOU'

I was overjoyed when the year 1991 drew to a close and we were to discover that 35,625 seafarers from 90 countries had signed into our club during the year. This was an all time record and we had no difficulty accommodating this number.

We had come a long way since 1975 when about 14,000 seafarers annually were using the club. Since then a Chaplain's apartment had been created on the first floor, saving the society many thousands of dollars annually. We had received a gift of 50 North Dunlevy Avenue from the port authority and no longer had to pay taxes on this formerly rented property. The building was adapted to our use, having first acquired the cash to pay for each phase before the work was commissioned. Fire protection and emergency lighting systems were installed when we had the money to pay for them. The basement was developed and a major refurbishing job carried out on the building, all paid for with a grant from the H.R. MacMillan Estate Charitable Trust. Two Endowment Funds had been established within the Vancouver Foundation. One contributed annually towards current expenditure and the society was now paying its way. The second fund was for the long term care of the Flying Angel Club as a heritage building.

Many people welcomed the creation of these funds within the Vancouver Foundation who would retain the capital for management and investment and pay the earned interest over to the Mission. This capital could never be depreciated by over spending. We owed much to those pioneers who had helped establish this foundation, especially people like Captain Bill Ellis and Ted Jones, who are no longer with us in the flesh.

On many occasions with a totally undisciplined sense of gratitude I felt tempted to try and honour countless people who had come to our rescue but wisely under the constitution of our society it was only our directors who were empowered to do this. They were empowered under the society's constitution to elect as Honorary Members 'Persons who have made an outstanding contribution to the work of the Missions to Seamen in the Diocese of New Westminster'.

In addition to those who fulfilled a leadership role in our major fund-raising drive the following persons were so honoured.

Mrs Alex Marsden – Canteen-shop volunteer.
Mrs Dorothy Kerr – Canteen-shop volunteer.
Mrs Sally Hames – Canteen-shop volunteer.
Mrs Geraldine Martin – Canteen-shop volunteer.
Mr Fred Spoke – Former General Manager Port of Vancouver.
Captain A. Cabot – A Director of many years standing.
The Rev. J.G. Gardiner – Vice President for many years.
Mr Vic Watts – Man Friday about the club for years.
Mr Brian Kaneen – Volunteer Receptionist-Telephone Operator.
Mr Jack Cunningham Q.C. – Legal Adviser & Director.
The Rev. I Shim Ro – Presbyterian Chaplain.
Mr A. Thompson – Our volunteer Magician friend.
The Most Rev. D.W. Hambidge – A former President.

The one who remembered

There's another name which should have appeared on the foregoing list but who made it into higher service before we could put him on this list – Jack Wilson, a retired Vice President of Canada Trust.

I recall him as the one who remembered: a supporter of many charitable causes who went out of his way to do so. Indeed in retirement he was almost as busy assisting charities as when full-time employed. The story of our plight on that fateful Christmas night when the toilets overflowed filtered through to Jack Wilson and he made a mental note of the fact that our basement needed developing but that we had no money. He was ill when invited to participate in our major fund-raising drive and deeply regretted that he could not do so.

He was a personal friend of the late H.R. MacMillan and a Trustee of his Estate Charitable Trust. The late H.R. MacMillan, he informed me, was a lifetime supporter of the Missions to Seamen. The society received an annual grant from another family fund. Jack asked to see our basement and enquired if we had any plans for developing the area. 'We could certainly use the space right now but as for plans we've lots of dreams but they will have to wait until we get some money.' Turning to me he said, 'Draw up your plans and submit an application to the trustees, H.R. MacMillan Estate Charitable Trust, for a grant.'

Later Jack was elected a director of the Missions to Seamen but by this stage his health was declining. His former company, Canada Trust, honoured him before he died by establishing an Endowment Fund in his name with the Vancouver Foundation. He informed me before his death that he had requested a portion of the income from this fund be applied to the Missions to Seamen in perpetuity. Those reading the society's annual financial statement and seeing mention of the name Jack Wilson now know who he was and how much he contributed to the society.

Many hands make light work

Many times I have said throughout this book that the foundation upon which our Ministry rests is ship visiting. 'The good shepherd knows his sheep and is known by them.' A ship going staff makes for club going seafarers. There is no substitute for ship visiting.

The Chaplain is a lightweight without the willing support of the shipping community and the volunteers who man the club. They are as much part of the work of the Mission as the Padre in his dog collar. Everyone has a part to play. We need each other if we are to do a good job.

When I served in the port of Vancouver, as most people will remember, a common sight from Stanley Park was the number of ships waiting to load grain. (I don't know who paid the cost of this, no doubt somebody did, but it went on for years at any rate and may still do for all I know.) We could not afford the cost of running a launch to visit and service these ships. Yet we knew that those on board must be lonely and would welcome an invitation to the Flying Angel Club when they came ashore by chartered launch.

In this respect especially we were indebted to the local Shipping Agents, Launch Operators and the Pacific Pilot Authority for their help and cooperation. We put together for each ship at anchor, a package about the club, and these in the appropriate language were mailed to the ships' Masters in the care of local agents. The agents would subsequently deliver them on board when they called on company business. This practice worked very satisfactorily thanks to the cooperation we received from the agents in this and in many other respects. The Launch Operators always displayed our brochures and maps for individual seafarers to help themselves. The Pilot Authority assisted us daily with information regarding the movement of vessels within the port, especially from the anchorages.

Really what I am trying to do in this chapter is acknowledge some of the countless ways, possibly not yet mentioned, through which people helped us achieve some of our goals. In other words the Missions to Seamen didn't just consist of Chaplains but of all of us working together for the seafarers' benefit. Working in this spirit there follows a list of what was achieved during the year 1992.

30,306 seafarers from 90 countries signed into the club.

211 seafarers enjoyed our hospitality for Christmas Day banquet, entertainment, etc.

130 seafarers on St. Stephen's Day (Boxing Day).

103 on New Year's Eve.

Our Chaplaincy staff visited 3,468 ships.

13,458 International Telephone Calls were processed for seafarers.

296 exchanges were made from foreign currency.

$17,610 worth of postage stamps were purchased to mail letters home.

15,884 pocket books were placed on board ships. (Not to mention an even greater number of books and magazines taken by seafarers from the club library of which no record is kept.)

66 Bibles were given to seafarers in a variety of languages upon request.

22 visits were made to hospitalized seafarers.

202 Worship Services were conducted in the Mission Chapel for seafarers – 1,805 seafarers attended.

UP WE GET AND AWAY WE GO

To all intents and purposes I am an amateur when it comes to writing this book. Of necessity I have had to be selective and my hope is that my readers will find what I've written interesting. In no way is it my intention to put forward my account of life as the only way. As someone once said, there are many roads to the throne of grace and this is but one of them. If this book stimulates others to look at life a little deeper than the surface then it will have achieved a purpose. It's not written for personal financial gain and what it earns is dedicated to help in life those who probably helped me more than I ever helped them.

I have deliberately excluded much reference to the time I spent on sabbatical leave in Northern Ireland following the tragic death of our beloved son Stephen, immediately before we emigrated to Canada. Our activities during this period were not specifically related to the waterfront and as such do not qualify for inclusion. Perhaps one day I may record an account of these days.

Before I conclude I want to reminisce a little about one or two of my duties which I may have overlooked. Over the years quite a number of ships were built in Vancouver Shipyards. My wife and I always looked forward to the launching ceremony when I was almost always involved by being privileged to bless the vessel. A reception would follow when the food was simply delicious. These occasions provided me with a wonderful opportunity to make the acquaintance of people related to the shipping industry which I would not have done otherwise.

I shall always remember the first side launch of a vessel I had just blessed. My heart stopped beating as it hit the water, rocking so far over from side to side that I thought it was going to sink before righting itself. A real test of faith.

I was fortunate to have been posted to serve with the Missions to Seamen in the Diocese of New Westminster and though we got off to a rocky start, we came to love Vancouver and Fraser Port. The shipping community and transport industry eventually claimed us as their own and were very supportive of our work. It was always my pride and joy to be invited to join them and say grace at dinner and other functions throughout the year.

The idea of retirement was something I had not even seriously contemplated when I was suddenly confronted with the idea. Oh, I knew the years were adding up and the date would soon be upon me; I hankered after the idea of seeking an extension but gave this no further thought. I loved my work which I had always found very fulfilling. Now after a struggle of some years, thanks to the support of the Port authorities, the shipping community, many friends of the Mission and the income generated from seafarers who patronized the Club, we were clearly out of the red.

In 1991 the income from club services reached the astonishing figure of $98,442. Overall our income actually exceeded expenditure by $12,649. In addition we had begun to plan for the future by establishing with the Vancouver Foundation a second Endowment fund, the income designated for the exterior maintenance of the club premises. The Missions to Seamen Heritage Endowment Fund was the name chosen and a sum of $10,000 was transferred to establish this fund. We had been stabilized and things were on the up and up. It had been a long haul and to remain in this solvent state in the future care would have to be taken to balance expenditure with income. Once in debt it is by no means easy to get out of debt. Responsible leadership was called for in the years ahead.

Suddenly my world was to change. I developed an eye problem which eventually gave cause for concern. The long term prognosis was good in medical terms provided I took early retirement which would ensure a greatly reduced work load. I chose to do as I was advised.

However, there was one very comforting thought. When I joined the Missions to Seamen I was given to understand that if I remained in the service of the society until retirement I would be provided with retirement accommodation for my wife and myself. The years I spent on sabbatical leave in Northern Ireland cost us every penny we owned and since we settled in Canada I never sought to earn more than my clerical colleagues who were being paid the Diocesan minimum stipend. By careful management of the resources at our disposal throughout my working life, the part-time salary my wife received from the Vancouver Public Library, and with pensions, while we would not be wealthy we would be comfortable. The Central Authority of the Missions to Seamen in London, England generously agreed to provide this accommodation in Canada in view of the tragedy we suffered in Northern Ireland.

The appointment of my successor was the responsibility of the Archbishop of New Westminster in consultation with the Secretary General of the Missions to Seamen in London, England and the Directors of the Missions to Seamen in the Diocese of New Westminster. It became clear that my successor would not be instituted before the date of my retirement. In the circumstances I felt that it was incumbent upon me to prepare three papers in relation to the position from which I was retiring. This was not the appointment of a Parish Priest; very different skills would be required. All those responsible for the appointment each received a personal copy of all three papers I had prepared relating to my work. I promised to make myself available to my successor for consultation if he felt I could be of help to him.

Position Papers

1) 'Behind the scenes'
   Briefly this paper traced the growth and development since 1975, highlighting certain important factors, launching and function of the *Flying Angel Review*, Operation Renewal, Gift of 50 North Dunlevy Ave., Sea Sunday, Ecumenical Co-Operation, etc.
2) 'Day to day operation of the Flying Angel Club'
   A detailed operational manual – what required doing and why.
3) 'Times, Seasons and Volunteers'
   This paper contained a detailed list of every activity, functions, services, etc. which required advance planning and preparation. Dates where known. Where necessary to set dates.

A detailed list of all volunteers, name, address, telephone number – a detailed description of what each one did and when. My wife who had coordinated all volunteers over the years updated this list to the day of our departure.

Before our final departure from the waterfront scene every day had a surprise, people and groups taking us out for meals and celebrations of one kind or another. They were memorable occasions.

When our daughter Karen was married, volunteers at the Mission gave a shower for her. As an emigrant this was a new experience for Dorothy who thought it was a lovely idea and she was most impressed. Vivian Murray, who took over Dorothy's role as coordinator of volunteers, arranged a reception a few days before our departure to give us an opportunity to say good-bye to them. A well kept secret from Dorothy and me was that this get-together should take the form of a shower. It was a truly memorable occasion shared with those who over the years had been so much part of our lives and without whose contribution we could never have managed.

Surprise of a lifetime. Joe and Dorothy Parker at Retirement Banquet with Roger and Karen.

Even today, almost five years later, we still use many of their gifts in our retirement home.

Man is essentially a social animal and apart from our daily work most of us enjoy social contact with those with whom we work day by day. Two of the highlights of my social calendar were the spring and fall banquets of the Plimsoll Club at which I was always invited to say grace. Everyone and anyone associated with shipping would be there. While I was not a member of the club, the hospitality and welcome I always received was boundless, though I was totally unaware of the fact it was to be here that my wife and I would say our final farewell to the Port.

Apart from the lady members of the club who were not numerous, one rarely saw other ladies at these functions. When my wife informed me that she would be a guest at the spring banquet and that she would be accompanied by Pat Stark, the wife of the President of the Port Corporation, and that she and Captain Stark would collect us a little early so that we could have a quiet drink before the banquet I was a little confused and not quite sure about what was happening.

We had hardly taken our seats when out of the woodwork came our daughter Karen and husband Tony. Now I gathered something was under way but a moment later I could not believe the sight my own eyes when my son Roger stood before me. He had to tap me on the shoulder and say, 'It's me, Dad, I am here.' My wife overjoyed to see him and just as confused as myself was in tears beside me. Roger, who had decided to follow me into the ministry, was attending University in London. A truly magnificent gesture on the part of the Vancouver Port Corporation, by its President Captain Norman Stark, was to fly him home from London for this great occasion.

A magnificent banquet was to follow. We were presented with a cheque in excess of $3,500 amongst other gifts for our retirement on behalf of the Marine community, acknowledging our contribution to the shipping industry during our eighteen years of service with the Missions to Seamen in the Diocese of New Westminster. Both Dorothy and I were very deeply touched that both Karen and Roger had been included, for in our struggling years they were part of our main support. In addition we received from Captain Stark, a framed letter of congratulations from the Federal Minister of Transport which reads as follows:

Ministre des Transports   Minister of Transport

CANADA

April 21, 1993

Reverend Joe Parker
The Mission to Seamen
50 North Dunlevy Avenue
Vancouver, B.C.
V6A3R1

Dear Reverend Parker:

While we have never met, I have heard of your devotion to assisting sailors passing through the Port of Vancouver. As the Minister responsible for the Port of Vancouver, I would like to congratulate you for all your endeavours on the eve of your retirement, and thank you for being such a good ambassador, helpful fixer and spiritual guide to thousands who crossed the door to the Missions to Seamen. I understand you are not one to sit and wait for those in need to come to you and that your presence and profile in and around the Port have been widely felt.

As you move into the next phase of your life you and your wife and family must be looking forward to a change of pace. It must be reassuring to know that you are starting a new chapter of your life having accomplished so much with the Missions to Seamen.

Congratulations on all your successes, and I wish you the best with your future endeavours.

Sincerely,

Jean Corbeil

A few weeks after I had retired my wife and I received an invitation to attend a conference of the Canadian Ports and Harbour Association which was being held in the Fraser Port, New Westminster. During the conference we were each presented with the Association's Medal of Merit by Captain Norman Stark, President. Such recognition would never have come about were it not for the loyalty and dedication of the volunteer workers of the Mission.

Time waits for no man and soon it was time to depart from our apartment above the club which had been our home all these years. By now William, one of our cats, had used up the last of his nine lives and had departed from us, but MacIntyre was still with us waiting to accompany us into retirement. We had been first tenants in this apartment and watched our furniture being moved in. It was a nostalgic experience to see it empty again when the furniture was moved out. Right away Dorothy decided the next tenant must find it as we did and she promptly left the money with Vicki, the Mission Secretary, to have all the carpets cleaned. We were sorry to leave for this building had been at the heart of our lives for many years.

EPILOGUE

This story began with a young couple who were happily married and had two beautiful healthy children. A reasonably successful business man at an early age, yet he could not seem to find in his work the fulfilment he craved until he eventually joined the Missions to Seamen as a lay worker which led on to ordination and a lifetime of service as a Chaplain with the Missions to Seamen.

On this pilgrimage there were rough paths to cross and no doubt we made our share of mistakes whether knowingly or unknowingly. I have come through this experience in life to have confirmed for me that real fulfilment only comes in life when we try to make God's purpose our purpose. As St. Paul once wrote, 'One plants, another waters, but it's God who gives the increase.' Whatever our imperfections as St. Paul would say called according to His purpose God will use any one of us and we will find fulfilment in being used.

When I listened to the conclusion of the Hon. Treasurer's Report paying tribute to my wife and myself at the final Annual General Meeting of the Missions to Seamen which we attended before retirement, this truth became a reality for us both.

'I will also take this opportunity to recognize just a small portion of the efforts of the Reverend Parker and Mrs Parker – he claims to "know nothing about accounting" and yet it is little short of miraculous how, during their term of service in Vancouver, the fortunes of the Missions to Seamen have turned around. Questions about the viability of the Society were valid when they arrived; today it is a well founded and very well run organization business. Certainly the future is far more secure and the financial standing so much better than when the Parkers arrived.'

In the face of this great drama of life in which under God's guidance we are all called to play a part, my mind is drawn back to an article I once wrote about a Sunday night in the Missions to Seamen in the Diocese of New Westminster. I quote:

Today was Sunday and as usually happens in the life of the seafarer most of those in port today will sail tomorrow. Invariably seafarers when sailing miss the celebration of many festive occasions which those of us who live ashore take for granted. Sometimes we juggle around with these dates for the seafarers' benefit and bring them forward so that they have an opportunity to celebrate with us. Tonight we observed two festivals, one sacred and one secular. Tomorrow will be Halloween and Tuesday All Saints Day.

We had a fair number attend our service in Church this evening. The hymns were sung with meaning and if one can say so with gusto. I'm not a singer, indeed I'm almost tone deaf, yet I love to hear other people sing. The sentiments expressed in the words of our final hymn are breathtaking and set to a tune which seems to span eternity.

> For all the saints who from their labours rest,
> Who thee by faith before the world confessed
> Thy Name, O Jesus, be for ever blest.
>
> Alleluia!
>
> And when the strife is fierce, the warfare long,
> Steals on the ear the distant triumph song,
> And hearts are brave again, and arms are strong.
>
> Alleluia!
>
> The golden evening brightens in the west,
> Soon, to faithful warriors comes their rest,
> Sweet is the calm of Paradise the blest.
>
> Alleluia!

A difficult hymn to sing but by the extent of the participation of this small congregation obviously the meaning was not lost on them.

The Halloween Party followed the church service as naturally as night follows day. Our Lightkeepers, a number of whom attended church in costume, had gone to endless trouble preparing fancy dress costumes for the occasion. Many a sight to behold. They also decorated the club as they do every year.

The Lightkeepers provided an excellent supper, garlands for the men to wear around their neck so that nobody felt left out, organized games, dancing and a pumpkin carving contest. There was a big attendance from the ships in port and throughout the evening a wonderful spirit of fellowship, enjoyment and camaraderie which melted the barriers of race, creed and culture. The Mission at its best.

These evenings provide church members with an opportunity to offer hospitality to the seafarer and the seafarer with an opportunity to enjoy their fellowship.

Thus my prayer for All Saints Tide has got to be:

'O God of Love, we thank and praise your glorious name for the memory and example of Chaplains, Lay Workers and Volunteer Workers of the Missions to Seamen, now Saints in the Light, into whose heritage we have entered. Grant O Lord, that in our generation and time, we may be inspired by the memory and example of all that has been true and good in their lives through Jesus Christ Our Lord.

Amen.

Whatever our disappointments and apparent failures in this life the closing words of this beautiful hymn remind us that as Christians we have a great hope.

> But lo; there breaks a yet more glorious day,
> The saints triumphant rise in bright array,
> The King of Glory passes on his way
>
> > Alleluia!
>
> From earth's wide bounds, from ocean's farthest coast
> Through gates of pearl streams in the countless host,
> Singing to FATHER, SON and HOLY GHOST.
>
> > Alleluia!
>
> Amen.